"Marañón's The Gringo's Hawk is a weaving of the many different threads - rich in texture, varied, and intertwined with both rough and delicate fibers that add interest. It is not a smooth, perfect life, but one that has crafted an interesting, beautiful tapestry for others to enjoy." Rated Four Stars: A very good read! You won't want to put the book down.

- Angie Ledbetter, Sandy Cummins Book Reviews

"The Gringo's Hawk is not a book to be devoured at a sitting. Like wine it is best sipped and savored a little at a time. Jon Marañón writes with a grace and fluidity that is seldom experienced in this era....he reveals himself as a gentle but gallant warrior, a Don Quixote of the rainforest, the beach and the reef. If there is justice in the world of books then Jon Marañón's The Gringo's Hawk will become a sleeper - an unexpected best seller. The more we read in it the better we like it. It wears well." Rated five stars.

- Rowes Reviews, John Culleton, Publisher

"Like Henry David Thoreau before him, Marañón exhibits an appreciation of wilderness that is always informed by the perspective of civilization and a view of civilization that is only achieved by freeing oneself from its comfortable embrace. The Gringo's Hawk is the story of one exceptional man coming to terms with one exotic place and the people who inhabited it...In the end Marañón's memoir is about discovering the world outside ourselves and trying to find our proper place in it..."

- Craig W. Allin, Ph.D., Author of Politics of Wilderness Preservation

"Here is someone who walked the walk, who witnessed the willingness of desperately poor natives to compromise their natural resources. Marañón understands the complexities of saving the rain forest and he was successful in helping establish some national parks and marine reserves."

- Tom Leveen, Associate Editor, "Today's Librarian"

"In The Gringo's Hawk...the reader is not given the standard "traveller in paradise" account...Here we meet Marañón's neighbors, workers, close friends, and family and become acquainted with the "drama" of their lives–the non-fantasy world of actual living in the tropics, confronting environmental change and dealing with the advent of a globalized world economy that was reaching into their corner of the world...Marañón built his house and life not in, but of Cantarana."

- **Dr. Sterling Evans, Author of The Green Republic:**
A Conservation History of Costa Rica.

"Marañón's sensitivity, compassion, and insight along with sound ethical values make him the quintessential "participant observer." He doesn't just dabble in another culture; he wades in deep and puts down a firm anchor. The result is a rich, complex, and clear-eyed story not just of a North American pioneer seeking harmony with nature and with himself, but of a country buffeted by the winds of change.... It is a tale well worth telling, and reading."

- **Martha Honey, Ph.D., author of Ecotourism and Sustainable**
Development: Who Owns Paradise?

"God bless Jon Marañón for being brave enough to do what most will not. This courageous story of the atrocities inflicted upon the rain forest and what Mr. Marañón has endured in order to bring these realities to light, is a great contribution in the difficult task of ending this out of control slaughter. It is true that one person can make a difference—here is the proof!"

- **Lois Tulleners, Founder of White Wolf Sanctuary**

The Gringo's Hawk

One person's long-term transformation,
adaptation and struggle with modern civilization,
the environment,
his own species and many others,
his own conscience,
and his own body, mind, and soul
in a tropical "paradise"

Jon Marañón

Library of Congress Control Number: 2017912867
ISBN: Hardcover   978-1-5434-4510-7
                Softcover   978-1-5434-4511-4
                eBook   978-1-5434-4512-1

Cover art by Kamel Kuradenk.

Rev date: 05/23/2018

To order additional copies of this book, contact:
Xlibris
1-888-795-4274
www.Xlibris.com
Orders@Xlibris.com
756294

Photo Credits

The following photos are used by permission and Copyright © Jon Marañón. All rights reserved.

xix   Going in
54   Humo's offspring

The following photos are used by permission and Copyright © Marco T. Saborio. All rights reserved.

xviii   *Gavilán negro* (black hawk)
32   *Playa del Tunel* (Tunnel Beach)
44   Lowland tropical rainforest flora
53   *Caucél* (nocturnal rainforest feline)
79   *Careto* (capuchín or white face monkey)
89   *Caimán* (Caiman)
105   *Mariposa azul* (blue morpho butterfly)
129   *Tortuga "lora"* (Olive Ridley turtle)
142   *Flor de bejuco* (rare flower from a rainforest vine)
153   *Rana venenosa* (poison arrow frog)
163   *Monos congos* (howler monkeys)
176   *Cola de ballena jorobada* (fluke of humpback whale)
192   *Ballena jorobada* (Humpback whale)
218   *Canopé del bosque lluvioso primario* (climax rainforest canopy)
226   *Cusinga* (fiery-billed aracari) in *guarumo* (cecropia tree)
227   *Gavilán blanco* (white hawk)
239   *Gavilán negro* (black hawk)

The following photos are used by permission and Copyright © Robert Goodell. All rights reserved.

43   *Perezoso* (three-toed sloth)
67   *Buey* (ox)
68   *Siete Vueltas* (Seven Curves)
191   *Jureles ojones* (big-eye jacks)
203   Destruction/construction of the Costanera Highway

Cover art Copyright © and used by permission of Kamel Kuradenk.

All rights reserved.

The Gringo's Hawk

Seeking Paradise in Southern Costa Rica
(before the highway)

Dedication

To my parents, no longer in this problem-plagued world, who helped me realize my childhood dream of exploring untamed jungles;

and to the Costa Rican elders, men and women who befriended me and shared their stories with me before they died;

and to all people who love God's creation enough to fight for it . . . even a little bit.

and to my friend the black hawk, who I am so very sorry I killed.

"A man is rich in proportion to the number of things he can afford to let alone."

- Henry David Thoreau

"No matter how much one may love the world as a whole, one can live fully in it only by living responsibly in some small part of it."

- Wendell Berry

Acknowledgments

I am very grateful for the help and advice of Peter Cohen, John Krist, Carolyn Rousseau, and especially Richard Haight in writing this book. I thank my parents, my brothers, my wife and children, and Nina Gaddis for being patient and encouraging me to complete the project. Thanks to Marco Tulio Saborio and Robert Goodell for their photography and friendship. And thanks to Roxann Spevak and Sheila Hart for getting the thing done.

Contents

Contents *continued*

Introduction

At age 21, but still a boy in 1972, when I first arrived in Morita on the southern Pacific coast of Costa Rica, the rainforests and offshore reefs were thriving, full of life in awesome variety. But the last local jaguars were being poisoned. The last harpy eagles were being shot and the last tapirs, red monkeys, and scarlet macaws were being devoured - we humans are so shamelessly omnivorous. Industrial-nation exploiters and more and more Costa Ricans were beginning an assault on the rainforest that would have disastrous consequences for the environment, the creatures that lived there, and the people.

While my two older brothers braved the cold academia of Harvard and Cornell, respectively, I felt blessed to be wearing shorts and a T-shirt and to sit on bamboo, enthralled by tales being told by smiling, wrinkled old men who were happy to have such a listener and questioner as I. Over more than a quarter century, I wrote down their tales and what their wives, children, and grandchildren said and did; what they showed me; and what I thought about the place, the people, the animals, and myself, and noted how we all changed. Now that the elders are no longer alive to tell their folk tales and life stories, I feel privileged that I was there to hear them and can pass on at least some of them.

For a privileged, sensitive, animal-loving gringo college student to jump into such a foreign environment alone, into such precious and threatened biodiversity, was staggering, and I felt I had to tell somebody about the experience. I was a de facto anthropologist, acting as a "participant observer" in the change from a hunter-gatherer/subsistence farming/horse-and- oxen culture to a distressed version of the all-conquering modern Western cultural extravaganza. I was an uncalloused, inexperienced book reader becoming a cattle rancher, chocolate grower, tourism operator, reforester, and furniture maker. I was a narcissistic young man marrying a much more savvy native and raising a family - and joining an extended family that connected me dangerously (for it can be dangerous to have a conscience while living among have-nots) with the Third World. And I was a college dropout dealing with witches, loggers, bureaucrats, hunters, tourists, politicians, and a Nobel Peace Prize recipient. I had become a marginal character, a man without a country, living as best as possible with highway crews, vipers, and telecommunication satellite signals, with God and children and himself.

I knew I was a witness to something amazing, something newsworthy and important. So this is why I felt compelled to write this book, to communicate something of my awareness and involvement with these issues of such importance to us all: symbiosis, adaptation, metamorphosis, evolution, sustainability - personal, biological, social, global. Life-and-death processes seem so accelerated in the tropics, more obvious, more spectacular, more diverse, more interconnected. There are more participants, more competitors, more complexities, more difficulties, and more uncertainties. How important on a human/ planetary scale are the tropical forests and oceans? What has our kind been doing there? What are we doing there now? What should we be doing?

Some people believe that we only truly perceive what we can imagine, which is circumscribed by what we are prepared to perceive by our conditioning and experience. Some speculate that this is why the indigenous pre-Columbian Americans were so vulnerable to the invading Europeans, why they could not grasp the meaning or the danger of the horse-and- metal-clad riders and the sailing ships, and the exploding sticks that blew them to smithereens, not to mention the far more deadly viruses and spirochetes the invaders brought with them. It was a breach of apparent reality that conquered the New World. And the invasion - the raping and pillaging and murdering and poisoning - continues today, only on a much larger scale, a scale that threatens us all.

I wonder how we can still be in denial to so much. We stand aside and allow the continued barbarism against nature and humankind.

Far more formidable monsters than mounted conquistadors are active among the clear-cut hillsides and over- crowded, squalid towns and cities of the tropics. I have engaged in some negotiations and skirmishes with some of the monsters, and with myself, and wish to tell of victories, defeats, and truces.

Though I have tried to be as accurate and truthful as possible, I have changed most of the names of people and places that might identify them - out of respect for privacy and the right to exist without interference.

"Jon Marañón" (the "o" pronounced as in "cone") was the name young children called me when they wanted me to act offended and chase or tickle them. Sometimes it was *Marañón* (which means cashew), sometimes it was *Tiburón* (shark), and when they really wanted to rile me up, they would call me *Chicharrón* (pork rind). Anything containing an "ón" ending worked well for their mischievous childish purposes.

This book is mostly a memoir - many years' notes put together, a conglomeration of reality and documentation of it, and also quite a bit of personal expository stuff, which I hope is okay. News and dates are not a high priority to me, and I apologize where I am inaccurate or ambiguous about them.

Gavilán negro (black hawk)

Going in

Chapter One

Wandering, wondering

Had I known how frequently those ancient Cessnas went down in Costa Rica, I'd at least have worn a helmet. But, of course, a helmet would have been merely uncomfortable on days when the plane did not crash, useless on the day it did. Wedged into the co-pilot's seat of a roaring, rattling, smoking, single-engine Cessna, I watched the dials of the instruments spin and jitter as we fought awkwardly through the wind currents swirling above a range of tree-carpeted mountains. I thought about asking the pilot whether there were parachutes tucked somewhere in the crevices of the plane, but the roar of the engine made conversation impossible.

At 7:00 a.m., I'd had second thoughts about getting on that six-dollar flight with my two fellow students. By then, we'd been waiting at the cold and windy hangar for two hours. Radio contact was lost with the first flight that had gone out that day. "Don't worry," they'd told us, smiling as if nothing at all was out of the ordinary. "We'll get this other one fixed right away and take you." A small, grease-covered mechanic smiled as he walked by carrying the two-blade prop to "our" plane, which we'd speculated earlier was something they might be using as a source of salvaged parts. Once the prop and wheels had been attached, we had to admit that flight at least looked feasible, if not assured.

As we cleared a 9,000-foot ridge, I relaxed my grip on the seat and loosened the seat belt; I realized it had been cutting off my breathing. Soon my anxiety yielded to appreciation of the Costa Rican scenery – bold mountains heavily forested with huge trees, some flowering lavender and others bright yellow, white waterfalls cascading from the dark-green cliffs, rivers rushing through steep valleys.

In the middle of the rainforest, the first tiny clearing appeared, with a thatched hut and some pigs loitering around. Where the mountains sloped nearer to the gray-blue sea, there were more clearings, more huts and pigs, as well as fields planted in corn, bananas, manioc, and beans. Then came, near the towns of Quepos and Parrita, a long stretch of a littoral and flat region planted in rectangular sections of rice and oil palm. After 40 minutes in the air, we could see our destination, Punta Morita, a sandy peninsula protecting a little bay that was to become Alcoa Aluminum's deep-water port for exporting bauxite.

To Alcoa, it may have been ideal for a port. More important to me, gazing down through the calm, clear, blue-green water, seeing tan patches of what must be healthy reef, it looked fantastic for snorkeling. There were no boats, houses, or people on the miles of surrounding beaches. It seemed like a perfect place for me to do some valuable research before Alcoa ravaged it.

The pilot suddenly dipped one wing and the plane dropped so much that I felt my stomach in my throat. He pulled out of the deep turn and headed for a narrow pasture where a few horses and cows were peacefully grazing. Scowling and cursing, he buzzed just over the heads of the animals, stampeding them, then circled for another approach. "What are you doing?" I yelled at him in Spanish, with pronunciation made poorer by urgency.

He yelled back something about landing, smiled enthusiastically, and pointed toward the pasture. I twisted around to warn my friends to brace for landing. They were pale-green with big white eyes. I tightened my seat belt and braced myself as the pilot cut the engine. The plane sailed ten feet over some weird-looking trees and plopped down, bounced, swerved, and skidded through grass, weeds, mud, and manure, which created quite a rural collage all over the plane.

The landing was as momentous in my life as if I were stepping onto the moon. In Robert Frost's words, I had just "taken the road less traveled," and for all the years of my life up to now I have wondered how good or bad a road it really was for me to take.

My journey had begun earlier that year, born in disillusionment. Natural sciences were my passion, and most of my life I'd dreamed of becoming, like Dian Fossey or Jane Goodall or Jacques Cousteau, an animal-behavior researcher out in the wilds. I abandoned this idea in college, however, when I found out my dream would require me to spend years studying math, physics, and chemistry – disciplines for which my spirit was not suited. When I found out what most zoologists actually did, such as paint giant fluorescent pink numbers on helicopter-harassed and drugged polar bears; fit tigers and pandas with radio transmitting collars; or collect live and dead specimens for universities, museums, and zoos, animal-behavior research didn't appear as romantic in reality as I had envisioned in my dreams.

I sought refuge in cultural anthropology, which I figured might be more humane and would possibly satisfy some of my passion for studying animal behavior. My first professor in that discipline at Colorado College (in Colorado Springs) – either because he liked me so much or because he wanted to get rid of me – rewarded my interest by selecting me to join the Associated Colleges of the Midwest Program in Costa Rica. Neither he nor I knew much about it. The previous year's Colorado College's sole participant got typhoid and her hair fell out. I didn't press her to tell me about the details of her trip.

The important things were that I would get full college credits toward my anthropology major for the term and my parents would finance it. Other young nerds like me who were without political connections or savvy lawyers were getting sent to some damned war in Southeast Asia.

So it was in my sophomore year that I found myself airborne, bound for Costa Rica. In those days, the drinks on the Costa Rican airline were free and the passengers took full advantage. Sometimes it seemed the pilot drank his share as well. We flew out of Miami, stopping once at Grand Cayman, in the middle of the vast mosaic of blues, greens, tans, and whites that was the Caribbean.

Costa Rica greeted us with long beaches, dense green jungles, smoking volcanoes, and a wonderfully nonrectangular pattern of multihued fields. On touching down, the passengers broke out in vigorous roaring, whistling, and hand clapping. Nationalism? Relief for a perfect landing? I had no idea, but it was very nice to be with so many celebrating people in an airplane, a unique phenomenon I later discovered was characteristic of landings in Costa Rica.

San José, the capital and the largest city – at the time it had half a million inhabitants – was the busiest, most people-packed environment I'd ever experienced. Endless lines of vehicles spewed thick black diesel exhaust. The streets were a confusion of buses and trucks and semis; horsecarts and peoplecarts; bicycles and motorcycles – all enthusiastically competing with horns and shouts for space and a chance to move. Policemen carried screwdrivers rather than guns because having your license plate removed was worse than getting shot.

After the two-week orientation required by the academic program, I grabbed the quickest escape route out of that mad metropolis. Once again I was airborne, but this time there was no alcohol to dull the panic induced by that rocky, swooping journey aboard that tiny, smoking Cessna.

As we disembarked after our spectacular landing in the manure-mined pasture, damp air filled our nostrils with unfamiliar scents. Barefoot people in ragged clothing stared as we unloaded our baggage. Gray-green, mossy, waist-high, mysterious stone spheres bearing hidden meaning – pre-Columbian artifacts left by ancient local people – lay in the weeds. Back among the fruit trees stood the largest building for many miles, a mildewed, two-story house that was to be our temporary headquarters.

A local man greeted us amiably and led us to the house, where he grinned widely, introduced himself as Luis, and firmly shook our hands. He then left us alone with a smallish, cutish, black and yellow-white chained monkey named Lola. Lola, he said, was known to grab and bite people she didn't like – which was almost everyone.

The sun seemed remarkably large and close and the humidity incredibly high, so my fellow "whities" and I changed into bathing suits and headed for the ocean a couple hundred meters away. The water was extraordinarily warm but cool enough to be refreshing. Taking a breather from body surfing, floating on the swells out past the breakers zone, letting the soothing sea penetrate, I allowed my mind to relax deeply after the stressful morning. Mesmerized by the gently swaying greens and blues of the beautiful, mountainous coast, assimilating the massaging energy of the friendly sea, I felt a tremendous sense of well-being. Amazingly, I felt I was in exactly the right place, as if I had finally succeeded in following my instincts along the right path. Was my gratitude and euphoria simply a relief for having survived the plane ride, or were there deeper reasons, perhaps of good omen?

When we returned to town, four saddled horses stood patiently under the palm trees by La Pichinga, Morita's only general store and saloon. Inside, the bartender was filling shot glasses with clear liquid from a bottle with a feathered Indian on the label. Four serious customers wearing dirty, wide-brimmed hats leaned against the worn wooden counter, smoking and staring at us in silence as we entered Morita's bat- and rat-infested social center. After an uncomfortable silence – we weren't aware that local custom required us (the arriving party) to greet everyone first – the bartender stretched out his hand and we shook with him and with the *vaqueros* (cowboys), who instantly became friendly and talkative with us.

I spoke adequate Spanish, and since my gringo companions (the term "gringo" had no derogatory meaning in Costa Rica – yet) could barely grasp anything that was being said, I suddenly became interpreter, a position I readily accepted as a prestigious honor and very quickly grew to dislike.

For lunch we could choose from the shelves and bins of La Pichinga – rum, *guaro* (a kind of white lightning), beer (warm), cigarettes, candles, matches, sugar, salt, rice, beans, lard, canned fruit juice, canned tuna, and soda crackers. We all ordered the last three. The next day our stomachs discovered the pleasant old widow, Doña Rosa, who offered to sell us our meals for ten *colones* (then about $1.20) a day per person, as long as we ate what she served us. Mostly it was rice, beans, tortillas, sour cream, and fried plantain, plus an occasional surprise like fermented fungus juice or pig's head stew (with hairy ears). At least I never found any eyes (other than those of fish) staring back at me or live things crawling around. Her two other local customers usually seemed to search their meals for something they feared to find but apparently never did – at least while I was observing.

Our weathered cinderblock house beside the pasture runway, generously loaned to us by the owner of the degenerated hacienda and airline, looked as if its occupants had fled suddenly. Pots of food covered with mold still nourished some of the less finicky rats. Closets bulged with clothes and hats and spiders in all shapes and sizes. The owner's father had died, leaving his once-successful hacienda and once-successful airplane company to his only son, a heavy drinker who didn't care much for work and allowed everything to deteriorate.

As the first night wore on, unidentified noises grew louder and closer. The flickering candlelight (there was no electricity) intensified the darkness and shadows. Frogs, lizards, cicadas, centipedes, beetles, birds, and who knew what else buzzed, screeched, clicked, and droned indoors and out. In the middle of the night, a scuffling sound kept advancing from the hallway closer and closer to my bed, so I lit a candle to investigate. A silky brown vampire bat was pathetically hopping and crawling toward my bed, and luckily for me, making too much noise. It was probably used to easy dining on horses and cattle but had made a fatal mistake with an insomniac gringo armed with a hefty, snakeproof Durango cowboy boot. I left the squashed bat near my bed as a negative advertisement for other would-be diners. Hopefully they would know that of the three possible hosts, I was the worst.

A multitude of belligerently territorial roosters clucked, and then a herd of emotionally desperate cows on their way to their calves in the corral mooed, to announce a new day. The Moritan day for humans began before sunrise and ended not long after sunset. Wristwatches, even the ones that worked, were merely a status symbol, not important like a pair of boots or a machete or a saddle and horse.

Luis, the hacienda foreman, could have been cast as a cowboy in a Marlboro commercial, only he wore a machete and smiled a lot and didn't smoke. He had the lightest skin and straightest, whitest teeth in Morita. He possessed some sort of magic with the animals, taming them and curing them and getting them to go peaceably where they were supposed to go. Chontales, the old helper who rode a burro, got the same jobs done only by spurring and yelling and whipping.

By observing Luis and Chontales, I began to learn a little about horses and cattle and how to use a machete. I learned to recognize which mud holes were superficial and which could swallow horse and rider. At first I laughed at deep mud, but I gained respect for it when the hacienda's 800-kilo Brahman bull, worth $20,000, got so stuck he died from exhaustion while rescuers failed to extricate him by hand, horse, oxen, and tractor.

I also learned about certain wasps, biting ants, thorns, and poison-sap trees; about hidden barbed wire, fast-flowing rivers, and fer-de-lance pit vipers; and about witchcraft. As soon as I thought I was becoming sort of savvy, a saddle cinch would break, or I'd get whacked across the face with a thorny branch covered with biting ants, or would bite into the wrong end of the same kind of fruit someone else was eating and burn my lips with caustic sap.

I was better at sea than on land, and a lot more comfortable. At that time, most Costa Ricans feared sharks much more than vampire bats or pit vipers or jaguars, and lobster had little monetary value, so the coastal reefs were still intact. I was the only one for miles with a mask and fins. Few people had even seen them. They called my snorkel a "chimney." After returning from a quick trip to San José with a spear gun (and flashlight), I began to provide seafood from the reefs near the point for some of the local people and in this way gained rapport with the subjects of my "research," becoming more a competent peer and friend than foreign tourist.

Strain developed between my fellow North American students and myself. They needed me desperately as interpreter and I needed desperately to have my own space, peace, and freedom. They were buddies from the same university, and I was the odd one out. They were going to do a joint project in human genealogical lines, while I was going to try to achieve some cultural insights as a "participant observer." This soon precipitated our separation, still friends, but on different teams. After about a month, the other students left for a cattle ranch closer to their subjects, and I went to live about a mile and a half away from "town" with my contact-friend Chinto, a 5-foot-3, 130 pound "jungle animal," as he laughingly referred to himself. He'd invited me to help him plant his rice crop in exchange for room and board plus seven colones (almost a dollar!) a day. He would have taken a loss by hiring me if it hadn't been for the seafood I now and then provided his family.

Stabbing with a pointed pole through the ground-litter of charred branches and tree trunks to make holes in which to plant five grains of rice, hour after hour under the unrelenting sun, caused me to give up on hygiene and frequently attack Chinto's water-filled gourd. The blisters that erupted on my fingers and palms made him laugh hysterically and gave me an acceptable excuse for resigning temporarily.

Chinto would have to finish alone, since the children of the farm were only big enough to work as little live scarecrows to keep the black *diablo* birds and the doves and the parrots from digging up and eating the seeds or sprouts. While the children banged on pieces of metal roofing, Chinto made war banners out of dead snakes, vultures, and a sloth. After the first bird attacks were repelled, it would then be a backbreaking struggle to clear the rice field of strangling vines and choking weeds.

Some herbicides could kill some weeds without killing the rice, but the worst weeds were immune and absurdly fast-growing. The more I learned about local agriculture, the more I learned about the epic battles people worldwide had to wage against weeds, pests, plagues, and the elements, which in my opinion were locally invincible but somehow had to be overcome if the humans there were to survive. The people of Morita, on the very edge of what could be considered their "niche," stubbornly insisted on battling the odds.

Watching Chinto return from his field late every afternoon, drenched in sweat, stained with ash, slightly bent over with backache and fatigue, with maybe a swollen cheek or eye or lip from a wasp sting, I wondered whether it was really worth it. Was human habitation in such a place desirable or even feasible?

I wouldn't have survived a week on my own. It was taxing enough for me sleeping with Chinto in the thatched *choza* (the small, typical Moritan house), up on the platform with the chickens, above the pigs, calves, and dogs. Chinto spent his weekends hunting for *tepezcuintles* (large, spotted rodents), which made for excellent eating, or harpooning fish in the rivers. At night, usually on weekends, he would often drink too much at La Pichinga, and then he would fight or run into unforgiving obstacles or say things that might cost him a friend. I felt lucky to avoid conflict with him during these times. Wild-eyed, he would pry the caps off the beer bottles with his canines (he had no front teeth) and insist that I drink from his offered bottle and then buy him another.

I became very close friends with Chinto's widowed mother, Doña Miranda, who loved to talk with a listener who hadn't already been numbed by her philosophies and advice. She also loved to cook for someone who would actually taste her food and complement her on her cooking. Chinto and his brother Tino and sister Rosi were too busy or frustrated or hungry all the time to pay much attention to her talk or to appreciate how her meals actually tasted.

Doña Miranda also secretly enjoyed letting her silvery waist-long hair down every evening in front of me, especially after I'd commented on how pretty it was. While brushing her hair, she would giggle and tell me a story or offer advice. "You know that can't be true about people visiting the moon," she would say, her deeply wrinkled brown face grinning with ancient wisdom. She was responding to the news that astronauts had landed on the moon in 1969 – three years before our conversation. "Not only could people never get there, but God wouldn't let them. A long time ago people built a big tower to reach the sky, and God knocked it down. Those scientists think they're so intelligent, but they're nothing to God. God makes the moon and the sun and the stars go round and round, and people would maybe like to reach them, but they can't, so they invent stories about it, that's all."

Doña Miranda gave me much more accurate advice on what company to avoid and warned me to be especially careful of any person with witchcraft. I believe she was particularly kind to me because she hoped I might strike up a relationship with her 20-year-old daughter Rosi, who had a 4-year-old son and no husband. When Rosi daily began to make it obvious that she was perfectly willing to treat me as more than a guest, I found my relationship with the family increasingly awkward.

One day Chinto's skinny brother Tino insisted I join him in a soccer game. Rural Moritan *futbol*, not to be confused with North American football, was a vastly rougher sport than soccer. Though the rules were those of soccer, they were often disregarded, and fierceness replaced sportsmanship. This "jungleball" was played to prove courage, physical stamina, daringness, and the ability to smash into another person and get up again.

I felt fortunate that, when the Moritan team asked me to play that day, I was fresh from college where I'd played varsity soccer. I forded the Morita River and walked a couple miles with Tino to the dark-green playing field/pasture. My confidence began to fade and I became nervous when I saw about a hundred saddled horses tied up under the trees. About as many people sat or stood in clusters and talked and laughed excitedly. Brightly clothed women arrived carrying parasols to defend themselves and their babies from the merciless sun. Wood fires sent up heavy smoke that smelled enticingly of pig fat and corn tortillas. By midmorning, many men beamed with the effects of *chicha* (fermented corn and sugarcane) or local guaro. I was the only light-haired, light-skinned person there, and I quickly gave up trying to be inconspicuous. I must have shaken 50 hands before the other team from up in the mountains rode in with their families. Like most of the Moritan team members, many dangled cigarettes from their hands or mouths and wore stern expressions.

It wasn't until midday that both teams were dressed and out on the field warming up. Young boys hooted and shrieked and chased the last cows, horses, pigs, and dogs off the playing area. During that time I tried to figure out how to compensate for the patches of thick grass and mud and the otherwise irregular surface of the field, which had just been "mowed" with machetes by 20 men and boys. It was decided by the team captains and a local policeman that the referee hadn't drunk too much guaro and could blow his whistle to start the game.

In college, I had been trained to pass the ball to the open man and get open to receive the passes, but in Moritan jungleball it was more like gang up on the guy with the ball, take it away from him, and kick it in the direction of the goal until somebody gets it in. After half an hour of this, my head was sizzling and dizzy, my vision blurry with sweat, my legs heavy and weak. Running hard after the ball, I stumbled in some loose dirt and lost my balance, clumsily fell forward with arms flailing, and ended with an unsuccessful shoulder roll. When I got up, I felt the complete attention of everyone and the sudden hush was followed by an explosion of wild laughter by players and spectators. They all thought I was acting! No one could be so clumsy! I joined in on the laughter, but at halftime I wisely asked to be replaced.

Besides fearless soccer players, deep mud, bloodthirsty bats, and bad booze, Morita had a few other dangers, as I discovered once while swimming in the ocean with a friend.

"Shark! Jesus, a shark bit me!" my gringo friend Mark, a fellow student, yelled in panic while standing right next to me in chest-deep water. I froze, waiting for my turn. He turned as white as a New England scholar in winter and thrashed frantically toward shore while I followed more calmly (or was I simply more petrified?), worried about attracting attacks on my own vulnerable self.

No fins, no swirly water, no abrasive skin against my legs. Mark's jumping was so energetic that I knew without a doubt that he still had both legs and feet. Up on the beach I made him lie down, which was easy since he was fainting anyway. I made a sand pillow for his head and pushed a lot of sand under his bad leg to raise it as much as I could. Blood poured freely out of one ankle and dyed the sand and his white foot red. The contrast disturbed me. A perfect dime-size hole on the inside of his Achilles tendon bled profusely. Surprise! The hole passed all the way through and out the other side! What could have done this? Examining the wound, I was so intrigued with the mystery that it surprised me when I suddenly realized I'd better take some sort of medical action.

Seeing a woman horseback rider coming our way, I ran down the beach toward her, waving my arms and shouting for help, thus frightening her so badly that she turned around and galloped back to

La Pichinga with a story about a wild gringo trying to assault her on the beach. Luckily, a friend of mine knew that I'd gone swimming and came with his horse cart to investigate. We helped Mark, who I feared was going into shock, into the cart and hauled him back to Morita.

Carlos, the local representative for Alcoa Aluminum, saw the wound and asked his wife Anita to boil some water. "This was a very big stingray," he said. So that was the mystery attacker! Carlos poured steamy water directly into the wound and I expected Mark to scream, but he didn't move. "The ray barb has terribly strong 'cold' that must be heated up." Carlos said. "He doesn't feel the hot water because he has so much cold *pasmo*. Not even the bravest man can withstand the pasmo of the ray, and I'm afraid your countryman will be hurting badly when the poison takes hold."

When Mark began to clutch his leg and whimper and moan with the pain, I decided maybe it was an emergency. Carlos enthusiastically agreed to get the hacienda's leaky aluminum rowboat ready to take Mark the 25-kilometer ocean route to Puerto Nuevo. If he could get some gasoline for the outboard, we could make it in two hours and get there just before sunset. There, we could hitch a ride to the hospital in San Cristobal.

The ocean was beautiful as the low sun highlighted the choppy surface with yellow and orange. Terns dived around schools of jumping bonito and mackerel. Dolphins came to play at the bow. We had loaded Mark with aspirin and acetaminophen, and he almost looked happy despite his throbbing ankle, which made him wince and curse now and then. Fortunately, the outboard didn't fail us, and we didn't run into any of the submerged shoals along the way. Once we reached land we were able to get Mark a three-hour ride to the San Cristobal hospital, where his wound was treated.

On the way back to Morita with Carlos, I realized there was something special about him. I thought I noticed it before – his piratical look, his small black beard, his charming grin, his penetrating black eyes, and the fact that he had a 25-year contract with an international company just to measure an occasional tide. Surprisingly knowledgeable about the ocean, he calmly guided us back through the moonless night past all sorts of navigational hazards. Bioluminescent plankton exploded in blue-white-yellow light as we cut through the horizonless sea. After he had skillfully piloted our boat past the Morita shore-break and into the estuary channel that led to La Pichinga, we celebrated at the bar with several beers. We began kidding each other about buying a decent vessel and going into business together fishing, diving, guiding, and transporting cargo and people by sea. The more we drank and joked, the more we realized that we both truly enjoyed entertaining such a remote possibility. From then on, only half-jokingly, we called each other *socio* (partner).

Chinto's mother, Doña Miranda, scolded me for even joking about considering Carlos as a socio: "You will find out for yourself, someday perhaps – it isn't good for a Christian to talk badly of others, and God forgive me, but I will warn you now – Carlos and his people are not to be trusted."

I didn't listen as much to Doña Miranda then as I might have. Scoundrel or not, Carlos kept doing me favors, got the bartender to give me from the small kerosene-run freezer cold drinks that were reserved for special customers, invited me to Anita's delicious meals, gave me a free haircut – Carlos was tops on my list, right up there with Luis.

After a couple of months in Morita, I felt ready to do some more serious terrestrial exploration alone. I'd been wanting to go south down the coast in search of the hidden Playa del Tunel, or "Tunnel Beach," Carlos had told me about. It bordered the forest his father owned. Luis loaned me a semidomesticated coffee-colored horse that "needed riding," and I took off jolting down the long Morita beach. Where the sand stopped, I dismounted and led the horse slowly up the steep, rocky trail that climbed through old overgrown fields and jungle up to Vulture's Peak, so named for the raptors that sunned themselves with outstretched wings on the trees at the crest. It was an amusing coincidence that at this point most animals and people arriving from below were exhausted and soaked in sweat and wanted just to lie down in the shade somewhere. The sight of patient carrion-eaters peering down from the branches encouraged renewed energy.

The climbing path stole my breath and replaced it with the hot damp aromatic essence of jungle, decaying vegetation, and very organic dirt. At the top, an opening in the dense growth let a precious breeze come through from the ocean, and I could see way back and down the long Morita beach. My meandering horse's tracks were the only ones besides those of two near-naked children who were fishing with hand lines by the estuary. Continuing on, I met a smiling young man coming from the other direction and eating a banana. He handed me one of the others he was carrying, and once again I felt wonderful to be among such friendly people who were so open to strangers. The wild banana, orange-red, short, fat, was exceptionally sweet, with a unique flavor that vividly reminded me of a special candy I used to love as a child and hadn't enjoyed since. That blissful taste caused recall of profoundly pleasurable scenes and people in California a dozen years earlier.

Dense green ferns and thick, smooth balsa trees shaded much of the trail on both sides of Vulture's Peak. Fluorescent, velvety red-and-black plush tanagers flitted from branch to branch. Shimmering blue, green, and turquoise hummingbirds with long white tails raced from flower to flower and hovered gracefully over each bloom. Yellow, green, brown, and black chestnut-mandibled toucans and fiery-billed aracaris flapped and sailed in single file, from treetop to treetop. Green and yellow parrots and parakeets screeched loudly at each other, competing greedily for the small, yellow, round fruits of a tree bursting with them. The filtered light that trickled down through the high, feathery branches of the *gavilán* trees was full of noisy, glittery insects. A giant, brilliant-blue morphus butterfly floated and flickered by silently, just a few feet away from me, making me stop still, hold my breath, and open my eyes and mouth wide with awe. When was the last time I'd done this, sitting in a classroom?

The trail leveled, and so I remounted, soon passing two thatch-roofed chozas with blue-gray smoke rising from their chimneys. A whimpering child stood in front of one. I asked him what was wrong, but he was too upset to respond. I asked where his mother was, in a loud enough voice to attract anyone close who might be listening. No one appeared and I reluctantly rode on; for the first time in Morita, I felt seriously unsettled, as if someone were staring at me intensely and disapprovingly. "There are eyes where you least expect," Doña Miranda would say. Later, I would learn that my sixth sense was operating perfectly and that Doña Miranda had not merely been overly protective in her words of warning.

Continuing on, I passed a field full of burned, fallen trees with the greenest, thickest stalks of corn I'd ever seen shooting up between them. Close by, I could hear the methodical whack of steel into the flesh of one of the gigantic old trees. I wondered how long it took a man swinging an ax to fell such a defenseless colossus. My sadness was somewhat diminished by the consolation that at least there were no chainsaws or bulldozers – yet. From the trail, looking above the flowering corn, I could see to the south a spectacular panorama of the coast – *Piedra Cachelote* (Whale Rock), *Isla del Faro* (Light Island), and the *Osa* (Bear) Peninsula. The ocean shimmered silver-blue, and the rising cumulus clouds shone dazzlingly white in the light-blue sky.

Soon after fording the swift and clear Quebrada Chica, I found the trail leading down a couple of hundred feet to the hidden beach Carlos had described. This "easy access" was crowded with vegetation and was hardly detectable to someone like me who had different notions as to the definition of "trail," but I found no other alternative. My horse didn't want to go first down the steep leaf-covered mountainside, so I had to lead him close behind me, which I disliked because often we would both slide down a bit on the loose dirt and rock. I wondered if there would be time to leap out of harm's way if my companion lost his footing.

The trail passed through deep shade cast by the canopy of majestic trees, draped with thigh-thick vines, pineapple-like epiphytes and bromeliads (both types of plants that derive nutrients from air and rain and use other plants as hosts), and flowering orchids. The forest floor was cool, damp, and dark and smelled strongly of earth and leaves, flowers, and fruit. Shiny little black and lime-green poison-dart frogs hopped away from our feet as we inched down the path. Blue and orange land crabs clicked their pincers and spread them out menacingly as they, too, wisely retreated. Small, dark forest birds flitted and chirped among the undergrowth. Now and then in scarce patches of light, my eyes caught glimpses of red legs, a royal blue cap, a yellow fringe around an eye, black-and-white striped feathers. Cicadas and horned beetles and six-inch grasshoppers tried to drown each other out in a great variety of sounds. Creatures scurried or fluttered through the leaves on both sides of the trail. Even though in many places the ground cover was sparse due to lack of sunshine, and even though I went very slowly, I could only hear, not see, the vast majority of the life that was present.

Never in my life had I been aware of the wonder and value and limits of human sensory perception. Near the bottom of the trail, high in a gnarly old mango tree, a troop of white-faced monkeys chattered and fidgeted. A few shook branches defiantly and made angry faces at me. Others jumped to other trees and scrambled away fearfully. Naively, I wondered why they feared me.

Under the mango tree, the trail ended in a swampy marsh where the grass was taller than a man. Guessing the closest route to the ocean from the sound of breaking waves, I chopped my way until I emerged into glaring sunlight glinting off sea and sand.

I stood there nearly blinded for a minute before mounting my agitated horse and galloping down the beach, which lay at the foot of towering cliffs and steep, forested hills. A small waterfall came down a shiny rockface, forming a small pool in the shade of a tree, where fragrant white flowers scented the area. The water, which Carlos had guaranteed was excellent for drinking, was cool and delicious. As I doused my head, I felt deep gratitude for finding such a place, with absolutely no garbage, no sign at all of humans, fresh delicious water with no trace of contamination, between incredible forest and incredible ocean.

A dark hole in a cliff jutting into the ocean turned out to be a deep, natural passageway the height and breadth of two people. I entered and followed its curve within the mountain. To my joy, the passage opened up to a new scene every bit as beautiful 20 meters down the beach. So this was the natural tunnel where Carlos facetiously said Captain Morgan had hidden pirate treasure. In a shady cove, I tied my horse to a branch, laid down on smooth driftwood, and slept.

When my eyes opened, I saw two brown, furry creatures – known locally as *tolomucos* – resembling a cross between a small brown bear, black panther, and mongoose. They stopped and stared at me, and when I moved slightly, they ran up a tree, looked at me again, climbed down, and scrambled noisily through the dry leaves on the hillside. Sitting on a big driftwood tree trunk, I ate the plantain, cheese, rice, beans, and tortillas Doña Miranda had wrapped in a banana leaf for me. I took in the surrounding scenery and found that I was deeply attracted to everything I'd encountered since my arrival in this corner of Costa Rica – the unspoiled ocean, beaches, reefs, forests, the thriving wildness, and the simplicity of the residents' lifestyle. It seemed as if I'd finally found a place that was real, where people knew how to live for life's sake, not for misleading and eventually disappointing diversions.

Life was somehow so rich, powerful, and rewarding here. And it was available to anyone who wanted to experience it, without (as I, perhaps unfairly, judged many of them) bored and boring professors, without thick, unfriendly textbooks, without artificially heated classrooms. In the little cove, half-formed ideas began to flower into conclusions that fascinated and frightened me. Quit college? With a brother getting his Ph.D. at Harvard and another brother at Cornell? And do what? What would I do here? How could I get my parents' blessing? Was their blessing necessary?

Whatever lay in store for me, I felt deep inside I was fast approaching an important crossroad. I'd even possibly discovered a niche on the planet that I wasn't even sure existed for me. I knew I was in some new sort of mental trouble. That wasn't really so surprising to me, as I'd been in some sort of physical, psychological, or spiritual trouble ever since I could remember.

I cut open a young, green coconut and lustily gulped down its clear, sweet water. After a short swim in the ocean, I rinsed off in the waterfall and headed back to Morita, a big boyish smile on my face and a welcome lightness in my heart.

Chapter Two

Fitting in (or not) – fulfilling my destiny (maybe)

Perhaps there was something intrinsically problematic about me . . . some peculiar hard-wired genetic material or program, or something that would make perfect sense to psychiatrists, psychologists, or astrologists upon hearing how I became enchanted by the ocean, the rainforest, and the people of Costa Rica.

Such a rowdy, gregarious, dirt clod-throwing kid – how did I end up so antisocial, anti-Vietnam, anti-military, anti-industrial, anti-plastic? I *loved* the material luxuries – the fast food, the supermarkets, and the rock concerts – of the United States. Why would I trade them for a non-air-conditioned Central American jungle?

Of course, I had no accurate concept of reality concerning exactly how very crazy it would be to try and hang on to the foreign paradise I'd thought I'd discovered, or how difficult it might be to protect it and keep enjoying it sustainably. I think I sensed from the beginning, deep down, that I, like many others, would learn what it felt like to think and plan and work, maybe for a whole lifetime, for a better life that I would never quite get to live. But wasn't that rather normal for humans?

Maybe, I thought, it was only natural for people to find or at least search for the kind of people and places that suited them. But then there were those like me (a Pisces) born in freezing, oceanless Ohio on the day that comes only once every four years who seemed to have a hard time wherever they were.

We moved to California when I was 2. There, while the other kids played with bikes and toy cars, I fooled around with fossils, bones, rocks, leaves, and plastic dinosaurs in our backyard, which was a big field where deer came to eat the licorice-tasting anise. Our black border collie, Nicky, ran after mountain lions. There were crystals and arrowheads; huge oak trees; a nearby ocean with life-filled tide pools, shells, and fossil whalebones. There were foothills and canyons, kumquats, persimmons, and poison oak. There were unexplored caves, and candy bars that we could buy at the fire station halfway out on our exploratory hikes. For me there was no better place, and I cried when we had to move to Illinois, where my father was going to work.

Somehow my parents and three brothers and I (number three) stuffed all our possessions into a small orange-and-white U-Haul cart and a station wagon, which my father called "The Blue Streak." My parents had a drink, hugged each other, and smashed empty wineglasses into the fireplace in a ritual they didn't explain to anybody. Nicky chased us down the road for an agonizingly long time and I knew his paws would be bleeding. He was my best friend, and knowing he was destined to live out on someone's ranch didn't make me feel much better.

The world we drove through – tall, green pine forests, snow-covered volcanoes, cold blue lakes, and endless scorched lava flows – got better and better, and when we reached Yellowstone, I decided I was going to be happy again, on the condition that I could pet one of those fantastic furry bears that we kept stopping for. I whined until my father yelled, and I became morose again. He wouldn't let me have any elk antlers because they were too big, but he finally did let me have some deer antlers.

I was always trying to touch and acquire nature and have it around me, alive and not. My collections slowly grew. When we moved to sunny Florida after a year in icy Illinois, I had my own room, and it became a museum with things I found or had been given, or bought from magazines with allowance money. I had shelves of rocks and shells, Indian artifacts, fish in jars of formaldehyde, a bird skeleton, a cat skull, a live boa, an aquarium with fish I captured on the reef, a live iguana, a stuffed iguana, live turtles, and caimans. I had a human friend who was like me. He was from India but thought he was really from Neptune or possibly Uranus. It made little difference to him or me. While we competed in acquiring new additions for our collections, our peers discussed cars and planes and guns and football and girls.

South Florida in the 1960s was a paradise because the natural environment was still so healthy. The reefs were full of colorful fish and lobster, the coastal waters still clean and clear. Spending blissful hours in the warm, calm summer sea, marveling at the awesome beauty of the marine world, I soon learned to provide easy lobster meals for my family. At first, I grabbed the spiny lobsters with gloved hands in waist-deep water right in front of the beach club where my neighbors and I went swimming, 20 minutes by bicycle from my house. Then I had to swim out to the first reef and learn to clear the pressure in my ears to get the "bugs" in the caves 15 feet deep. Then I had to work hard swimming way out (never alone) in shark-infested waters to search for them on the third reef at 25 feet. Eventually, as the crustacean population continued to dwindle, even that grew fruitless, and we would have to travel four hours by car to reach the nearest good lobstering.

Fishing was similar. The huge tarpon, which once thrashed through exploding schools of silver mullet right next to shore, moved elsewhere. "Empty" fields thickly covered by natural sea grape, saw grass, and Australian pines were leveled and covered with concrete high-rises. Gray fossil sand was dredged up from between the reefs and spread out to extend the eroding natural beaches. The tourists didn't know the difference, but we did.

When I was older, my parents sent me away to boarding school in Massachusetts. Kept indoors by frigid weather, I sought adventure by playing drums (which I'd practiced with teachers for several years) with a "rock-blues" band, privately and publicly. Conforming to the then-popular style of anti-establishmentarianism, we played Hendrix, Cream, Doors, Blues Project, Grateful Dead, Buffalo Springfield, Jefferson Airplane, Country Joe and the Fish, and Beatles. A man from Boston offered me a future of money, lights, and fame. Did I want to be a rock star? I wasn't a night person, doubted my resistance to possible personal corruption, and feared the probably violent reaction from my parents and disappointment from my brothers, so I stayed in school instead, got good grades, and stayed out of trouble – for quite awhile.

A friend from the neighboring all-girl's school visited me in my dorm room one night, and, according to the authorities, I was guilty of failing to slam the door in her face and telling her to go away. We didn't get caught (we didn't "do anything" either, but maybe we would have), but got ratted on, so she was booted and I was put on probation "for my own good." My father pulled me out at the end of the year and decided on my behalf, "Well, maybe it's better to be a big fish in a little pond than a little fish in a big pond." He enrolled me in my old school in Florida and then sent me that summer to Colorado Outward Bound – which first I hated, then loved.

My father had been a hotshot pilot in some war in Europe. He wanted me to learn to fly, like my older brother Kevin. I took a friend along on my first (and last) lesson. My instructor insisted that I fly the plane alone, and after a series of exhilarating vertical climbs and falls, my greenish friend started screaming in the back seat.

My father had also been a hotshot football player back in the Middle Ages when they wore leather helmets. By strongly encouraging me to play varsity football, he probably wanted to have all the "Northeast crap" kicked out of me; for my part I wanted to show him I could get out there and do the manly meat-mashing thing, too. When I wasn't warming the bench, I was tackling around the neck, clipping, getting ground up by others' cleats, seeing stars, etc., but I stuck it out. The highlight of my football career came during homecoming game when a star player begged me to lend him my belt. I had little or no chance of playing in that game anyway, so I took it off and gave it to him. Five minutes later, our tobacco-chewing coach, who used to spit and yell, "Play like you got peach seeds up your rear!" (and later would just spit and yell "Peach seeds!"), called me and sent me in to play, laughing with the other coach about my beltlessness. I didn't care. Out I went, pants falling down, bleachers full, roaring crowd, on my way to achieve glory. The coach had to call me out after a few plays, not out of consideration for me, but to keep from dying of laughter.

For two years, I enjoyed the fantastic companionship of a girl I dreamed of someday marrying, but after she went to college in Connecticut and I in Colorado, she became irretrievable and I tried earnestly, but failed miserably for longer than was good for me or anybody, to fall out of love with her.

At Colorado College, I realized that the mysterious qualities that attracted me so much to the natural sciences were treated by my fellow students and the faculty as mere physicochemical mechanics. To them, zoology, biology, and ecology were merely academic disciplines like geology, chemistry, and physics, devoid of that extra dimension linked to the magic of life. Their easy acceptance of this – and my inability to join them – reinforced my feeling of separateness.

In my first months at Colorado College, I lived in a dormitory on campus, but I soon found it to be noisy, uncomfortable, and stifling. I decided to move off campus, but this change required the blessing of the college psychologist. I puffed out my intellectual feathers while pleading my case during my one unforgettable 20-minute session with her, but she was apparently unimpressed. After I eloquently (I imagined) described all the ways my decadent dorm neighbors had trespassed against me, she locked her clear, unblinking eyes on mine and said prophetically, between frighteningly pregnant pauses, "Don't you think it's really *you* who needs to change? . . . *You* are the one who needs to learn to adapt, to work it out with your roommate and the others on your floor . . . because all of your life you're going to run into similar situations. . . . You can't keep trying to escape from your problems . . . or keep blaming others. . . . You must learn to confront your problems and deal positively with them. . . . We all have to learn to adapt to the world and society we live in."

This was not what I'd been hoping to hear. Confrontation brought out the coward in me. I hated arguments; hated getting almost drafted to Vietnam (I declared myself a conscientious objector); felt too many butterflies in my stomach around fist-fights; distrusted police, doctors, and dentists; felt a grudge against the authorities who had power over me. What I wanted most was to be left alone, to decide on my own what was best for me.

In any case, with or without permission, I moved off campus to seek more benign and less depressing surroundings. At first it didn't help my situation nearly as much as I'd hoped. Drinking beer and smoking on weekends with other lost souls grew old fast. Then I fell in love with a beautiful place in the mountains where I could drink the cold stream water, hear the aspen, smell the vanilla-strawberry ponderosa pines, and see the Milky Way in 3-D. Sometimes I'd go with one or more friends, sometimes alone. Sometimes I'd hike in too far. Sometimes I'd forget something important like my sleeping bag or Fig Newtons. Sometimes it would snow, and the next morning there would be no trail. I had important things on my mind and a wonderful suit of down.

Being a member of an upper-middle-class American family with generous, loving parents, burdened me with the freedom to choose my own path. Of course, I didn't expect to find much empathy with such a problem, and in fact I learned to lie about it in order to adapt more easily in the highly class-conscious world.

Adapt to the world – that's what the college psychologist said I would have to do. Struggling to adapt happily and healthily had been my family story and my own, too. We'd faced a succession of problems, demands, desires, opportunities, to be handled appropriately, to be learned from, to be avoided or adopted, to progress and digress and regress and hopefully progress again. Wasn't this the human drama, the human condition, the human comedy, the human experiment – trying to adapt to a world we neither created nor chose? Or, if life was, as some believed, the way we projected it, shouldn't we learn better methods of projection?

The psychologist was right about having to learn to adapt, but she underestimated my capacity for discovering coping mechanisms and for choosing alternative situations to adapt to. The natural sciences department, inside its huge stone, steel, concrete, and glass box, treated life forms as complex organic molecules marching out of the primordial soup. I couldn't adapt to that all-of-a-sudden-magic "soup" business (I wanted to know who the cook was!), so I changed to the anthropology department, which had more ivy growing around its domain.

Shortly thereafter, I embarked on my first trip to Costa Rica. There I met Luis, Chinto, Doña Miranda, Carlos, and the other Moritans. They introduced me to a strange, beautiful, and fascinating world I would never have imagined, a world that attracted me in ways I couldn't explain.

After three months in Morita, I had to return to San José to satisfy the academic demands of the program that had made my trip possible, to submit a report on my fieldwork. It was probably one of those common, absurd days when I was seeing the cement- and exhaust-filled world, and envisioning my place in it, as ridiculous. I was bored by the other students' oral presentations and decided to attempt a different approach. After explaining basically where I'd been and what I'd been doing, I asked for the audience's participation, to please question me about any aspects of the Moritans they were particularly interested in. After one question on archaeological sites, there were no more questions, so I knew I was in trouble. Instead of attempting to continue by reducing my Moritan "subjects" into categories that would satisfy the concise mechanistic methodology of the professor, I floundered and said slowly, hoping for someone to bail me out, "Well, if there are no more questions . . . thank you," and left the podium to take my place among my fellow students. My irregular presentation seemed to leave some embarrassed and others pleased.

For most of my educational career, I worked hard to achieve high recognition in the form of grades. Though my written report was rewarded with an A and the personal congratulations of the program director, my oral fiasco landed me a C for the term. It made me realize that something really had happened to me back there at Playa del Tunel. Could it be that I no longer cared so much about how the lords of the status quo judged me? Could it be that I was steering away from the established channel of "finish college, get a good job, make good money, become somebody"? If I was no longer so interested in "becoming somebody" in the U.S.A., then who would I become? And how and where? I did know this – I was in trouble. But that wasn't really so surprising to me. I was getting rather used to it.

I needed to follow this experience with something new and exciting, so on returning from Costa Rica, I applied and was accepted to the University of Hawaii, where I planned to study the cultural anthropology of Oceania and Pacific Ocean marine biology, about which I was extremely enthusiastic.

After three months in Costa Rica, the United States seemed so luxurious, with, for example, its giant, comfortable cars cruising smoothly over superwide highways, highways that were fenced, lighted, patrolled, and lacked potholes. Supermarkets offered all kinds of food and drink, plus tools, clothes, fishing supplies, Pepto-Bismol, binoculars, tennis balls, videocassettes, lawn furniture, and suitcases – all in one place! Lots of people worked indoors in air-conditioned offices and factories, no sweat, no bugs, no mud.

What a difference between industrial countries like the United States and agricultural Third World countries like Costa Rica. But even though Costa Rica seemed *too* organic and *too* chaotic, I felt my most serious qualms about having to find a neat and sterile desk job in one of those hermetically sealed buildings with reflective windows and wear a full set of ironed clothes and hard shoes – every day they said – and try to make sense out of the papers my boss gave me.

One day my father, who'd been drinking, gathered my mother, two of my brothers, and me around his giant illuminated globe and asked, "How'd you like to go somewhere?" The last time he did that we went to Alaska. My poor mother (she was the only female in the six-member family and so suffered terribly amidst us often-inconsiderate macho brutes) said, "Well, I know you don't want to go where I want to go, anyway, so I might as well keep my mouth shut."

"Where do you want to go, Mom?" I asked.

"Paris."

"Ugh. Too populated," I said, speaking selfishly. None of us except my father had been to Europe, but by my other two brothers' silence (my eldest brother was busy in Cambridge at the time), it looked like no one besides my mother was interested in Europe. On the other hand, we males had something in common: We were all curious to explore the South Pacific, to see if there really was someplace resembling Bali-Hai on Earth. My mother was outvoted, again. My older brother agreed to work it all out with the travel agency, and we eventually left for Fiji, our first serious stop.

In Bora Bora, I met a yacht captain who was down one crewmember due to an ear infection. He was heading for Honolulu via the Tuamotus and Marquesas. On the slim chance he might accept an inexperienced crewmember, I offered my services as fisherman, diver, and dishwasher. He told me what he most needed was provisions and beer money and that if I could get him $800 I could go. After a remarkably peaceful pow-wow with my parents, it was agreed upon, with the condition that I arrive in Honolulu in the fall in time for registration at the University of Hawaii. The captain said he would do his best and my father signed over the $800 in travelers' checks and wondered, probably, whether he'd ever see me again and whether it would be his fault if he didn't.

My family took off from Bora Bora by plane for the United States while I waited for the yacht Irish Mist to depart. Those two weeks in Bora Bora were hard on me since I spoke almost no French or Tahitian and the wahines were so beautiful and amiable. Passage to Ahe and the Marquesas was like most great adventures: sometimes uncomfortable and dangerous, usually so-so, and occasionally so exhilarating that it made all the rest worthwhile. Captain Gordon considered me his cabin boy, since I was seven years younger than the next youngest crewmember, the Mandarin-American navigator. I washed dishes, pumped out the bilge (manually), stood my watches, caught fish, cleaned fish, and tried to stay out of Gordon's way. His young and beautiful blonde wife (his fourth) was the only woman aboard, and though she was very friendly with me, she didn't help matters at all by sunbathing nude and by being totally ruthless when she applied coconut oil to all that exposed skin.

I spent long hours every day on the bowsprit looking out, being sprayed by the vast, warm Pacific, wondering, thinking, trying to plan. I was headed for another dormitory, more classrooms, with more buzzing fluorescent lights that I was particularly allergic to, more professors; I hoped they wouldn't be so boring. Two more years, and then what? What was truly worthwhile in life? Why had my father given me Herman Hesse's <u>Siddhartha</u> for the second time? Who *was* my father really – wounded war hero or detoured seeker, or both? Who did he really want me to be, a business executive or a man of virtues? He wasn't an example of someone in whose footsteps I wanted to follow (nor did he wish me to), so why, it being *my* life, did I care so much about what went on in *his* mind?

After nearly two months of high-seas adventure and misadventure, we pulled up at the Ala Wai Yacht Harbor in Honolulu. Everyone left to eat and drink, but as if completing my on-board responsibilities and trying to make up for putting a sail on backwards and nearly killing the captain with a flying boom I couldn't control with the winch, and offending everyone by farting toxic gasses after eating a flying fish that I'd collected on the deck and mistaken for a fresh one, I stayed to clean up the barbarously messy yacht before I left. I finally gathered up my old rodent-chewed backpack, the sun-bleached shark jaws I had cut out of an oceanic whitetip I caught and ate in the Doldrums, a one-piece sculpted wooden saddle I had purchased in the Marquesas after successfully riding on it all day to and from Typee Village, and a few Marquesan rosewood bowls and cowries for my family, and debarked.

I checked in at the YMCA and called Mark, an old Florida surfing/diving buddy who was living out on the North Shore with his parents. He told me to quit school and help him and his family build a fishing boat on the beach. I told him that I wasn't going to become a derelict dropout surfer bum like him, but that I would visit him as soon as I had the chance.

The following day at registration for classes at the university, I was fairly sure that everything was perfectly normal for normal people; but for me it was a nightmare. Although still rocking on my sea legs, I was able to locate the computer printouts of the classes and the students in each one. Out of the five courses I signed up for, the enrollment lists for the three that were my top priority – the ones that were my reason for being there – did not include my name. In the administration office, everyone was too busy to talk to me, and I was just one of 25,000 students (or was it 125,000?). I learned eventually that for that fateful year there had been a computer malfunction that accepted people like me into courses that were supposed to be reserved for "priority status" juniors and seniors. They told me that all of us duped rejects could get full refunds on our prepaid registration fees if we insisted. Instead of reacting with all the rage dictated by my rising levels of anger and testosterone, I took advantage of my plight as a good excuse to flee the crowded campus and city and do some serious surfing.

Mark picked me up the next day, drove me an hour and a half out to Mokuleia, and started me out right away, in green uniform decorated by a hundred burn holes, teaching me to operate the acetylene torch to cut pieces of steel for his family's 70-foot "ark." Mark's father, Carroll, had all the plans for the future tuna boat in his head. Though the neighbors sometimes thought he was crazy, they also highly respected him for his vision and courage, except when that vision involved early-morning or late-night grinding or sandblasting.

Juggling the demands of his landlady, navy surplus auctions, loan agencies, the local municipality, and the Environmental Protection Agency was much more demanding on Carroll than the design and construction of his vessel, which he did in his "spare" time after working every weekday as a nuclear submarine engineer at Pearl Harbor.

I think my contributions to the construction of the Day Star averaged out with the destruction I caused. Two years later, welded to a sled, the boat was shoved down the beach by five bulldozers and sent over the reef into the Pacific. I felt proud to have played a small part in the albacore boat's extremely successful career. The owners and crew of the Day Star would eventually prove that commercial quantities of tuna could be caught profitably by trolling with lures, a method that led to the capture of more target fish than the use of nets and didn't harm dolphins or other nontarget species.

When I had called my parents to inform them of my latest detour from academia, they sounded resigned to my waywardness and weren't nearly as upset as I'd imagined. Though the prospect of my becoming a college dropout bothered them, they were mostly relieved I survived the trip from Bora Bora. It was at times like these that I realized how fortunate I was to have such supportive parents. More for their sake than mine, I planned to return to college – I didn't know where – for the next semester, but in the meantime I would work and surf, eat and sleep, party on weekends, and try not to think or worry too much about my future.

Nevertheless, I still thought and worried. Every day that passed, I wondered how I would pull out of my pleasant entropic slide. As I became closer friends with the little tribe of local surfers, part-time artists, musicians, and carpenters of the North Shore, most of whom received welfare checks, I became dangerously comfortable. They drank much beer, smoked much pot, and cared little for the status-quo existence of money-and-success-oriented overachievers. Why care so much for the future when the present was so pleasant? But I couldn't help it, I did differ from them: I was concerned with stability, long-term growth, and security. I wanted to achieve something more. They called that "up-tight, paranoid, haole talk," and I knew they were at least partially right.

Around that time, I received a stained and wrinkled letter from Costa Rica. Barely able to decipher it, I understood it was from Carlos and that he was telling me that his father lived near the beach that I liked so much and wanted to sell his land because he was old and sick. The old man wanted the equivalent of $50 an acre for 60 acres. Carlos also mentioned something about a suitable port for a small boat in front of the property. That sounded enticing to me in ways I couldn't pinpoint, and I wrote back and told him not to sell it to anyone for at least three months until I communicated with him again.

The more I thought about it, the more it interested me. The investment was small, the financial risk small, and the general potential great. Maybe I could go live there for a while, search for some way to live, and if it didn't work out, sell later for possibly a large profit, since the Coast Highway and Alcoa Aluminum were soon to descend upon Morita.

I had enough savings to buy the land, and I decided it would be better invested in Costa Rica than in a car or bank or the Mustang Saloon in Las Vegas. I'd never spent $3,000 for anything, but this might be worth it, and I decided to investigate seriously. To do so, I coaxed my parents to give me their mixed blessing, and after six weeks of intensive language study in Cuernavaca, Mexico, I headed on down to Costa Rica, a lot more self-assured, partly because of the language study and also maybe because I'd had more experience of the world than when I'd first gone to Morita.

When I found myself once again clutching the co-pilot's seat and sweating as we swooped down to land on the Moritan grass runway, I appreciated again the fragility of life and the vulnerability of my person. This time, though, armed with better communication capability, some money, and foreknowledge of the people and place, I felt much better. My Moritan friends seemed glad to see me again (I shook a hundred hands in the first couple of days back) and were genuinely excited with the gifts I brought – blue jeans, pocket knives, boots, nylon rope, snorkeling equipment, soccer balls. Most things from the United States were considered almost sacred, and news of my gifts spread quickly over an unbelievably large area. Luis, thrilled with his Buck knife, explained to me that nobody, not even the richest ranchers, gave away things like those, much less to poor people. That made me feel rather important, which was nice for a change.

Carlos, as Alcoa's representative in Morita, was able to offer me one of the two small, empty houses next to his, which belonged to Alcoa. I gladly accepted. He and his family were very pleased with the gifts I brought them, and his wife Anita gave me my meals without charge. Carlos borrowed horses from Luis and took me to his father's house near Playa del Túnel between Vulture's Peak and the Quebrada Chica stream. His parents, Don Arturo and Lucía, welcomed me very warmly. Their small choza looked as if it would collapse in a moderate wind, but it was shady and cool inside, which made it very valuable. After I had shaken hands with everybody, Carlos's handsome younger brother Javier, who was Don Arturo's spokesman, took my horse and unsaddled it, washed it by the stream, and led it to a small, weed-filled pasture.

Don Arturo, thin, old, and gray, lay in a hammock made of sacks tied with vines, puffing a corncob pipe he had fabricated. Now and then he would cough and spit. When he spoke, he usually said things he thought out beforehand. Carlos told me how years ago his father was lying in a hammock when an enemy came and slashed him deep across the chest and head with a machete. He lost so much blood that no one thought he would live, and ever since he had been bone thin and sickly. His wife Lucía, about 15 years his junior, was ostentatiously full-breasted, strong, usually smiling, and loquacious. Both treated me very respectfully. Don Arturo explained that he wanted to sell his land because he was too old and sick to work it and because he needed money for medicine and other things of necessity.

Javier took me down to the stream and explained that the water never dried up in the dry season, which is what made the land around it so valuable. He took me through the dark rainforest and showed me many immense trees that he said were ideal for lumber. He took me beyond his choza through pasture and weeds down to where the main stream entered the ocean amid shady coconut palms and smooth black boulders. Yellow, red, and black butterflies fluttered by without hurry. A blue-and-white kingfisher sat on a branch looking down at the stream, watching for a careless prawn. A large flock of pelicans skimmed the surface of the ocean in single file. The soft sound of cool rushing water from the stream blended with the gentle whoosh of waves of the sea dissolving on the boulder beach.

Javier climbed a palm tree skillfully and knocked down a few young coconuts, whose sweet water we drank with deep pleasure. The canopy of branches over the stream opened up at the ocean and allowed a cool breeze to flow through from the forest. Reveling in the cool air and the refreshing drink, I felt as close to paradise as anywhere I'd ever been. I had never seen a place like this on any coast – virgin rainforest sloping down to the sea; fast-running, clear, fresh water flowing over boulders into the ocean; abundant wildlife – and all of it for sale, cheap! I could actually own this if I wanted. Well, not really, not land and trees, rocks and streams and living things – these were not things any human could truly own – but I could have a temporary human authority over them if I so desired.

"You know the real reason this land is exactly what you want?" Javier said in his smooth, deep voice. "You see this boulder beach? You may think that since it's not sand it's no good, but I tell you that it is much better than the sand beaches for loading and unloading people and cargo. About 15 years ago, a man lived here and had a choza on the hill, where he died. He planted these palms. He had a boat here, was a good seaman, used this little port a lot. You could anchor your boat out a ways, because the waves never break there, even when it's rough. You could bring in supplies here when the sea is calm and go fishing whenever you wanted."

I spent that night on a very uneven bamboo bed, scratching the bites of obnoxiously persistent chiggers, and wondering what I was getting myself into. I was tired of being wishy-washy. I had to do something with my life, and this looked very promising. Overriding the negative impact of the miserable night, I decided to buy Don Arturo's land and told him so in the morning.

There was a problem, the first of many. Don Arturo had no title or deed, just a dirty smeared letter of sale signed with an "X" by the man who had sold the land to him many years ago. My brother Kevin recommended to me a supposedly reputable law firm in San José where I had already talked with one of the less important, less expensive lawyers. I purposefully chose Don Manuel because he didn't wear a $300 three-piece suit and drive a Mercedes like the big shots in the same firm. He spoke no English, so he didn't deal with many North Americans. I figured he might not be a rip-off artist, and I was right. I often saw barefoot clients in his office. What I could not stand about him was his infuriating way of always making me and everybody else wait so long to see him. When he told me to be at the office at 9:00 a.m., I wouldn't get to see him until 11:00, or later. He accepted no fault, offered no apologies, felt no shame, and persisted in this frustrating custom.

I soon learned what was known as "tico-time" – the normal delay in everything. When a Costa Rican said, "I'll be right there," he might show up an hour later. When he said, "It will be ready this afternoon," it might be ready the following day. Most Costa Ricans didn't consider punctuality appropriate or praiseworthy, and most North Americans like me could never learn to tolerate it very well. And the poor English and Germans who tried to accomplish something efficiently in Costa Rica always seemed to be steaming and on the verge of exploding.

Don Manuel said that getting clear title to Don Arturo's land would take several months due to the inefficiencies of the Costa Rican bureaucracy. "Several months" probably meant a couple of years. Should I trust Javier and Don Manuel? For all I knew, either one could pull something and leave me with nothing. I knew that in Mexico anything was possible, that the police and the bandidos were equally suspect. In Costa Rica, however, I seemed to perceive a lot more honesty, respect, and fair treatment on all levels. If I was going to go very far here, I had to depend on a lot of people to help me, like Carlos and Javier and Don Manuel.

Don Arturo felt too weak to go to San José to sign the necessary documents, so I arranged a date for Lucía, Carlos, and Javier to help Don Arturo make the three miles by foot and horse to Morita, where Don Manuel would come by plane with the papers to be signed. The plane arrived only two hours late, and Don Manuel did materialize out of it, which made me very happy. While the pilot waited, Javier guided Don Arturo's shaky hand to make a scraggly mark on the letter of sale. Two witnesses signed, and I paid Don Arturo half the total price in cash and signed an agreement to pay the rest after Don Manuel had completed the transferal.

To conclude the personally historic ceremony, everyone shook hands for the second time and prepared to depart. I told Don Arturo and Lucía that they could continue living in their house as long as they liked. I asked them if they would mind if I moved into the extra room in their house later on and they laughed long and hard, which I figured was mostly a reaction to being handed more money all at once than they'd ever seen before. "Of course! The house is yours! If you don't mind living with us oldies, we surely don't mind living with you!" Don Arturo said in as strong a voice as I'd ever heard from him.

As the little manure-splattered Cessna noisily fought its way into the sky, Don Manuel waved back at me and smiled from the co-pilot's seat. Squinting into the bright sunlight and trying to smile, but failing, I waved back, wondering with mounting anxiety what had just happened and where my life was leading me.

Playa del Tunel (Tunnel Beach)

Chapter Three

Initiation - the testing gets tough

The land Don Arturo sold me stretched from the beautiful, sandy Playa del Tunel along several hundred meters of rocky coast bordered by virgin rainforest to the mouth of the Quebrada Chica and followed the stream up the mountain to the trail crossing. I shared the cool, shady watercourse with my neighbor, whom I didn't know yet. Across the Quebrada Chica, close to the ocean, sat a relatively level cornfield with a few charred and rotting tree trunks in it, about three slash-and-burn planted acres surrounded by 150-foot *ajo* (ah-ho) trees teeming with dangling vines, parasitic plants, toucans, and white-faced monkeys. After lamenting the striking loss of primary forest, I envisioned the cornfield as a beautiful coconut grove and felt a great desire to protect the pristine forest that surrounded the clearing. I wanted both sides of that beautiful stream as intact as possible. I very strongly did not want to see any more of those giant trees being felled by my neighbor, who was killing them one by one.

It seemed interesting to me that, while across the ocean my countrymen were sacrificing limbs and lives in the Vietnam War, I was getting all worked up about saving some trees. But, truly, they were such beautiful trees, wonderfully indifferent to human barbarism, and had been for hundreds of years. Now, though, they needed a human like me to protect them from other humans who didn't care for trees.

When I asked my friend Javier who the owner of that land was, he laughed and then scowled. "That's Oscura's land. She probably wouldn't sell it anyway, and you shouldn't even deal with her at all," he said with a strange grimace.

"Why not?" I asked impatiently.

"Do you know what '*Oscura*' means? 'Dark one.' She's not that dark on the outside, but inside she's black. Everyone here knows she's a *bruja*," he said, smiling, anticipating how I'd react to the news that I had a witch for a neighbor.

I laughed at him and said, "Oh, I see, and just what makes you think she's a bruja?"

Javier replied very slowly and politely: "My friend, I know you don't believe there are witches, just as you don't believe in many things. But here, I think you will learn a lot about things you never believed in. I myself have witnessed a neighbor woman in a fit of convulsions spit up two flies and a little frog and cry out, 'Oscura!' and that cured her. Oscura put those little creatures inside of her somehow to do her harm, and it took a *curandero* [healer] to get them out and learn who had done her this evil."

"Javier, you give me your word that you saw that?" I asked in disbelief, wondering how much I could trust this person I'd taken such a liking to.

"Yes. I was there when it happened. And so were others. . . . No man can stand that woman, and those men that she has had have all run away from her and become drunks. She often whips her children with a branch and makes them do things only grown men can do. She knows black magic. She can turn herself into an animal and go spy on people without being noticed. The dogs don't bark because they can't see or hear or smell her. She keeps a sloth in a tree by her house, a sloth that never goes away. The people think that sometimes at night she puts herself in the sloth and goes spying. . . . You have to be careful if you deal with her. She always has problems with neighbors and lawyers. Her land is very good, but she is very bad."

"Will you help me deal with her?" I asked him, getting to the point.

"I'm not on the good side of her, but if you really want, I'll try to help you."

When I met Oscura, I realized with uncomfortable embarrassment that she was the same woman on the horse who had galloped away when I had run toward her on the beach seeking help for my stingray-injured friend. She didn't *look* like a witch (what did witches look like?), and at first she seemed friendly enough, even though for some reason I couldn't look at her eye to eye for more than an instant. Then she began to speak in her peculiar, sarcastic, nasal voice.

"I understand you want to buy my property," she said, snickering slightly.

"Well, yes, I was thinking about it," I admitted. I already felt like I had to defend myself.

"That's too bad, you see, because I really have no desire to sell. The Coast Highway will be passing right by here very soon, and so the land here is going to be worth piles of silver."

"Well, if you decided . . ."

"I already told you I don't want to sell, and even if I did," she said, snickering again and looking at me confidently and mercilessly, "it would be for more money than you'd probably want to spend."

"Fine. Nice meeting you. Adiós," I forced myself to say, but I felt offended at the discourtesy and stubbornness of this woman who owned something I now felt an obsession for acquiring. I couldn't stand to own *half* a stream, and I didn't think I could stand the everyday sound of her ax in that precious forest, which she planned to gradually chop down and burn so she could use the cleared ground for rice, beans, corn, and plantain. Oh, God, those trees! The monkeys, parrots, toucans, ocelots . . . all the animals would flee or die. And the stream. . . . Her pigs would take over.

After two months of encouraging Javier and Carlos to work their charms on Oscura, Carlos finally told me she would sell her 30 acres, but for 10 times what I paid per *manzana* (1.7 acres) for Don Arturo's land.

In trying to squeeze into the local niche as a respected landowner and neighbor, I suppose the testing was inevitable. Whether the testing was consciously carried out by the locals or was the work of my own mind terrorizing itself, I'll never know. But the effects were all too real and unpleasant and seemed to mercilessly exploit my greatest weaknesses and fears.

At the time I learned that Oscura might sell, I began to sleep poorly. The nights were starless and moonless; the tides especially large; the ocean I loved so much was rough, dirty, and strangely unfriendly. Don Manuel was supposed to fly in one day for me to pay what I still owed Don Arturo, but he didn't show up, and I felt bad about bothering the old man in this way, the trip to Morita being hard for him. That night in La Pichinga, two dark, furry vampire bats flew in and the bartender killed them with a broom. He showed me one with blood in and around its mouth. "This blood is not his. I killed it softly. This blood is from another animal," he said, smiling for reasons I didn't know.

Late that night I woke suddenly to some soft sounds outside my room, like a cat walking around brushing against things. Then above me I heard two huge rats hiss and scramble and fight viciously. At the same time, I heard what sounded like a whirlwind outside the house. I slept little after the weird noises faded into silence.

In the morning, I went to buy batteries for my dead flashlight, but there were none for sale at La Pichinga. That night I woke with a cold apprehension as I heard the broken metal latch of the door to my room rattle as if someone on the other side were gently trying to open the door. Fully awake, I heard this three times and then no more – heard nothing except for the thumping of blood pounding through my head.

The next night I was invited to pay respects to a man who had died that day. I was told his wife would feel honored by my presence. Perhaps I was being accepted into the community. I walked with Chinto's brother Tino nearly 3 miles over a muddy trail and waded across the Morito River to get there. About 50 people were standing outside the choza talking and laughing. Inside, illuminated by candles all around, casting exaggerated shadows on the four bare, adze-hewn wooden plank walls, lay an elderly man, dead, gray, on a board bed, with a red scarf tied around his head in an unsuccessful attempt to close his gaping mouth. Most people spent the night there, as was the custom, socializing and taking advantage of the free coffee, rum, and snacks, but I didn't enjoy the scene at all, so I walked back in the dark by myself.

That night I woke in frozen fear again and heard what sounded exactly like a person breathing heavily in the darkness just above my face. Chills shivered up and down my back. I barely forced the question "Who is it?" On hearing the breathing continue, I realized that I was in too much danger to hesitate any longer. Overcoming the strange leadenness that had seized my body, I grabbed my machete and swung out with it, hitting against the top bunk bed. I jumped out of bed and swung again, cursing in English to help defend myself from the foreign darkness. I lit a candle and discovered absolutely nothing.

I spent the following day walking on the beach, wondering what to do. Was someone trying to rob me or scare me? Was I hallucinating as a result of stress? I needed to get more sleep. I took my hammock and headed up into the mountains to where my friend Chinto was planting corn. There, I thought, I could sleep peacefully. I stopped by Doña Miranda's farm for a while, where she told me that a strange black man with long black hair and beard had recently been seen again, the fifth time in about as many months. They said that he ran around naked. "He's as smart as a wild animal and as powerful as three men," she said seriously. "One day we saw what looked like a man run right over a fence and keep going. We never knew what it was for sure."

Suddenly, the cord of Tino's hammock snapped and I fell to the ground, hurting my hip. Everyone laughed but me. "Great!" I said loudly in English. "Just great." This place is getting too weird for me, I thought to myself. I'm going to have to do something fast before I go nuts.

I had no one to talk with about my worsening situation. Those I thought were my friends just laughed at my stories and didn't seem to believe me, except Javier. He said that maybe Oscura or someone was doing this to me to scare me away.

"I think you have already made an enemy here and I think it is probably Oscura," he said. "If it gets worse, either you'll have to leave or look for a curandero to help you."

I wondered about the things Javier had told me while I hiked up to Chinto's cornfield in the hills. I wondered how I could have been having such bad luck. I felt there might really be an evil conspiracy against me, maybe as a way to frighten me away. Or maybe this was some sort of bizarre initiation, a cruel, mind-tormenting ritual that I would have to endure or flee from. Everyone I saw, even my friends, seemed to know a secret that made them smile at me in an unnerving way. Or was it my imagination? Crossing the river, I found a deep pool that lured me for a swim. Later, cooled off after the walk under the burning sun, I felt wonderfully refreshed and relaxed. Then I felt a sharp pain in my foot as I stepped on a rock. On inspection, I saw something black embedded deep in the callous on the side of my foot. The foreign object made walking very painful, but I made it all right to Chinto's mountain house.

Chinto and his young wife Nora greeted me very nicely and said they would be happy to let me stay there for a few days. Chinto took me back to the river to look for prawns. At the river, I explained to him that I preferred not to walk around on the rocks because of my injured foot. He laughed as if calling me a weakling and took off by himself. While waiting for him, I saw a sleek otter swimming gracefully, which I took as a welcome treat and hopefully a good omen. When Chinto returned in an hour he said, "You wouldn't believe what I just saw! – The monkey-man, downstream, crouching on a rock, searching for prawns. When he saw me, he took off running!"

"Chinto," I tried to say calmly, "You're my friend, right?"

"Of course!" he said, as if I were crazy.

"Look, as a friend, I want you to do me a big favor. I want you to tell me the truth. Did you *really* see that?"

"Yes! I'm not kidding," he replied, smiling strangely, but not as if he was lying.

You bastard, I thought, you probably wouldn't tell me the truth anyway, for all I know. My feelings of friendship were turning to hatred.

By the time we had reached his choza, my foot was red and throbbing. My eyes, sunken in their sockets, burned with fever. I showed the little round black object in the sole of my foot to Chinto, and he said that it was the lip of a snail shell broken inside of me. "We'll have to heat it to get the pasmo of the river out so you won't get an infection." He placed a little grease on the wound, lit a candle, held it to my tender foot, and burned the crap out of me.

"You crazy! You burned me!" I screamed and laughed as I yanked my foot away from my friend-turned-enemy.

"I know!" he laughed hysterically. "It's the only way to get the pasmo out! Don't be a coward. Believe me, this will cure you." His wife nodded in agreement that it was the right thing to do – to burn out the "cold," the pasmo.

I stood as much "curing" as I could, which, according to Chinto and Nora, was very little. Later I enjoyed Nora's delicious meal of rice, beans, sour cream, tortillas, prawns, and lemonade and then went to lie down in my own hammock. After about a half a minute, my hammock fell to the ground. My arm hurt badly from the fall, but this time no one was watching (or so I thought), and so at least no one laughed at me. I inspected the ropes of the hammock and saw that on one side almost all the strands were half-cut or frayed by malicious rats or people. I showed the hammock to Chinto, who was closer by than I thought, and he and his friend Cachiro laughed hard and looked at each other conspiratorially, saying it must have been the rats.

I fixed the hammock and tied it again between the two trees about 25 yards from the choza. I was so tired that I went to sleep right away, but in the middle of the night I woke with a terrible cramp in one of my calves. Simultaneously, I was seized by the same nightmarish fear I had experienced for the last three nights. What was up? Footsteps in the tall grass several yards away, slow and sure, a two-legged creature, coming toward me! My heart pounded audibly as I lay there feeling completely vulnerable, eyes bulging, throat swollen and thick, trying in vain to see something besides darkness, with a cramp that screamed for relief. It was like one of those childhood nightmares in which I desperately wanted and needed to escape from an ill-intentioned pursuer but couldn't get my legs to respond or my mouth to scream for help. The footsteps stopped, and I felt or imagined a malevolent stare bearing down on me through the pitch-black night. Could it be that wildman? Was it Oscura? A thief? A prankster? After an interminable time, which I spent in agony and fear, praying for help from God, whom I wished I knew a whole lot better, the footsteps resumed, but heading away from me, retreating as slowly and surely as they had approached.

I lay there a long time, a victim of fear more acute than I'd ever experienced, defeated and defenseless. Little by little I stretched my cramped leg. Then a cold wind came and brought a rain that soaked me. I got out of my hammock and went to wake up Chinto, who prepared me a place to sleep on some boards beside sacks of husked corn. I told him what happened, and he just laughed and said it was probably an ox that scared me. I covered myself with a canvas tarp and managed to get a couple hours of sleep.

The blast of a transistor radio woke me at 4 in the morning – getting-up time for most local farmers, who were proud of their work-courage-manliness-vigor. Nora had already been up for 20 minutes lighting the fire and preparing breakfast in pots and pans hovering over the flames. She had made no noise at all. But when the man of the family got up he had to turn on the radio full blast, in the same way, I thought, that a rooster tries to make the loudest ruckus possible as early as possible.

I packed up my wet hammock, ate some breakfast, thanked Nora, and left limping, enduring an infected foot, a swollen lymph gland in my groin, a fever, and a blemished face. Red-eyed and with no one to talk to or get consolation from, I made my way back to Morita, where I told the man at La Pichinga to sign me up for the next plane out of there. He said he didn't know exactly what day it was coming, since a couple of the planes were being repaired and another had crashed a week earlier.

"Shit!" I said loudly in English, and headed for the ocean. My condition didn't allow me to enjoy any body surfing, but I was able to relax in the ocean and try to put myself back together. I prayed to my unknown God for help and prayed there *was* a God that listened and did care and could help.

I dreaded the night and drank a few shots of rum before trying to sleep. I also borrowed a good flashlight from Carlos. "This time, I'm going to find out the truth of this," I swore. The entrance to the house I was sleeping in had a door, but no operable latch. I figured that if someone was really entering the house he had to come through here to get to my room. So that night I closed the door, which opened inward, and placed an enameled drinking cup on the rough, cratered cement floor right next to it. I opened the door as a test and the cup grated loudly against the floor. I put it in place again and went to sleep with my flashlight and machete.

Late that night I heard the cup move, and to make sure I was really awake, I opened my eyes wide, opened my mouth, touched my face with my hands, and said the words almost out loud, "Okay, I am awake." The cup was moving slowly across the floor and in a way I felt relieved because I knew I wasn't crazy. Careful not to make any noise, I sat up, flashlight in my left hand, machete in my right, ready for action. But as I strained my ears and eyes, I could neither hear anything except the rushing of my own blood, nor see anything except splotchy hints of colors in pitch-blackness. I decided to take the offensive. I jumped up, turned on the flashlight, and rushed out of the room, shivering with fear chills but ready to face my enemy in battle.

I shined my light on the door and felt a shockwave in my heart and brain when I saw the cup right where I had left it. Nevertheless, as I ran toward the door, I heard what sounded like someone barefoot brush against the outside corner of the house and run away. I yelled, *"Hijo'epúta!"* (the equivalent of screw you!) and ran out of the house, but saw nothing. I woke Carlos in the house next door and told him what happened, and he just said to quit worrying and go back to sleep. No one could have entered or left through that door and left the cup in the same spot, yet I could have sworn I heard it move just as surely as if I were wide awake. "Damn it, I'm going nuts," I told myself out loud. "I need help. Someone or something's screwing me up. I gotta get out of here."

Exhausted from fear, anger, and defeat, I left the door wide open and opened the window, too, in defiance. I laid down on my bed, sweating, and transmitted a soulful plea for help to God, Jesus, Buddha, Bahaullah, Krishna, Moses – whatever God or saint or divine being might be listening – saying I was losing to something evil and didn't know how to defend myself and to please help me out. I slept well the rest of the night.

In the morning, I told my story to Don Ramón, who ran La Pichinga, and he seemed slightly sympathetic. "You're not the only one who's been spooked in that house," he said. "I know people who have slept there once and wouldn't sleep there again if you paid them to. Maybe it's just the rats, or nerves – I don't know."

The next day a plane came and took me to San José, the lymph gland in my groin still swollen and painful. I also had slight nausea, an infected foot, and diarrhea, which threatened to embarrass me at any time. The following day, after a night spent visiting the shared hotel bathroom way too many times, a friendly pharmacist gave me some antibiotics for my infection and some awful-tasting charcoal tablets for my stomach, which rumbled and growled constantly (were there weird creatures in me?).

I stayed in San José for four days to recuperate before flying back to the States. The evil spirit or enemy or hallucinations or whatever it was didn't bother me after I left Morita, so I slept wonderfully. I realized that I hadn't beaten the thing that was hurting me, but I had at least endured without giving in. I acknowledged its power, realized that it could overwhelm me, but never did I respect it or ask mercy from it. It could give me bad luck, make my friends seem like enemies, make my body shake and shiver in fear, deceive my senses, and cramp my leg, but it couldn't get into my soul. I'd been able to keep strong a power inside me, one I hadn't been sure existed, and when finally I relied totally on this power and on the benign forces in the cosmos, leaving doors and windows open, leaving myself physically vulnerable, my cure began.

Of course, all this was mere speculation. I wasn't sure of anything. I wondered what really would have happened if I had stayed in Morita a few more days. How much more would I have endured?

After flying back to recover at my parents' home in safe, witchless (or was it?) Albuquerque, I fought with myself over whether I could continue in Costa Rica. My parents helped me decide to try to make a go of it.

"You sure that Pan Am highway's going right next to your land?" my father kept asking. "And Alcoa's going to build a port there?" To the best of my knowledge, both projects were being planned very seriously on all corporate and government levels.

In the fall of 1973, I visited my "tribe" in Hawaii and got some advice from Bruce, the wood sculptor. "Look, if that witch ever gives you a hard time again, take a couple hits of acid with you and slip them in her coffee or something so she can see what kind of medicine *you've* got! Yeah, some good white *gringo* medicine! Maybe she'll quit messin' around with you!"

Though it sounded like a great idea – had I been sure Oscura was really the culprit – I didn't take back any LSD. I did return with something that was much more valuable in the short and long runs: the solid backing and almost unconditional blessing of my parents. Now I could relax more and try to sink some stronger roots into "my" place, and if I failed, if the witchcraft got too heavy, if I decided to bail out, or if I simply lost my shirt, it would be sort of okay and I could go back home and change trajectories. Maybe I could become a college drop-back-in.

Perezoso (three-toed sloth)

Lowland tropical rainforest flora

Chapter Four

Settling in – surviving

Don Arturo's choza, in the midst of Lucía's colorful ornamental and herbal jungle, had two bedrooms, an open sitting area, and a kitchen. Lucía kicked the chickens out of the spare "bedroom," swept the corroding, low, tin roofing, bamboo walls, and clay dirt floor and did her best to make me comfortable in my new home. Her cooking, which she accomplished over three rocks strategically placed on a raised wood, clay, and hardened-ash platform, was delicious. Mostly simple rice, beans, corn, cheese and plantain, in varying presentations with local herbs, the meals were served in enameled bowls and plates with an aluminum cup of juice and an aluminum spoon. Now and then I had to chase down a mostly wild chicken for the pot, but that was nothing compared to the professional job she must have had to do to make the tough birds so palatable.

During those first crucial weeks in early 1974, I would learn whether or not the local people, especially the brujas, would let me be, whether or not I could even consider being a safe and happy camper there. In the daytime, cheerful Javier and his good-natured friends would guide me on free tours and teach me about the forest, the critters, and how to keep out of harm's way. My biggest concern at the beginning, besides the nocturnal brujas, was snakes.

Manolo, an expert of forest lore, with uniquely large and charming brown-black eyes and long, straight, shiny black hair, lectured me about snakes as he sharpened his machete with a file. "If you run into a bad one [poisonous and/or aggressive], run downhill and then give a quick turn to one side so the snake will keep on going until you can get away. If you meet one on level ground and it is following you fast, throw down your hat or shirt or anything and the snake will stop and curl up nearby in striking position. This gives you time to cut a branch and come back around to kill him. It must be a green branch that bends, because if it breaks, the snake will rise up unharmed and come after you madder than ever. If you cut him with your machete, don't cut him completely in two because the part with his head can jump a few yards by itself with its mouth open and grab onto whatever it hits, whether it be a tree or your leg.

"A big snake, like a *platonegro* [bushmaster] has enough force and weight to knock you down. If this happens, get up and get away because you can be bitten again. If the snake gets you and stays hooked, since some of their fangs are very curved, you must pull it off and throw it away.

"They say – I don't know if it's true or not – that the best thing you can do after getting bit by a snake, if you're far from help, is to take three steps backwards, and, without looking, grab the first plant you touch with your left hand and eat it. They say it tastes as bitter as bile, but you have to eat it. It's a secret – you can't tell anybody or it won't work. And if you look around to see what the plant is, it doesn't work. I guess it's the faith that counts. Also, they say eating the ground-up *jabillo* seed is good, at least until you get to the hospital."

I told Manolo and Javier that I had anti-venom serum and that at least 40 cc's had to be injected in the hip of the snake-bit victim, after first testing to see whether the person is allergic to it or not. Manolo laughed and said, "That might be the best thing, but many people would rather die before having such injections!"

As I walked around the property with these friendly guides, most of whom had never conversed with a foreigner and obviously enjoyed the opportunity, they would point out different plants and flowers, name them – often with more than one name – and explain their value in human and animal terms. They showed me in the forest which vine to cut for a drink of water, and which vines not to touch. Once when I cut my finger fairly deep with my machete, Javier took me to the *cedrillo* tree, whacked it with his machete, and smeared its bright yellow sap on my cut. The bleeding stopped, and in a minute the sap had hardened into a plastic-like bandage. Following his advice, in three days I pulled off the flexible bandage and saw with satisfaction and amazement that my cut was healed and my finger wasn't at all puckery as I'd expected.

One day when walking a trail with Carlos, he said calmly, "Ants." I looked around but saw no ants, so I asked, "What do you mean, 'ants'?"

"Don't you smell them?" He smiled at me and sniffed the air.

"Ants? *Smell* them?" I asked incredulously.

"Yes, there must be a lot of them," he replied more seriously, sniffing and scowling.

Continuing on the trail about 20 yards, we found thousands of army ants crossing the trail, some with little white burdens on their backs. "Those little white cargoes are the ants that haven't been born yet. They are the future of the colony. This colony is moving from their old home because it's probably going to rain so hard today that they decided their home was in danger of flooding. You see how high the vultures are circling today? Did you hear the *congo* [howler] monkeys howling this morning? And the *guacos* [laughing falcons]? Rain. Do you see the dark gray-blue of the ocean? Two days from the new moon? I'd bet you all I own, which I admit isn't much, that it's going to rain tonight, long and hard."

I chuckled, looking at the cloudless, pale-blue sky, but that night it rained long and hard as Carlos had predicted. The next day he said he was glad he hadn't lost his reputation as weather forecaster, and that if it had rained any less, he would have lost.

I was particularly impressed with the necessity of learning the ropes of the place when one day, after defecating in the forest, I wiped myself with the wrong kind of leaf. The itching made me dance, and my companions cried with laughter. Fortunately the discomfort passed quickly. From then on, Javier and Carlos would try to broaden my education by teaching me to identify the leafiest local plants in terms of their usefulness as toilet paper. There were so very many that looked practically the same that I decided from then on to pocket a little paper on long hikes, just in case. It would soon be damp with sweat or foliage water or stream water, but it was better than having to take my chance with tropical botany.

At night, Don Arturo's old-timer friends would usually congregate at his choza to smoke and talk of times past, of adventures and witchcraft, sharing "Indian" tales, exchanging stories they had told probably dozens of times. Luckily, instead of inhibiting them, my presence seemed to inspire them, and they warmly welcomed me. Though a foreigner and young, I was genuinely interested in what they had to say, which was becoming increasingly rare among the generation of local youths.   Listening and later recording with pen and paper, I felt curiously like I did with Oscura's old-growth forest. Here again, I found myself in the presence of something very valuable that I could save or let disappear forever.

When it was Don Arturo's turn, he would speak slowly, pausing to catch his breath. "One day, late in the afternoon I was on my way home when I heard a branch snap behind me a little ways off the trail. I wasn't sure what it was, so I kept going. Then to my left side in the forest, I heard another movement. Later I heard something ahead of me. The sun was going down, and the trail was getting dark, but I could see on it the fresh footprint of a mighty *jaguar* [hah-gwar]. Then I knew what was happening. The creature was circling me, like they do their prey. My choza was still pretty far away when I heard the loud snarl and saw the animal on the very path about 20 *varas* [1 vara = 33 inches] away. You know the roar of a big *tigre* [tee-gray] is one of the most powerful things there is, and it can be a very frightening thing. There he was, just sitting there staring at me. Of course I couldn't keep walking on the trail, so I started off through the forest, but now and then I heard sounds around me. He was getting closer, so I headed back for the trail, thinking that if I had to do battle with him, I would have a better chance on the trail. This happened some 20 or more years ago, when there was nothing here but forest and more forest, nowhere to flee. This was jaguar territory and it was the *people* who had to flee from *them*. I remembered something my father taught me, the way they defended themselves against a tigre if they had to. I had no gun, just a machete. I picked a bunch of weeds and put my machete in the middle of the bundle when I saw the jaguar in front of me again, this time he was growling and hissing, mean and brave. This time he ran toward me, in a charge, and as he sprang for me, I fell on my back holding the machete with both hands, the weeds disguising my weapon and also protecting my forward hand from being cut as I held it out as stiff as I could. And thanks to God, in that way I was able to wound the tigre in his breast and thereby save myself, though I was scratched deeply and bleeding a lot. The jaguar lay right next to me, panting, and before it could attack again I chopped off both its hands, which are its most terrible weapons. The tigre died, and the next day his pelt was taken.

"Twenty years ago this was a dangerous place to live, there were so many wild animals. The most dangerous was the tigre, which hunted at night. You couldn't go on this trail at night. Of course all this was pure forest, and to go up or down the coast you had no choice but to pass though this area, which was the home of big jaguars, like the one that attacked me, the one I was lucky to be able to kill. Those big animals killed to defend their territory; they never ate anyone. In the forest you could see trees all scratched up higher than a man could reach, where the jaguar would sharpen its claws and make signs to scare people and other jaguars away. Playa del Tunel was sometimes covered with the tracks of jaguars that went there to play at night. Now they're gone.

"When the white people with their cattle and pigs moved in, and the jaguars learned to eat these easy prey, the people poisoned them and shot them. There are no more except for one big black one up on the ridge back of Cachelote, but they'll kill him, too, because he's been killing cattle on the hacienda."

Between the daytime explorations and nightly talks, I felt like a perfectly satisfied student, learning from the immense wealth of the old ones' first-hand knowledge about the environment, the wildlife, the people, the history. For months, I was as interested in the acquisition of fascinating local information as I was in the purchase of Oscura's land.

I unintentionally outwaited her, for she finally contacted me and said she would sell for three times the dirt-cheap going rate rather than ten times. Though I still hadn't gotten clear title for Don Arturo's land, I trusted Don Manuel when he said it was merely a question of time and assured me that Oscura's similar bureaucratic title mess could also eventually be sorted out. Over the phone, from Don Manuel's office to Albuquerque, my parents said yes to the Oscura property and urged me to secure another property upstream, and then another one, slowly trying to join a significant chunk of the mostly forested steep hills surrounding the Quebrada Chica stream from sea level to a thousand feet above.

By the time we purchased some 400 acres from a dozen different owners, most of whom didn't live there after a few years, I became somewhat skilled in the local real estate business, at least the buying end. I felt somewhat guilty about taking land from the few people that lived there, but I encouraged them to stay for a year or more while they got settled elsewhere. Besides, the way they were squandering the sparse topsoil by constantly slashing and burning more forest, they would not benefit much longer there.

For more than a year, I had to travel frequently to Don Manuel's small office in San José and wait hours to see him and then accompany him to hopelessly crowded, hectic government offices, trying to properly establish first that the property sellers were the legal owners of their farms and then to transfer their properties to my name in the Institute of Colonized Lands and the Public Registry. What was supposed to take months, took years and my older brother, Kevin, who at first was my valuable partner in the Costa Rican venture, came down to try to help me out of the apparently hopeless mire but soon decided, probably wisely, to sell his share back to me (with the help of my parents) and thereby avoid a potentially mucky business and personal disaster with me.

So many flights between Morita and San José, so many windy passes, so many times when the plane plummeted in free fall, so many one-wheel landings – each time I swore I would let two months pass instead of just one before going back to wrestle with the slippery heavyweights in San José. Jostling my way through the masses of so many people with urgent missions, I struggled to accomplish all my errands and meet all my appointments as quickly as possible, to be able to escape as quickly as possible. Maybe that's what everyone else was doing, too.

Tools, parts, favorite groceries, letters, stamped documents, and medicines for myself and for others back in Morita – I learned where and how to get them in the most efficient ways. I learned where and what I could eat and still survive, what hotels were inexpensive but nice and not dangerous or too noisy, which strangers to ask directions from and which to avoid, how to get discounts, how best to avoid being run over by drivers who seemed determined to do so, and how best not to get my pocket picked.

San José offered surprising rewards, like clean, cool movie theaters showing American films in English with Spanish subtitles. In the small, classic National Theater, I sat in rapture listening to Ravi Shankar, Stan Getz, Weather Report, and several excellent classical music performances, a luxury fit for royalty, yet available to me for only a few dollars.

Sometimes I sat in for percussionists at nightclubs and soon made quite a few friends who always welcomed me whenever I was in San José. Staying up drinking and smoking until 1 a.m., after a day of errands and erratic eating in exhaust-filled San José, would throw my body out of balance every time, and my visits to the big city began to make me sick. Like an alcoholic who drinks even though he knows the nauseating consequences, I was addicted to the same neurotic over-indulging every time I returned to "civilization."

There was a long period, two or three years at least, when I felt truly comfortable in no place. At the farm, I often felt like a researcher and a tourist, with a lot of land I didn't know what to do with; in San José, I was a nervous carouser and runner of errands; back in my home country, I was an ex-college student and a visitor with business elsewhere. I found myself in the lonely predicament of so many other expatriates: feeling like a foreigner wherever I was, in limbo socially and culturally, with no friends close enough to satisfy my real need for close companionship.

What would the college psychologist have said about the unenviable social situation, not of the "normal" expatriates who hauled their sociocultural baggage along with them wherever they went, but of the officially declared "misfit" expats like me? If "birds of a feather flock together," where was my flock?

Maybe we were more like fin whales. They mostly live alone, sometimes traveling thousands of miles before meeting a fellow fin whale. There were friendly expats just as isolated as me all over the world. Perhaps our society was simply a sparsely populated group of space-loving individuals? We most enjoyed each others' company on a hike, scuba diving trip, after a couple of beers, or via letters that took weeks to reach their destination. We usually had to be semidrunk in order to dance. We almost always adored nature. We liked weather, whatever it was, and we liked to get up early in the morning and to go to bed early at night. We were normally awkward with the opposite sex. We often carelessly spoke the truth. But yes, our type, though often lonely, did exist.

Thanks to my parents' financial and emotional interest in "our project" in Costa Rica, I had to leave to one side my chronically unproductive soul-searching and concentrate on what I planned to do with our investment down there. The highway and other major developments slated for the area would someday surely bring financial opportunities, but what would we do with the land in the meantime?

Though we were mostly considering a tourism-related business, which my parents knew something about, since they had run a very successful small motel in Ohio, Carlos and Javier and the general local public had suggested we start by raising cattle on the hillsides that had already been degraded by unsound farming. Unlike the dry western United States, where every cow needs 20 acres, in warm, rainy southwestern Costa Rica, where the grass grew fast all year round, a cow needed only one or two acres of grazing land. Cows could also walk themselves through the swift rivers and over rough terrain to market, eliminating the need for complicated transportation arrangements.

What did we know about raising cattle in the tropics? About as much as we knew about raising cattle anywhere – almost zero. But it was the best and cheapest idea we could come up with; it was the local people's number-one choice; and for the time being, it would keep possible squatters away from our land. We decided to try it for starters.

So, instead of pursuing the life of tropical explorer, researcher, ecologist, anthropologist, photographer, sustenance farmer, surfer, or spiritual seeker, all of which I had at times envisioned, I was going to become a *cowboy*? Yahoo!?

Focusing my energies on a single goal was never my forte.

Caucél (nocturnal rainforest feline)

Humo's offspring

Chapter Five

Cattle business – me a cowboy?

Doing *something* with those jungle-weed fields suddenly gave me improved status in the area, and although I knew better than anyone how young and touristy I still was, I greedily soaked up the clearly enhanced respect and acceptance the people showed me. Maybe it was just my imagination, but everyone seemed somehow relieved after hearing my plans to follow their advice by raising cattle. Maybe they were happy with all the employment that decision signified. Maybe they were happy I wasn't going to plant marijuana. Maybe they were happy I wasn't so insane as to let the jungle take over the hard-earned cleared areas (which was what I really wanted to do).

These parcels, once parts of the glorious rainforest, had been cleared with enormous effort by ax, machete, and fire; planted with rice, corn, and/or beans several times; and abandoned to the rapid recolonization by "junk" trees, vines, and weeds – which were apparently worthless to man but were the only vegetation besides grasses that could prosper in the mostly humusless clay soil.

Grasses could feasibly be encouraged to form pastures for grazing animals. In 1975, there was a continuous and rising international demand for meat and dairy products. With no need for extra feeding or fattening as was necessary in the United States, and with low wages and low costs of veterinary supplies, cattle raising in Costa Rica could be more lucrative than in the United States. Of course, this was all theoretical, and there was no shining model in the neighborhood to follow. Of the 400 acres, we planned not to touch any of the 200 or so acres of forest and to make orchards and pastures out of the rest in order to make it "productive."

How naïve I was to think the forest could remain pristine! We needed wood, and lots of it, to build fences, a corral, and houses for the cattlemen, machete men, fence men, chainsaw men, carpenters, and their families, all of whom had to live there to work there, since there was no convenient labor source or transportation for 20 miles in any direction.

Wood - that ancient building material- didn't come from lumberyards but from forests. To get it, trees had to be felled. It wasn't nearly as simple as it sounded. Parts of the precious forests would be damaged selectively, carefully, and on a small scale, but nevertheless damaged. Grudgingly following the prophetic guidelines of the college psychologist, I went along with the popular, rarely seriously questioned, human custom of compromising nature for progress. At the time, I was too gung-ho to worry about it very much. The concern was there, firmly rooted inside, but I was too cowardly or too busy or too much in denial to give it much heed. Besides, we were modern people in the tropics, and we were going to *do* something. Of course, there was going to be some messiness.

Which of the hundreds of species of trees were suitable for our purposes? The *cedrillo* with the yellow healing sap? The giant, thick *vaco* with its copious white, drinkable "milk" and the smooth bark early indigenous peoples made into cloth? The blood-red *zapatero* (cobbler) with "crystal" in it? Or the *ojoches* that were so hard that axes bent and bounced off them? Or the 10-foot-diameter thorny *jabillos*, which were prized for making dugout boats? Gradually, I would learn so much about the local tropical trees and their qualities that my knowledge of them would displace large areas of useless academic software loitering lethargically in my gray cells.

"Ajo is eternal," Enrique, the old mestizo carpenter, swore solemnly.

"Nothing's eternal," I corrected him, smiling.

"Ajo is as close as you can get around here," he smiled back. "It's the best wood, besides *manú*, which is too hard to get, for fences, corrals, and foundation posts for houses. In the ground it never rots, and it's so bitter that termites take one bite and vomit!"

Green-eyed Tito, the 40 year old oxen-driver, chainsaw cutter, butcher, and fence and corral builder, added, "There are lots of really big ajos all over your land, many already fallen but still perfectly good, a few accessible with oxen, making a good path, of course."

Ajo it would be then, to start with. Tito, all 5 feet and 120 pounds of him, was eager to get his deafening, smoking chainsaw (which I helped purchase and bring from San José) cutting into the largest and oldest of the climax-forest trees, of which there were more dead than living. I would use the dead and leave the living, no matter how much Tito, who was twice as old as me and ten times as experienced, tried to persuade me to take closer and easier live ones. Ajos were apparently becoming locally extinct, since the only live ones were old giants, and their garlic-scented tiny yellow flowers never seemed to produce viable seed.

We made a verbal contract for a thousand fence posts and a hundred corral posts, each six inches square and 3 varas long, measured by Tito's experienced hands and eyes. The posts could also serve as house foundations. Tito would take charge of the fence and corral building, and I would provide him with several helpers to carry the 100 to 200-pound posts to where the oxcart could penetrate the forest to dig the holes and plant the posts, to carry and string the barbed wire, etc. To adequately house these workers and their families, another chainsaw operator with a special rig for producing building-lumber began exploiting other softer woods for house construction, the few existing chozas being mostly rotted and devoured by termites.

People with families came to help me "make the *finca* [farm]" while I helped them by housing them and offering them steady wages, which at the time was equivalent to $2.50 a day. Houses for these families, corrals and fences for the cattle, and a few rustic cabins for adventurous tourists – the foundations for everything we built were made of ajo wood.

"There are two types of termites, one of the air and one of the ground," Enrique and Tito explained to me, telling me not to worry about the mud tunnels that I discovered one day going up some of the ajo posts. "Those are air termites and can easily be killed with poison or kerosene long before they do any damage." After a couple of years, I began to look into the termite matter more closely and found that "air" termites, when given the opportunity, would secretly insert themselves into the slightest crack or fissure or joint and quickly penetrate other wood next to the ajo. In a short time, they could inflict incredible damage on the inside of a board with absolutely no outward manifestation. Then they were called "ground" termites, "the bad ones." I began to suspect my informants were perhaps not so well-informed. I should have realized that most of the local people built thatched chozas on pole foundations, which they generally abandoned after five years to move in search of more fertile land, and that they had no interest or experience in truly permanent construction. Panicking one day, I ordered a confused worker to dig up five ajo fence posts and to saw them into pieces. What relief when I saw no sign of rot or termite damage. I wished to prolong that relief.

In the tropics, we humans use quite a bit of poison. I didn't wish to succumb to the temptation, but I did. Maybe if I could put wood preservative or some sort of repellent on the foundation posts it would prevent the termites from climbing them and getting into the other wood. Seeking professional advice in the small town of San Cristobal, about 30 miles away, I was introduced by the "engineers" of the Ministry of Agriculture and various farm supply store owners to the strange world of toxins, so deadly and so available, spilling out of their plastic bags, leaking from bottles and jars and 55-gallon drums.

"How about a few pounds of aldrin?" "Ten kilos of chlordane mixed with creosote ought to fix 'em, or you could apply a coat of pentahexachylorophyl ["penta"]. Sorry, we don't have DDT right now – your countrymen are making problems about it for some reason." "Why don't you go for dieldrin with diesel?"

I didn't know. Nobody did at that time, nor would anybody really know until much later. I used "penta" and malathion, which seemed slightly less evil than most of the other products, some of which gave me a strange tingling, burning sensation on my face without even touching them. I mixed the white malathion and penta with kerosene and asphalt paint and slopped the dark, hideous concoction on the house foundations. That would surely do the trick, I thought. At least the red clay termite tunnels were more obvious against the black background.

But those soft little, white, helpless, blind beasts got tough and must have mutated a few times, too (nature is grand!), because after a year of slopping them with penta, just the thought of which made *me* wither, they were *playing* in the caustic, carcinogenic crystal residue and, equally incredible, were boring from the ground up *into* the ajo wood, which was, according to everyone, something they would *never* do, not with ajo, no señor.

After a termite swarm, which was fairly common and probably had been for hundreds of millions of years, thousands of dead winged male termites covered the beaches. I realized that if they could spare so very many of themselves, if the competition for the queen was that keen, then I was obviously facing a formidable enemy, one that would never yield or compromise to the likes of me.

After eight years, all the ajo posts were showing signs of rot. They were fine above and below ground level, but where they contacted the soil they were deteriorating, and quickly. Some had nearly broken. Then there was an earthquake. All the buildings swayed with the land in that local section of the Ring of Fire, up and down, side to side with the jolting shock waves. Luckily no foundation posts broke, but I could no longer procrastinate. The labor and hassle involved in changing all the foundations of the buildings struck horror in my mind, but it wasn't the first time, nor would it be the last, that I would have to face a monster there and deal with it as best I could.

"Nothing is eternal, Enrique, not in this world anyway," I repeated to the old carpenter.

I considered fabricating reinforced concrete posts but shuddered at the prospect of transporting the tons of material required for the job. I finally decided on trying the teak-like wood called manú from high up in the steep mountains. Manú was considered by the wood authorities I trusted as the most termite and rot-proof wood available.

The exhausting and dangerous work of cutting those manú posts and hauling them down the steep mountain to the ranch was not the most difficult part of the job for me. It was knowing that I was damaging pristine forests for the *manú*, and for the *maría*, *manglillo*, *alazán*, *cedrillo*, and *zapatero* that I was taking for all our lumber needs.

At first I would accompany the tree cutters, and I couldn't help smiling in awe while watching them work. The deafening buzz of the chainsaw would suddenly grow silent. I'd see the men removing themselves and their equipment from harm's way, nervously looking up and shouting and laughing in disguised fear. The passive giant, so slowly creaking, cracking, splitting, the birds shrieking away, vines and leaves a hundred feet and more up on the canopy moving, slipping – loose leaves and flowers raining down; unidentified animals scurrying. The giant, of unknown age, in slow motion, yielding to the rude cuts in its trunk, succumbing to us young, sneaky little ground creatures with our diabolical machines and schemes. Time becoming more dense yet stretching and allowing us to savor the nobility of the ancient and magnificent living being, to ponder its grace, to ponder its perfect condition as an individual and as a part of the forest, as a rightful and worthy inhabitant of planet Earth. Our excitement and wonder turned to dread and guilt and misgiving as the tree gained momentum, bringing down tons of vines and breaking branches of neighboring trees, crashing, roaring, rumbling. Yet, as the tree thundered down and shook the ground with its impact, under the rain of debris and insects, I clung to the façade of boss/macho man with a project, rather than yielding to my impulse to cry like a child and beg the tree and forest and planet for forgiveness. Compensating for my acute sense of wrongdoing, I converted my exhilarated awe into smiles and shouts like those of the other men.

We seemed to need to reassure each other that we shared membership in a powerful and mysterious species, and that the deed we had done was somehow a triumph for humanity. I wondered and wondered some more, but was still unsure of myself and tended to go along with the wishes of others. Wasn't that the way life was? Didn't "growing up" mean adapting to the expectations of others? What would my college psychologist have to say on this? Would she be proud of me for learning to get along? I tried to remember what she looked like. I thought she was pretty, but all I could recall were her confident dark eyes and her cruel, moving, painted lips, which kept forming words I didn't want to hear.

The cattle business, like cutting trees, further subtracted from my peace of mind, personal integrity, and sense of moral and spiritual well-being. As with the sacrificing of trees (what else could I have built with?) I had to keep reminding myself why I was getting involved with cattle: to do *something* with the junk land, which was too degraded for anything else. Grow crops? I'd need tons and tons of calcium carbonate, potassium, phosphorus, and magnesium to build up the impoverished soil. There was no practical way of getting it there, and besides, it rained so much it would mostly wash away. Terracing? Way too costly. Besides, what would I plant? What were the locals doing with their land? Cutting and burning forest to plant a few subsistence crops, then turning it into pasture. Cattle could walk to market. Crops could not.

I told myself there was value in what I chose to do. The birth of a calf was such a wonderful thing, a positive, beautiful, right thing. To watch them jumping and kicking in the air, running fast and freely over the grassy hills, chasing and playing with each other . . . they obviously were happy to be alive. The milk, cream, and cheese we produced nourished so many people on the farm and in the neighborhood. The steady paid labor involved in maintenance of the pastures, fences, and corrals helped support many families.

On the other hand, these Brahmans weren't at all like the comparatively stupid, over-domesticated Herefords that I had been inclined to ridicule in the United States. These creatures, with their long floppy ears and their more African herd-animal appearance and instinct, seemed at times noble, nice, intelligent, worthy of respect. It would have been emotionally easier if I could have seen them as mere eating machines, unalert and unfeeling. If I had overwhelming obstacles, diseases, or catastrophes like those that occasionally afflicted other people's herds, if there were cattle-rustlers or anthrax or anaplasmosis or something, I might have been able to give up cattle raising gracefully. Actually, there were very few problems, until I had to sell my first bull.

"Humo" (Smoke) was a massive, old, humped gray-and-white bull I had purchased from a distant neighbor with our first ten cows. Humo had given us our first calves. After two years, when Humo's daughters became adults, Javier advised me to sell him to avoid inbreeding. Humo's large, buffalo-like head, with thick black horns and thick velvety folds of short-haired skin drooping from his neck to his chest, showed his Brahman ancestry. His 700 kilos were elegantly distributed, and he could clear a fence if he wanted to, but at 9 years he was aging, and it took more and more effort to get his increasing weight up steep hills or over rocky places.

The biggest problem with that powerful hulk was that he was my respected friend. He was more powerful and more potentially dangerous than any creature I had ever known, but so docile that I could feed him bananas, pet him all over, and grab his horns. He would sometimes even allow children to sit on his back.

I didn't want to appear the soft, oversensitive gringo, not then, when I had to do my best to maintain the respect of the workers who were mostly much older and tougher and far more experienced than myself. I couldn't afford to screw up on my first cattle deal. I had to sell Humo. The cattle dealer, called Panchana, was fat and swore and spit a lot while constantly smiling. His horse's ribs bled where he jabbed his spurs in, and still he jabbed them in the wounds. When I asked him why he did this to his horse, he said, "Oh, that doesn't hurt him because he's used to it, and besides, I need a horse that'll take me where I've got to go, and sometimes that's all day over bad trails." He smiled the charming pseudo-sincere smile I would learn to associate with *los comerciantes* – the animal dealers.

Walking slowly around nervous Humo, Panchana then frowned on the basis of years of experience and said with self-assurance, "Around 600 kilos."

Macedonio, my cowboy-employee-friend-teacher, had taken it upon himself to protect my interests. He chuckled and told Panchana, "If you're a good judge of Brahman bulls, esteemed friend, you can see for yourself that this animal is weighing no less than 700 kilos."

After a pause, Panchana said, "You know the bull's too old to sell for breeding or to get the best price for meat."

I nodded in acknowledgement of what I knew was true. Macedonio scowled privately to me and then smiled, cocking his head to convey tolerant disapproval. "The *most* I could possibly pay for him, and still make enough to cover my own costs," the comerciante continued, barely hiding the smile provoked by my inexperience, "is 3,600 colones [about $300]."

At this, Macedonio laughed as if it were a joke, took me by the arm, and led me to a corner of the corral, saying to the comerciante, "Excuse me, please, so we can discuss your offer." I realized he was trying to save me from accepting the unacceptably low price. "Boss, be careful of this guy," he whispered with his back to Panchana. "He's too smart. Humo's all of 650 kilos, probably a lot more, so don't accept any less than 5,000 [$450]."

After the coaching, I went back to the ring and said, "We figure the bull's weighing at least 650 kilos and so is worth 6,000 colones [$500] in San Cristobal, but since the trip to San Cristobal is going to take some weight off him, and since it's hard on you, too" (I glanced at Macedonio who was grimacing to one side again), "we figure he's worth 5,000 colones [$450] right here, but no less."

Panchana looked at me, concealing his mounting sense of victory, and said sadly, "Well, señores, I thought you wanted to sell this animal today, so that's why I came so far, but at that price, no one's going to take him. But since I'm here and don't want to lose the trip, I'll make you a final offer, seeing as it's our first time dealing with each other. I'll take him off your hands for 4,000 colones [$340], pay you cash, and you don't have to worry about getting him to San Cristobal."

This time I called Macedonio to one side to hear what he had to say. He said in a hushed voice, "Listen, boss, I don't like this guy, but there aren't many buyers with cash around here, so maybe you can settle for 4,500 [$400]."

I turned back to Panchana. "What do you say we split the difference? But on one condition, that you walk him out by way of

Puerto Nuevo, because he's heavy and I know he'll have a hard time getting over the ridge. It's too steep and rocky for him, and he's not used to it."

Panchana thought about it a minute and then extended his hand in agreement. "All right, 4,500 [$400], but you remember to notify me when you have more animals for sale. Deal?"

"Yeah, sure," I said, correctly suspecting I'd sold too cheaply and that Panchana knew he'd come out way ahead in the deal.

He gave me the cash and mounted up with his two helpers, who hadn't said a word the whole time. They separated Humo from his cows and calves and started to walk him away. The bull soon realized he was being led by strangers, alone, away from his home territory, and he stopped, despite the urgings of the cattlemen, who were shouting at him and whacking him with ropes and thick green branches. I was looking at him when this happened, and he looked back at me, withstanding the cowboys' energetic abuse long enough for me to feel deep inside what it was to betray a friend.

The bull struggled as the men roped him. Humo nearly pulled them off their horses as he ran into a barbed wire fence, which cut into his sides. Finally he quit trying to return and ran away furiously down the trail away from his domain. I separated myself from the others and went into the forest to suffer my emotional anxiety alone, wanting to be able to cry and purge my feelings. I tried to rationalize it, to ignore the visceral burning of guilt, but I would never be able to feel right about the incident, a lesson that was probably the only good thing to come of it.

Later I learned that Panchana had taken Humo over the 3,000-foot ridge where, I was told, the bull became so lame he could barely walk. There was nothing more to do for Humo, whom I had sent to a cruel death, but what about all the other animals I would be selling? Should I quit the cattle business after two years of hard labor and planning? Everyone would ridicule me, think of me as crazy, and lose their respect for me. I would have to fire a lot of workers and abandon the pastures. I would be a failure just when I was getting going. What would my parents and brothers say and feel? How would I feel later?

I procrastinated and tried to douse some of the coals burning within. Maybe I was being oversensitive, I told myself. But no, I knew Macedonio was bothered, too, by Humo's painful departure, though he wouldn't admit it. When I asked him how he felt, he replied, "Neither you nor me can afford to get too close to the animals we work with. I learned that a long time ago when I had to sell the best milk cow my mother ever had, and to sell an ox that has worked so hard for you for years – now *that's* the worst."

Other animals went more gracefully, less dramatically, less knowingly, and I was less affected by their departures. Most animals coped best when accompanied by other fellow animals. My ignorance of that simple fact had cost Humo and myself much suffering that could have been avoided. This seemed to make the deed even worse.

Time separated the dead bull from me little by little. A bit of rum at night worked nicely in that respect. Still, I would never condone the mistreatment of animals, and Panchana stayed away from our ranch, knowing how furious I was with him for taking Humo to his death in the hardest way. I fired workers for throwing rocks at cows or leaving horses tied up for hours in the sun, or running them too hard; at the same time, I didn't hesitate to whack the tail off a dog I found attacking a wild animal in "my" forest after warning the owner several times to keep his hunting dogs out of there. My moral stances seemed increasingly prone to wobbliness.

When the herd of breeding cattle grew to 180 head, and we (my parents, brother Kevin, and I) had become "successful" with the operation, I was hit again, hard. All this time, five years or so, I had been under the impression that the cattle I sent to market were slaughtered with those electric or gunpowder-fired devices that zapped the animal in the forehead and killed it immediately. I'd seen them used on TV and knew they were used in the United States, and it seemed a very humane way of killing. Well, I should have known the difference between the United States, with its legions of animal lovers and an active Humane Society, and the Third World, where most of the people were too busy worrying about taking care of themselves and their families to spare concern for animals who couldn't vote or state their complaints. What I discovered was that they were slaughtering the cattle with a sledgehammer.

Actually, the method wasn't bad as long as the killer was a good one, strong and accurate. However, the killers weren't always so good, and on inspecting the severed heads of cows in the butcher shops in the closest town, San Cristobal, I discovered heads with as many as three rude indentations. The butchers told me the big bulls were the most abused, since their skulls were so thick that they sometimes required up to five blows before they fell completely unconscious and their jugulars could be cut. Sometimes, the butchers told me, the killer would break off a horn, puncture an eye, or smash the nose before felling the poor animal. With renewed horror and guilt, I wondered how Humo had fared.

When I learned that the municipal slaughterhouse had once used a .22 rifle but quit for lack of bullets, I supplied the bullets. Then some of the butchers complained that too much damage was done to the brains, which were of commercial value, and the sledgehammer killings resumed. I brought back from the United States a special hand-held cattle killer that thrust a blunt, rounded point into the skull without damaging the brains and dropped the animal immediately with minimal stress. After a few months, however, they ran out of cartridges and didn't get any more or inform me about it. The head "veterinarian" kept the handy cattle killer for himself. When I found out, I acquired more ammo from the United States and made a stink to force the man to return the gun to the slaughterhouse.

This seesaw battle continued, with various "problems" prompting a return to use of the sledgehammer. Eventually I learned that the big export slaughterhouse near San José was using high-powered .22 rifles that worked wonderfully, so I purchased one for the local plant. At first, neither the municipality nor the butchers wanted to pay the 20 cents per bullet it cost to kill each animal, but eventually the municipality gave in. I could only hope the sledgehammer, *not* the rifle, would be lost or stolen.

During all this time, I searched for more satisfactory alternatives to cattle ranching and its attendant slaughter. I looked into vegetarianism; in the literature of one Eastern religion I discovered the admonition that "he who harms or causes the death of a Brahman cow will rot in hell for as many years as the cow has hairs." According to that and other accusers such as the Hare Krishnas, I was no less a demon and obviously in deep manure.

I could laugh at it, but just the same I much preferred to stay on the safe side of hell. My Christian and Baha'i friends tried to calm my guilt by saying that meat-eating was normal and acceptable to God. That might be so, but I knew that cruelty to the animals that were slaughtered would not be acceptable to the Chief, and as cattle raiser and seller, I was an accomplice. Why did I always seem to end up being an accomplice to the very things I was against?

The storm that raged inside of me finally produced an attack of joint pains (psychosomatic or not, they hurt like hell), which one doctor (I hoped he was a real quack) apparently misdiagnosed as degenerative rheumatoid arthritis and another doctor (who I believed knew what he was talking about) as Reiter's syndrome – a malady that affects only one in 10,000 males. Whatever it was, it hurt for about a year and then left just as mysteriously as it had come.

Maybe it left me when I ceased being so hard on myself, after I discovered the Hare Krishnas in their Honolulu center consuming milk from a local commercial dairy, which, like almost all commercial dairies in the United States, sold its old cattle and male calves for slaughter. It also helped when one of their popular spiritual leaders told me either to free all my cattle in the forest or not kill any more, but to keep clearing new land and making new pasture for all the new ones born. When I told him that I thought he had no accurate conception of reality, much less of reproduction dynamics, he responded with something like, "God will provide."

The overall effect of these conflicts and the inner turmoil they produced was that once again, I felt acutely marginal, unable to join the millions of happy, normal, hearty consumers who so confidently and enthusiastically gobbled down their Big Whopping Mega-Burgers without any concern about all that was in there between the ketchup and the bun, not to mention the pickles, onions, lettuce, flour, processed cheese, and of course, the supporting cast of nitrates, emulsifiers, enhancers and thickeners, fat, sugar, salt, corn syrup, monosodium glutamate, BHT, PCBs, growth hormones, herbicide and pesticide residues, artificial flavoring and coloring, and all that kind of stuff that made them taste so damn good.

Eventually I made some decisions, or at least rationalized my way to some peace of mind. I'd share my burgers with my dog, and I would cut the herd down to half the size, try to reforest the abandoned pastures, and be particular about the people to whom I sold my animals. I also decided to accept the possibility that I had a lot of bad karma to work off someday – hopefully not in Hades.

My decision to compromise was based on several facts, and probably on a few denials of fact. Protein was valuable nutrition in the Third World, and with careful management, cattle were an appropriate source of protein when raised on otherwise unsuitable land. A hundred people or more usually benefited from a single cow. Cows grew old and died anyway, so taking good care of them until they were killed and eaten, and then using their hides for leather goods and grinding up their bones for fertilizer and feed seemed reasonable. Most domestic cattle, at least in Costa Rica, lived very healthy lives in very beautiful places, and the entire ordeal of their deaths lasted a relatively short time.

Comparing these last couple of facts with the lives and deaths of most humans, I wondered if maybe I'd been investing too much emotional energy in the wrong species.

Buey (ox)

Siete Vueltas (Seven Curves)

Chapter Six

Visions of palm trees – flirting with paradise

If my little paradise was not destined to be a cattle ranch, what should be done with it? Wasn't there something better we could do than raise animals for slaughter?

In the late 1970s I thought I'd found a partial answer in the graceful swaying in the breeze of green coconut palms. Not only did they gratify my aesthetic sense, but I loved them also for all the good things they meant to humanity in terms of food, construction materials, and kitchen utensils. Palm wood, heart of palm, coconut husk, coconut shells, coconut meat and water at all their different stages, palm fronds, coconut palm roots – every part of this magnificent plant had multiple uses and probably many more not yet discovered. No wonder the coconut palm had been deified in places like the South Pacific atolls, where many creatures, including humans, owed their very existence to them. I wanted to walk in shady groves with these symbols of tropical paradise gently swaying around me, to hear the occasional drop of a frond or a coconut, to revel in seeing their luxurious green against the blue sea and sky.

The half mile of coastline of which I was steward was mostly steep, rocky, and still in its naturally forested state, but in the cove where the Quebrada Chica stream poured its sweet water into the ocean, the slope of the land was relatively gentle. Here, the first non-"Indian" colonizer, who lived and died there 30 years before, planted a dozen palm trees, which were now very tall and distinctive against the riotous background of other vegetation. They proudly marked the small natural port, which was what most prompted me to purchase land there in the first place.

Puerto Pedregal (Rocky Port) was the safest and most convenient year-round site for getting in and out of the ocean for several miles, yet at first glance this could be understood or appreciated by very few people. Who would consider an unprotected "beach" of large rounded boulders as any sort of a port? Puerto Pedregal's secret was its natural effect of significantly absorbing and dissipating the crashing punch of the waves, the same waves that pounded violently on the sand beaches a half mile north and south and on the rocky coast in between.

At Puerto Pedregal, the bottom dropped off quickly offshore and allowed no waves to break. When the ocean was at its most violent, the swells would rise and threaten but never break top to bottom. For many years the port for me was the theme of frightening dreams in which waves *did* break and swamped my boat where I left it moored, stranding me on some strange, foreign shore inhabited by strange people and creatures. I would wake up on stormy nights when the ocean roared and have to reassure myself that my boat was still safe, that the waves wouldn't break over it, that it would still be there in the morning, even though it might be full of water.

Behind Puerto Pedregal and across Quebrada Chica were two acres of gently sloping land that had belonged to Oscura, much of it already partially cleared, ideal for palm trees. There was a problem, however, one that launched a heated internal debate. A tribe of white-faced monkeys used the dense trees and vines lining the coast as a highway to reach the many different fruit trees in the area. If I cut the trees whose limbs and parasitic vines formed the "highway," I would be doing my monkey friends a great disservice, since they were arboreal creatures who hated to be forced down to ground level except to drink. According to a local man named Modesto, they drank with their eyes closed to avoid seeing their own reflection.

If I didn't cut the jungle, however, I would not be able to plant the palm trees to the edge of the ocean, which would be the most aesthetically pleasing and also the best for the palms, since the salt breeze was especially healthy for them. Once again, it came down to the moral issue of whose rights were paramount, the monkeys' or mine.

My employees/advisors were, as usual, all in favor of human enterprise, eager to chop down the jungle and energetic in their vote against the monkeys. "Those white-faced *caretos* are smart little devils," Joaquin told me one day, "harmful to the ultimate! Your cornfield is never safe as long as they're around. They love corn, young and old, and maybe you won't believe this, but I swear to you that when a group of white-faced monkeys raids a cornfield, first they put up scouts in the tallest trees to see if any person is coming with a rifle. As soon as they see someone coming, they call out an alarm and all the little thieves haul off their bundles of corn. You probably think they just carry a few ears of corn each – no. No, señor! They husk the corn halfway and tie two or three ears together with the husks! I've seen it! And so, when a bunch of caretos raids your field, you can count on them hauling off a lot. That's why we kill them when we can. Some people eat them, but they're not nearly as good as the red monkeys or the howler monkeys."

But I wasn't going to kill them or eat them. I really liked them. I enjoyed watching them jumping and swinging through the trees and was amused by their angry faces and the varied gestures they made. To me, they were a definite plus, these "people of the forest," as Joaquin sometimes referred to them. I left their coastal highway intact and cleared just the junk growth behind it.

The closest coconut grove lay hidden by a swamp behind Morita's overgrown graveyard. It was the only place where we could acquire enough sprouted coconuts for planting. Carlos knew the place well. His grandmother planted the coconut grove and now it was nobody's, so we needn't ask permission.

The idea of possession of land in Morita was strange to me. No one, for example, ever coveted the coconut grove in question for many years. Then, newcomers would purchase it from squatters, who appropriated it from the government, which took it away from Alcoa Aluminum after Alcoa purchased it from the ex-hacienda owner, who inherited it from his father, who acquired it from an unsuccessful banana company and poor subsistence farmers, who purchased it for pennies an acre from the original squatters, who, a mere 40 years ago, colonized the area after the indigenous people retreated to more remote mountain areas.

To get to the palm seeds, the coconuts, we hacked a kilometer of jungle trail for the oxen and cart. We then took all we wanted, several hundred of the largest variety there, called *chocoano*. So the young shoots would not be damaged, we took only 50 or so at a time, which was plenty enough cargo for the oxen, considering the poor condition of the trail. Each water-soaked coconut weighed between five and ten pounds. Tito and his huge curved-horn oxen took them three kilometers down the sand beach at low tide when the breakers weren't so powerful, and we next loaded them into our invaluable 22-foot jabillo-wood dugout (for which I paid $80 and then reribbed and caulked it with tarred coconut husk). We called the dugout *Siete Vueltas* (Seven Curves) because of its sun-warped sides. Powered by a 25-hp outboard, the trusty dugout hauled the coconuts back to Puerto Pedregal while Tito went back with the oxen for another load.

Unloading cargo on slippery boulders required all our agility, strength, and attentiveness. It was an operation that forced me to learn to make quick, serious decisions. When the ocean was calm, I could usually relax, but when it was rough our success depended on my judgment of the sets of waves and the intervals between them. Once we had committed to rush the dugout toward shore, it was difficult and dangerous to change the loaded dugout's position.

Our goal was to wedge the boat stern-first onto the boulders on shore, where it would be held securely. To do so, we aimed the dugout backward, pulled up the outboard so it wouldn't hit the rocks, and then two oarsmen riding an incoming swell paddled hard toward shore. Others, feet planted as solidly as possible on the rounded-boulder beach, received the boat and pulled and pushed it up as high as possible, aided by the waves. Three or four more would unload the cargo.

When particularly large swells approached, I would alert everyone. The big waves would knock Carlos, the intrepid bowman, around some, but if he didn't let go he wouldn't be hurt. The wave would often wash over us, the boat would take on up to 50 gallons of water, and some dry cargo would get wet. A few times – fortunately very few – we would all get knocked around. Bowmen other than Carlos would often panic and scramble for safety when a big wave approached. This allowed the wave to wrench the heavy dugout from us, the backwash banging it against boulders, putting it in a catastrophic broadside position to the next wave. At times like these I would have about 30 seconds to issue new orders and have them executed successfully to avoid the destruction of boat, loss of cargo, or injury to someone.

The most important thing was to keep the bow pointed into the punch of the sea. So when I would see one of those strong, foamy white backwashes rolling some of my helpers over the shiny black rocks, with Siete Vueltas broadside to the next powerful swell, I would have to see first who was still ready on his feet and get them to make a mad ankle- and shin-banging scramble with me to push the boat around and point it out to sea. This was one of Carlos's specialties, and I convinced him to quit Alcoa and help me – forgiving his troublesome drinking habit – largely because of his phenomenal competence with Siete Vueltas, his steadfastness at the bow while unloading at Puerto Pedregal, and his superior knowledge of the local sea. Truly, Carlos was irreplaceable.

The only time I saw anyone really close to being broken and crushed, was when we were transporting a ton of cement and sand taken from the sandy Punta Morita for the water-holding tank we were building. Those of us who were in charge of keeping Siete Vueltas steady and in correct position usually wore diving fins, for two reasons: At low tide, when the wave action was least violent, our fins protected our feet from the razor-sharp "take-a-bite" barnacles, which always seemed to tax somebody for a chunk of flesh. We often worked in chest- or waist-deep water and had to swim by the boat to guide it in and out.

A diving fin fit perfectly in a vertical position in the space between two particularly large boulders, and once in, if you panicked you couldn't get your fin or foot out, no matter how hard you pulled. The trick was to relax and seek the particular vertical position to gently pull the fin out. But we all tended to panic and yank in every direction but the right one. Of course, irregular boulders with take-a-bites, knee-deep water with oncoming swells, sucking backwash, and a boat full of cargo didn't comprise optimum conditions for relaxation and calm action. The hole wasn't something I ever pointed out to anyone or told them how to perform the magic trick that would free them because I never really knew where it was myself.

When I saw José sitting in the water behind Siete Vueltas' stern frantically pulling on his ankle, the whites of his black eyes growing larger and larger, I knew he was in it. Siete Vueltas was not very well cradled on the rocks and was full to capacity, a ton; the ocean was in a bad mood; and I had just told one of the holders to help the others with the 100-pound sacks of sand. And a series of big waves was approaching. For what seemed like much too long, I hesitated, not knowing what to do or yell. I couldn't give up my position to rescue José, who was laughing nervously and looking at me in utter frustration. I knew how the hole was. It wouldn't let go. "Throw them down on the rocks and grab the boat, quickly!" I yelled at the holders I had told to help with the sacks of sand. José was only a couple of meters behind Siete Vueltas, where a big wave could easily push the boat on top of him. Big waves were just about to hit. "When I say 'out,' everyone push out, and I mean out!" I shouted. Those who had been hauling the sacks of sand didn't realize José was stuck or in danger, yet I needed their outward pushing strength to save his life. In any other circumstance – big waves coming, boat full of cargo – my order would have been an emphatic "In! Up to the rocks," but there was no time to explain.

"Now! Out!" Just as the pounding swell surged under Siete Vueltas and lifted it off the rocks and shoved it toward José, we shoved hard back and sent it with the violent backwash out to sea. José was washed over and knocked around a bit by the strong surge, but without injury. Between waves, we helped him out of the hole and went back to work.

Unlike the tons and tons of barbed wire, nails, roofing, food supplies, salt for the animals, sand, cement, etc., that came through Puerto Pedregal, the sprouted coconuts were easy cargo. The Ministry of Agriculture people advised us to bury the coconuts in the ground four meters apart in "chicken foot" formation, which was theoretically accomplished by plotting out equilateral triangles and planting at the corners. The land was very irregular, however, and many of the corners formed on tops of rocks too large to be moved, so the chicken-feet business failed. This didn't bother me, as I wasn't so enthusiastic about even spacing in the first place. Carlos wanted to "do the job right," but after a couple of hours trying to comply with the engineers' specifications, he surrendered to the land's.

Instead of burying coconuts, we only half-buried them in loosened dirt, following the advice of Chontales, the old hacienda cowboy who had been born on the coast and claimed "100 percent more experience with coconuts than any *ingeniero agrónomo* from San Cristobal."

The palms grew frustratingly slowly at first, when their roots were just taking hold. Every couple of months the grass, weeds, and strangler vines reached a person's height while the palms stood only waist high. A year passed and they still looked small and insignificant against the rambunctious weeds and tall grasses, but two years after beginning our coconut palm planting in 1974, I could say, "Oh, what beautiful little palm trees." After another year, some of the fronds reached to twice a person's height, so we could let up some on the weed and grass cutting.

At this time, a particularly severe dry season came and the milk cows weren't giving half as much milk as they could for lack of adequate pasture. Carlos suggested we let the cows eat the plentiful natural grasses around the palm trees, and I optimistically agreed to go ahead and leave the cows there after corralling the calves that afternoon. The next morning in the milking corral, Carlos told me with his charming smile, "You know, it seems the cattle like the palms." My Costa Rican Spanish and psychology still had a long way to go, so I wasn't quite sure what he meant by "like" in that context. Distracted by a cow trying to squish me against the side of a corral, I forgot about Carlos's remark. When the milking was finished and he asked me whether I still wanted the cows to pasture with the palms, I pointed to the extra gallons of milk and laughed and said, "Yeah, of course! We've got cheese again!"

The next afternoon I helped Carlos take the cows back to the pasture where the palms were. I felt a volcano erupt in my stomach when I saw the battered, ripped, and mangled trees. Gazing stupefied at what appeared to be the obliteration of three years of costly nurturing and intense emotional input, I wanted to curse and scream. I must have at least turned red. Adequate words were nowhere available. A groan and a long string of English cussing helped, but I lost control of my temper and took it out on poor Carlos.

"Don't you see the cows are eating the palms? Why didn't you tell me?" I shouted.

"I *did* tell you, yesterday morning, and you said it was all right," he replied slowly, with obvious restraint, offended by my outrage. Luckily I saw this in time, barely. I didn't want to lose Carlos and my palms the same day, so I tried to cool down. Superficially I succeeded, but my insides were still a bubbling cauldron.

"I remember you said the cattle *liked* the palms. I thought you meant they liked to graze around them, not that they liked to eat the hell out of them!" I tried to laugh. "If I'd known, do you think I would approve? After so long caring for them?"

"They're not going to die, anyway," Carlos said defensively, looking down at the ground, probably still debating whether or not to resign. "It doesn't matter so much that they ate the fronds as long as they didn't eat the hearts . . . a few might die, but not too many."

A dozen or so died and the rest would need a year to recuperate from being ravaged by the cattle, who I now knew didn't just like palms but *loved* 'em! Unfortunately, traumatic experience seemed to be the most common way to learn important lessons there, or perhaps anywhere. To eliminate the psychological trauma was the secret, to learn to control my temper, to practice smiling in the face of frequent adversity, to take life on as a challenging sport – I thought of it as "jungleball." Then and only then could I roll with the complications and disappointments of tropical reality.

Five years after planting coconuts, I learned with a tiny bit more grace that horses, too, love young palm trees. But at six years in 1980, when the weevil plague hit, I realized how poor a sport I still really was. This palm weevil beast, the *picudo* with its shiny rock-hard black exoskeleton and state-of-the-art tools for digging and boring, outclassed any defense I could imagine. Weevils – I had seen little ones boring perfectly round holes in corn and beans, and I'd heard of the U.S. farmers' dread of the cotton weevil and the boll weevil; now I had evil weevils of my own, about the size of half a thumb.

I wasn't sure how they bored so fast and well into the earth and wood unless it was with the anteater-like proboscises, which were perfectly pivotable and too hard to break with one's fingers, as were their thoraxes and abdomens, which were ingeniously welded together. Each pair of legs and feelers and whatnot was different, specialized, with hooks and barbs and cutting edges fascinating to behold and stronger than those of any other insect I'd known. To observe such a creature, all metallic-black and apparently seamless, open up its back and take off in slow flight, was like watching a Transformer Robot I saw on a TV in San José do a similar stunt, only this was for real. In fact, these weevils made me tinker with the sci-fi speculation that insects could be of extraterrestrial genetic origin.

The palm weevils' eyes were black and immobile and showed no sign of intelligence. What they did show was simply a perfect adaptation to their environment, assuring them of survival as long as their habitat existed. Poisons of the nastiest sort were of no use unless the weevils could be persuaded to ingest them. There were too many of them to trap them all. For them to sacrifice a palm tree for the sake of producing dozens more weevils required only two conscienceless picudo adults, the male to fertilize the female and the female to wreak havoc. They could fly in and bore down from the top of the tree or dig into the earth and bore up from the bottom. Strong systemic poisons killed the trees before they killed the weevils.

When the tough picudos shunned the harder forest palms to feast on the succulent hearts of coconut palms we so conveniently imported for them, we had about 700 trees, half of them already producing. I hadn't yet been acquainted with the destroyer when I first saw the drooping yellowing fronds and the prematurely falling coconuts. It took a few weeks for the first dozen trees to die. We cut them open with ax and machete and discovered many fat, white grubs finishing off the rotting hearts of the palm. We also discovered a few almost-mature picudos, and then understood the life cycle of the creatures.

I'd seen the fat larvae somewhere in anthropologists' pictures of foods eaten by remote tribes of South America and Asia, but by the feel of them and the way they lurched and wiggled in my hand, I was repulsed by the thought of eating them. Later, after seeing the enthusiasm with which our turkeys gobbled them up, they seemed less nauseating to me. Fried, maybe, I mused. Yes, I could eat them, I finally decided. Perhaps sautéed in coconut oil, sea salt, and cilantro – not a bad lunch, perhaps, for a nuclear wintry day.

For the just-yellowing palms, my instructions to the workers were: cut them down; if the heart was still good, bring it back for us to eat, if not, chop it up into pieces and poison with malathion; bring back the grubs for the turkeys; kill any adult or juvenile weevils. For the healthy trees, the drill was to cover the lower trunks with calcium carbonate (lime), clean the ground of weeds and grass a yard around them, and fertilize with salt. When that didn't work, I took the advice of several agronomists and resorted to one of their recommended systemic poisons, sprinkled copiously around the trunks.

Like so much of modern technology, its effect, the "cure," did more harm than good. It scared off the weevils for a while, all right, but it sickened some of the palms. After learning more about this particular poison – which I discovered was one of those banned in my home country but was still produced there and exported in enormous quantities to the Third World, where ignorant farmers like me contaminated our land and ourselves with it – I lost my taste for the coconut water or coconut meat from those trees.

After inadvertently poisoning what were the very symbols of tropical paradise to me, I became disappointed with myself once again and this time vowed to give up on poisons – at least on plants. When the weevils returned, vengeance in their hearts, I gave up on palm trees, too, and on my plans to produce dried coconut chips for export. I drew small comfort from the knowledge that in Florida, where palm trees waving in the ocean breeze were a priceless tourist attraction, authorities had waged a futile, multimillion-dollar, high-tech battle against another even nastier little tree-killing devil, the yellow-mottle virus.

We continued to chop down the trees showing signs of infestation, hoping to prevent the larvae from metamorphosing into adults – and wanting also to eliminate the depressing sight of the dying palm trees. By 1985, half of the trees originally planted remained, and most of the survivors were closest to the ocean. Salt breezes seemed to fortify their defenses or repel the invaders. This left me pondering what to do about the thick stand of native trees and vegetation I left standing for the benefit of the monkeys. Their "highway" was blocking the ocean breezes from the largest grove of palms, leaving those trees susceptible to weevil infestation.

In the endlessly debatable matter of who had more "right," of what was "correct" on a cosmic level, I generally sided with nature and almost everything indigenous. But this was impractical if "nonprimitive" humans were to live and work and be happy in that environment. Nature and its human progeny often seem incompatible, especially in the tropics, where it seems people must compete constantly with so very many better-adapted plants and animals. Maybe it would have been best to fence off the whole finca, give in to all the creatures, and keep out all the humans. But where would that have left me?

In the conflict between monkeys and palm trees, and in many other cases, I was torn by warring emotions and my own confused attempts to chart a logical path. I felt young, naïve, foreign, and inexperienced, and in my quest to be accepted by those around me, I often allowed them to influence my course of action. This was the case now.

Down came the trees, vines, and shrubs lining a large part of the coast, opening up a beautiful view of the ocean. In rushed the salt air. Away went the weevils. And away went the monkeys.

Soon, it became uncommon to see a sick and yellowing palm. I knew the weevils could return, but for the time being I could lay back in the hammock on the porch and look out at dozens of coconut palms swaying gracefully in the sea breeze, the healthy green of their fronds contrasting beautifully with the blue ocean and white clouds. On Sunday afternoons, I could walk through shady groves and perhaps hear the thud of a big chocoano coconut dropping to the ground, and I could say, "Oh, my beautiful palms."

In my heart, though, I still felt that the very best things were those found free, the ones that had been there in the first place, the ones left as they were.

Careto (capuchín or white face monkey)

Chapter Seven

Getting along with our fellow creatures

It must have been a coincidence that, while my conscience was still punishing me for obliterating the monkey highway, a friend in the small nearby town of San Cristobal took me to a neighbor's house and introduced me to another monkey problem. This turned out to be one more of many similar problems that created the huge personal problem of trying to discover a benign role for man in the tropics and on Earth.

A distraught housewife presented us to a lanky 10-pound *mono colorado*, a red (spider) monkey, in a dirty little cage of chicken wire and scrap wood. The animal sat with a soiled little blanket over his head so he couldn't see the world, or so the world couldn't see him, or both. The only giant that didn't poke at him or bark at him or throw things at him or make horrible faces at him was the woman. And now her husband, for unknown reasons, was hounding her to get rid of him. The husband was the one who had captured the animal in the first place, after killing its mother while he was hunting with friends, which was the usual way people acquired pet monkeys. But Lolo had grown a lot, wasn't so cute anymore, and was no longer welcome. Many of the husband's friends suggested he should be killed and prepared, and although the wife undoubtedly was aware of its excellent culinary possibilities, she loved the poor creature.

The problematic relationship between these people and the monkey was a fairly common cause of tension in households in the region. Although they lived in close contact with the many wild creatures of the forest, animals that people in urbanized countries like the United States could visit only in zoos, the people of rural Costa Rica alternated between concern and abuse in their treatment of their nonhuman neighbors. The pet monkey dilemma seemed like one of those situations in which a naïve, animal-loving gringo could really come in handy.

"His name is Lolo," the woman said, trying to smile, then frowning in sadness and frustration. "You see how much he loves his blanket. It's that he's not happy around here. He needs to be free, to join his fellows. My husband just doesn't like him anymore. . . ." She paused uncomfortably as I waited politely for her to make her point.

"I hear you live on the coast . . . and have a lot of forest on your land. . . . Could you take him and let him go there for me?"

I was obviously dealing with a kindhearted person and a pet that was more than a pet to her. Apart from the minor inconveniences I envisioned in taking the creature on the 20-minute plane ride to Morita and then traveling the five kilometers to my land, I was unconcerned about what I might be getting myself into and told her, "Sure, no problem."

"Oh, wonderful!" she exclaimed, as if surprised by my easy acceptance. "He's no problem if you just remember a few things; Lolo likes his coffee with milk in his little red cup, with rice and beans in the morning. Don't watch him eat because he won't eat if anybody's watching. Don't make faces at him. And whatever you do, *don't* take his blanket away from him."

That sounded simple enough for me, especially since I figured on simply releasing him in the big banana grove bordering the forest. The woman cried and Lolo shrieked when I took him away in a wooden fruit crate. Between San Cristobal and the farm, by plane, horse, and on foot, everyone I saw insisted on poking at Lolo or making faces at him or trying to take his blanket away. When Lucía – whom I sometimes kidded and called "my Costa Rican mother" – saw my cargo, her cheerful welcome turned into an intimidating, tight-lipped frown. "Hear me good," she said in a very uncharacteristically serious manner. "It's either this creature or me. It goes and I stay, or it stays and I go."

"Oh, relax, it's just a little monkey, Lucía," I laughed, unsuccessfully trying to soften her.

"Just a little monkey, sure, but it's a little *male* monkey, and I've seen too many things in one life to have anything to do with such little devils."

By her expression and tone of voice, I could tell that Lucía was upset with Lolo, yet despite knowing her well, I couldn't figure out why. At 60, she was still strong and canny. She had been one of the best hunters in the area, and the men had begrudgingly accorded her quite a bit of fame for her bravery. She was known to take her single-shot .22 rifle and her dog and venture alone into the forest and return with a tepezcuintle as if it were her daily business. She once caught a cubeira snapper as big as herself after a three-hour fight from the beach with a handline. She defended herself well against wild animals and wild drunken men. One time when my dog was barking down by the stream a little harder than usual, I saw her drop what she was doing, pick up a big machete and run toward the barking. I arrived in time to see her rescue my dog from the incredibly strong claws of a large anteater. So why the fuss over a sad little monkey?

Don Arturo, old and sick and without energy, couldn't contain his convulsive laughter. He loved to see Lucía so riled up, but he still came to her defense.

"Once our neighbor had a pig, a big sow . . . and then they got a pet monkey," he said. "Every day the monkey would jump on the pig's back and make her run until she was so tired she couldn't run anymore. She would just lay on her side panting, so they had to kill the monkey or the pig would die. But Dimas has a better story, like the ones Lucía must be worried about."

He laughed until he broke down coughing and gasping for air. He motioned with his hand to Don Dimas to tell his story.

Don Dimas, who was nearly as old as Don Arturo but in excellent physical condition, was my most loyal and most consistent employee, with the smile of a boy and the manners of a saint. He always became innocent-looking and serious when it was his turn to tell a story – so as not to lose credibility.

"This is true," he began. "A man was riding along in his oxcart with a big barrel of guaro he had brewed and was taking to sell. He took his pet monkey to keep him company, because it was a pretty long journey. It was night and the man was half asleep. The monkey was in a playful mood and began to unscrew the stopper on the side of the barrel. All of a sudden there was a gush of guaro, and when the man woke up he found the monkey with his hands over the hole, trying to prevent the guaro from escaping. The man saw what the monkey had done, but seeing that he was trying at least to help, the man forgot his anger, laughed, and petted him, even feeling grateful that his monkey had been so smart and brave enough to prevent more guaro from spilling out. He tapped the barrel and continued on his way, until he arrived to where he sold his guaro.

"When he got home and his wife found out that they had lost money because of the mischievous monkey, she said to her husband, 'That animal is becoming too much of a problem. Maybe we should get rid of it.' But the man convinced her to forgive the creature.

"A few days later, the monkey discovered the woman urinating in a field behind a bush, and thinking he was doing the right thing, ran over to her from behind and put his hands up there to try to prevent any more from escaping! Of course, the woman jumped up and screamed, and then the man had to get rid of the monkey."

Amid the men's laughter, Lucía shouted, "You see? Monkeys and Christian women never get along. And male monkeys are the worst of all!"

I sensed unanimous agreement with Lucía, and when Don Dimas saw the confusion on my expression, he said to me, "Look, *patrón*, say a man comes across a troop of monkeys in the forest here. No problem. The monkeys stay up in the trees and maybe make threats, throw some stuff down, or go away frightened, afraid of a gun or rock thrown. But if it's a woman, those little guys will not only threaten to come down and attack, they *will!*" He laughed, but was serious.

I couldn't imagine such things and only found out by seeing them myself or having them spelled out for me by people I trusted. Maybe Lucía had had a frightening experience with sexually indiscriminate and aggressive monkeys while on one of her forest excursions. Still, I won a compromise: I could keep Lolo prisoner in the old chicken house, as long as it took for him to adapt to the local environment, after which I would let him go.

Had I known how difficult it was to reintroduce long-time captive animals to their native habitat, I might not have expected too much of Lolo. I always assumed an intelligent primate could learn basic survival techniques without too much trouble. I was foolish to suppose that Lolo, who had lived in a small cage for years and whose meals had always been brought to him, could find food in the wild while avoiding predators, snakes, and poisonous plants. Maybe if he was younger and I had enough time and patience – but the truth was that we were both too set in our ways.

Lolo was like a stubborn little child who didn't care to learn anything of practical value, like identifying a ripe banana on a banana stalk and pulling it off, peeling it, and eating it. He showed no affinity for any of the stages in the eating process except the last, and that only if I put the peeled banana up to his mouth. He did enjoy my company, but when I wished to go he would clutch my arm or leg and threaten to bite me if I abandoned him. Invariably, each time we finished a lesson, it was with violent shrieking on his part and vigorous cussing on my part.

He wasn't a model houseguest, either. Once Lucía found him in the kitchen after he'd spread lard all over it. She threw some hot water on him and he ran away, terrified. I found him in a weed-filled ditch, hiding under his blanket.

Sometimes when I returned after a weekend trip, I'd discover that someone had further traumatized him. It almost seemed to me that some of these people were trying, desperately at times, to prove their vast superiority over poor Lolo. When this kind of tormenting became more frequent, I began making Lolo's lessons in survival more frequent and more strict.

Finally I told Tito, who was very knowledgeable in handling wild animals, to take Lolo up to the high banana grove by the thickest forest and let him go. I hoped that he might join up with some of the rare red monkeys that had been seen in that area. Hopefully he would survive among his fellows if not alone. Later, the boy that accompanied Tito told me that Tito couldn't refrain from taking Lolo's blanket away from him to see what the monkey would do. Lolo did nothing, just cowered catatonically at the base of a banana plant. Tito then covered him again with the blanket and left. Then it rained.

Weeks later, I heard the rumor that Tito had not really taken Lolo to the banana grove at all, but to Oscura's place, where they made an excellent dinner of him. At around the same time, a more reliable neighbor told me he had seen a healthy lone red monkey in the forest behind his property. He remarked that it was too bad he hadn't joined up with another monkey tribe, but the truth was that people had eaten all the others of Lolo's kind in the area. "You know, those colorados really are tasty, and now the people who ate them are starting on the *congos* too!" the man said.

When I saw Lolo's human "mother" again in San Cristobal, she asked me with much hope and enthusiasm how her Lolo had made out. I put on my con-man smile and said, "You did the right thing. Now Lolo is free in the forest." She took my remark very positively, as I had hoped, smiled widely, sighed with great relief, and thanked me sincerely for my help.

Things could have been worse for Lolo. Dead or alive, he was better off than most lab monkeys. Nevertheless, I felt bad about my apparent failure with Lolo until years later, when I heard from some people who hadn't known about him that they had seen a colorado that curiously had become an accepted member of a white-faced monkey troop that frequented the same area where we released him.

If Lolo taught me anything, it was that wild animals and cages are not compatible, and so when a gringo couple came to the area "to be in the jungle with wild animals" (in cages), I listened disapprovingly to what the neighbors told me about their progress. They seemed like a really nice couple, the bearded seaman who was most of the year on the high seas, who could drink more beer and smoke more cigarettes than anybody had ever seen, and his friendly wife who recently had to have 12 stitches in her scalp due to an unruly ocelot they kept in San Cristobal.

They built a small tin-roofed house, which was actually a series of wire-mesh apartments to accommodate their white-faced monkey, their black tolomuco, two green-and-yellow parrots, and one scarlet macaw. The female monkey, who was in the best shape of all the creatures, was allowed to share living space with the humans. She constantly opened jars and made messes and jumped spectacularly all around, knocking things over. The old, dusty, flightless parrots squawked and pooped. The beautiful tolomuco, feline-like, paced continually back and forth in her little muddy enclosure.

These interesting temporary neighbors entertained ideas of expanding their zoo "to protect endangered species," and apparently sought help from some local people – who told me the newcomers particularly wished to acquire one or more howler monkeys from the small troop inhabiting "my" most remote forest area. Fortunately, things didn't work out as the interesting couple had hoped.

In order to attract other white-faced monkeys, they let their female loose. She did bring other "caretos" close to their zoo-house, but then she decided to take off with her new friends and learn to live like a real monkey. She never returned. I was pleased with this news and realized that this was the best way to reintroduce primates to the wild, to get a local tribe to accept them and teach them. I felt fairly sure that Lolo would have fared well with a troop of his kind, but since there weren't any remaining locally, he must have had a hard time. If he really had been accepted by a troop of caretos, then he was an exceptionally lucky monkey. Kind of like me, I thought whimsically, a lone gringo among friendly and hospitable ticos.

One time when the neighboring saviors of endangered species were away, as they usually were, a large, beautiful brown-orange-black-and-white boa constrictor came from the forest to visit the zoo-house. It devoured both parrots but made the mistake of hanging around to digest them. The local man who was left in charge of caring for the animals discovered the lumpy serpent in the parrots' cage and dutifully hacked it to death with a machete. A couple of weeks later, driven by hunger, the sleek tolomuco sneaked into the macaw's cage and made a satisfying meal of it. The man in charge killed the tolomuco for this unpardonable crime. When the owners returned, the only creature they found alive in their zoo-house was the man in charge.

The local people enjoyed having pets as well, but usually with the same typically tragic results for the animals. Parakeets and parrots were squeezed too hard by children or devoured by cats or dogs or snakes. Domesticated curassows (turkey-sized arboreal game birds) invariably wandered off and were killed and eaten by other people or dogs. Tame tepezcuintles and *pizotes* (coatimundis) met similar fates. The animal that survived best among humans, the dog, was tolerated because of its value as hunter and warning device, and because it was not considered edible and could withstand tremendous abuse and hunger. Cats were less interested in people than in the rodents attracted to people's dwellings and were therefore tolerated because of their pest-controlling abilities. Adult humans rarely, if ever, touched their cats or dogs unless necessary, not necessarily because of lack of affection, but because they had a good sense of tropical parasitology and pathology. Dogs and cats made great hosts for a lot of bad stuff.

One neighbor exhibited a very special relationship with animals (and with people, too). Santos, who was dark and lean, with black eyes and strong indigenous genes, was the only young neighbor male who never asked me for daily work. He hardly worked himself, in the conventional sense. More than anyone else in the area, he was still almost entirely a hunter and gatherer, and a first-class one. He never wore shoes or shirt, and he was often seen with a big iguana or pizote or giant fish dangling down his back. He could catch plump doves with his bare hands and return from a short visit to the stream with a bunch of shiny, large prawns. Amazing things were always happening to him.

Santos could harpoon *robálos* (snooks) up to 30 pounds in the estuaries as if it were his profession, which it could have been had he wanted to make the money. One day while he was fishing in knee-deep brackish water in the estuary near my finca, Santos was grabbed by a ten-foot crocodile that had appeared to be nothing more than a mossy log floating among the other debris. The huge reptile lunged at him, grabbed him around one thigh and dragged him under. A normal person would have panicked, gulped water, drowned, and been carried into the reptile's cave to rot and be devoured.

After about half a minute, Santos said, he observed a dark hole surrounded by roots in the side of the bank, which must have been the croc's underwater cave. The beast chomped down on Santos' thigh and shook its head and tried to push Santos into the cave. Nearing the end of his air, Santos reached out desperately and grabbed a strong root at the mouth of the cave. With the other hand he tried to drive his harpoon into the hard, leathery skin of the creature, which seemed unfazed. Then, risking piercing his own legs in the murky water, he jabbed his spear at the croc's head and eyes, and the animal loosened its jaws.

In that instant, Santos pulled on the root with a great surge of energy and rose to the surface, where he gulped for air while still jabbing the persistent attacker with his shattered spear. He lay on the bank for a long time, struggling not to faint, keeping an eye on the dirty water of the estuary, wary that the croc might attack again. Unable to walk and bleeding heavily, he dragged himself a kilometer to the public trail, where he was found and taken by horse and then bus to the hospital in La Palma, a four-hour trip south. The bite scars around his thigh reminded me of ones I'd seen on TV on the back of an Australian who'd survived an attack by a great white shark.

Santos was known to disappear for days at a time and when asked what he did or where he went, would reply with a big smile and raised eyebrows, "Oh, just wandering and sitting in trees."

A fascinating middleman between the human and nonhuman world, Santos amusingly referred to people's body parts with animal terminology. Hands were paws, feet were hooves, noses were snouts, hair was a mane, fingers and toenails were claws, stomachs were bellies, skin was hide. He devised animal nicknames for his acquaintances and used them instead of their "Christian" names. At one time, I had employees called Skunk, who'd been caught stealing a chicken;

Lizard, whose ribs protruded; Little Monkey, who had a small face and protruding ears; and Buzzard, who once consumed a half-cooked monkey after being lost and starving in the forest.

While Lolo was still in captivity, he regarded Santos as the devil himself. Santos never even had to make a move; but, when he looked at Lolo in a peculiar way, even from quite a distance, even for a moment, Lolo would go completely berserk and Santos would laugh and laugh. He was the only one who could provoke such violent reactions from Lolo, who would begin biting the chicken wire and shaking and jumping hysterically. Since Santos achieved this with no apparent effort, people brought Santos to Don Arturo's place just to observe the phenomenon, which I admit was mysterious and thought-provoking.

It was obvious to me that Santos possessed special qualities and valuable knowledge. He could have taught me many things about the local environment, but when it dawned on me that he would have eaten Lolo without any qualms – and may have done so, according to Tito – I lost some enthusiasm about becoming his apprentice.

Caimán (Caiman)

Chapter Eight

*Closer to nature – learning about good
and bad, right and wrong*

Who were the "Indians"? By "Indians" I mean the Native Americans whom Columbus, completely lost, so misnamed; but, was somehow able to convince everyone after him to follow his folly. I kept receiving new information about Costa Rican Indians, new ideas, and new evidence, which usually raised new questions. Were they like Santos in that they could prosper barefoot in the rainforest? Were they as fit as wild animals? What were their feelings for their environment, for other animals, for each other? Could they teach us how to prosper peacefully and nondestructively in the tropics?

Don Arturo, Don Aurelio (Lucía's brother), Don Dimas, and a distant neighbor, Juan, of particularly strong indigenous ancestry, all told me corroborating stories that depicted the vanished and extinct "dark ones" in surprising and unexpected ways.

Don Aurelio was 60-some years old when I first met him. Tall and thin with a gaunt face, resembling popular images of Don Quixote, he seemed to be an expert on the local indigenous people who had long since fled the area. Besides helping me with his carpentry skills, he was an honored regular at the nightly talks in Don Arturo's choza.

"The problem with the young people of now is that they don't care for the old wisdom of the Indians, who lived here, right here where we are now, for thousands of years, only God knows how long. But since the white man has come in such numbers, the Indian, the *real* Indian, has gone deeper into the forest, far into the Talamanca Mountains, and has taken his wisdom with him. When I was young, this area was mostly inhabited by Indians. My grandmother was an Indian who, they told me, was captured with the help of hunting dogs, along with some other females, by my grandfather and his friends, who didn't have women. My best friends were Indians. They taught me all I know. I could communicate in their dialect fairly well, but I've forgotten a lot now.

"They used to come to where we lived; as many as 25 would come and sit down and spend the night. They would ask for a pig or a few chickens, and of course we had to give them whatever they wanted. If a white man [mestizo] didn't give them what they asked for, say a pig, then that pig would be found dead the next day or a few days later. And if the white man asked for something in exchange, a clay pot or a spear or something, they would never return. They liked to ask for things but never gave a gift if you asked them for one.

"Where we lived, they used to come and collect dirt for their weapons. They had long, hollowed out *vizcoyol* [bamboo-like] rods that they blew little dirt bullets out of. It wasn't just any dirt they used for their bullets. It was a special clay that they found near our house. They would choose it carefully, roll it into perfectly round balls, and put them in a fire for many hours. These bullets of the Indians were hard as rocks. With these blowguns, poof! They could knock any bird out of a tree. I borrowed one once and blew as hard as I could and the ball fell out of the barrel on the ground just in front of me. But later I learned to catch fish with spear and bow and arrow so well that I could almost do it better than the Indian who taught me. The Indian never killed for pleasure like the white man sometimes does, just for meat. They ate everything and used the bones and hides for many things.

"It used to be that a person they knew could go to their village and trade pieces of cheap red cloth for a little golden frog or a little bell or something. Now the Indians are clever, though. They know what things are worth in terms of money, not like the poor *indio* who went into a white man's town and saw everyone wearing shoes on their feet – the story goes that the Indian wanted the best shoes he could get for the gold he was willing to trade, so he demanded that the owner of the store give him the very biggest shoes he had, which he put one under each armpit and walked away through town smiling and content with the deal. No, there aren't any more Indians like him!

"Indians are the most tranquil people. They don't worry about anything. They are happy drinking their *chichamuhosa*, the fermented drink that they make from plantain and corn, with the help of sugar cane. They used to eat all their meat raw. In fact, the oldest Indians used to eat meat a few days old. They liked it better just like the dogs, vultures, and crocodiles prefer their meat a little rotten, maybe because it's much easier to chew. It is said that they even smeared themselves with the old meat as if it were perfume! We may laugh at them, but they never had stomach problems like us, and their teeth didn't rot like ours. They didn't suffer from hunger, either. They only ate one big meal a day, but were stronger and healthier than any white man. They could go to the river and come back with enough prawns for a meal for several people. In the forest, they were fine. They cured themselves with plants. In many ways, they still know a lot more than anybody what you call 'natural knowledge,' which is the most important. They didn't need sugar, lard, coffee, cigarettes, or guaro and didn't depend on anyone else. Besides necklaces, bracelets, and other jewelry, the oldest Indians didn't wear clothes and didn't cut their hair, but the ones I knew wore beaten bark cloths around their waists which we whites used to call *tapa-rabos* [butt-covers]. The chief and police wore special feathers on their heads, depending on their rank. They used mostly feathers from toucans, macaws, and pretty forest birds.

"They didn't have to work much because they didn't try to grow the things we need to eat to be happy, like rice and beans. Instead, they used their energy to make fine gold figures of eagles, birds, jaguars, frogs, and alligators. They made tools and jewelry from the hardest green stone, jade. They also made perfect pottery and played drums and clay whistles and danced. Different tribes worshipped different things – some the sun, others idols of stone.

"In the old days, not many Indians grew to be very old because there were still ferocious tigres that killed them. Some Indians used to rub their newborn children with the leaf of the *pringamosa* plant that itched and burned but protected them against many dangers in their lives. They knew all kinds of natural medicines that many of us still use today. For instance, if I get bitten by a poisonous snake – I hope God doesn't wish it – I won't go to any hospital to inject myself full of that serum they say is so good – but really isn't. I just grind up the seed from the *jabillo de culebra* tree, which I always keep in my house, and eat the powder, no matter how bitter it is. That's what the Indians did, and they never died of snakebite or lost any limbs. When I have a stomachache, I go and look for some *mozote* or *zorillo* plants, pick some leaves, squish them in water, and drink the water. I don't need those pills and powders that they sell you and say it's so good. It's not. The Indians knew what was good. For deep cuts, they cured themselves like the monkeys, with chewed leaves that they put in the wound. For any serious stomach problem, they drank a little oil of *bequer* [boa-constrictor] or alligator. This is great for ulcers.

"The Indians were powerful. They knew the earth so well that they could use its power. If they had used their powers against the conquistadores, they would have easily defeated them. In fact, I asked an Indian friend why his ancestors had let the conquistadores beat them, and he replied, 'I don't know why they let that happen.'

"When the United Fruit Company was building the runway in La Palma (30 miles south), an Indian who lived there showed his power when the Americans told him, 'Your pigs are going to be a bother for us. If you don't enclose them, we're going to have to kill them.' The Indian replied, 'You kill my pigs, your mules die.' The Indian didn't enclose his pigs, so the Americans killed ten of them. The next day they found ten dead mules. Not to tell you the whole story, there was a slaughter of pigs and a mysterious death of mules. There was a giant old *ceiba* tree on one side of la Palma runway, which, when the Americans were making room for their airplanes, they were going to cut it down. The same Indian told them, 'The man that puts an axe to that tree gets sick.' And that's how it was. Many men tried to cut down the tree and they all got so sick that they thought they were dying. No one could cut the tree down. As a matter of fact, I think the tree still stands.

"The 'dark ones' were and still are the most powerful brujos and curanderos. I learned a lot of plant medicine but very little of the other, even though I do know how some witchcraft is done. A man from Guanacaste [northern Costa Rica] came looking for me some years ago, offered to pay me to tell him some things, but no way would I tell him because he was looking to do bad. There was a bad Indian that, any woman whom he desired but who didn't want anything to do with him, he would harm in this manner: he would go into the forest and catch a black toad with the similar markings of a *terciopelo* [fer-de-lance snake]. He would go to a certain spot, dig a hole about a yard deep, and put the seed of a gourd in one of the toad's eyes, put the toad between two boards, fill the hole, and sit there for six hours. I won't tell you any more, but the victim in his mind got sick and could even die. It takes a wise curandero to discover the reason for the person's sickness, and then he has to figure out which *contra* [counter] will be effective. Some Indians are experts in black magic. That's why you should never make enemies with an Indian, or with anyone who knows the black magic."

Many visitors to Costa Rica are disappointed with the apparent scarcity of "Indians" and "Indian culture." Unlike most of Latin America, Costa Rica's gene pool is far more European, Arabic, and African than "Indian." The reason for this, as I understood it, is that the natives here were very proud, intelligent, and hostile and therefore unwilling to yield to subjugation. The resulting conflicts were lost by the indigenous peoples, not due to lack of gunpowder or armor or military superiority, but because of lack of defenses against influenza, yellow fever, chickenpox, measles, tuberculosis, and venereal disease, which were the most powerful means of conquest the newcomers had.

If there still remain pure-blooded "Indians" who are comfortable in the rainforest, as their ancestors may have been, they have taken their mysteries into hiding with them.

With the change from the indigenous people's way of life to that of the newcomers and their descendents, the face of Costa Rica also began to change. The "Indians" merely took what they needed from their habitat, and as long as they were able to protect their hunting territory from encroachment by other tribes, they could prosper within their territory by rotating from place to place their small crops of *maíz* (corn), *pejivalle* palm, and manioc. Increased population, however, generated increased competition for resources and led to agriculture as an alternative to warfare and nomadism.

Modern agriculture-dependent inhabitants of rain-forest areas rely on non-native food plants that are poorly suited to the natural forest environment. In order to produce their photosynthesis-reliant rice, beans, and corn, Costa Ricans have to chop down a forest to let the sun penetrate. They kill doves, parrots, coatimundis, and monkeys that come to eat from their fields. And after they plant in the same ground and burn the weeds a few times, the thin topsoil washes away in the heavy rains and the land loses its fertility. Then they make pastures, grass being the only thing that can survive besides weeds.

It's a familiar history in rainforest lands: to plant more rice, corn, and beans, people destroy more forest. They want to have their cattle and pigs, so they kill off the jaguars. They want to have their chickens, so they have to kill the predator ocelots, tolomucos, skunks, opossums, hawks, eagles, and snakes. About this history, Don Aurelio said, "The Indian was a friend of the forest and the animals. The white man is the enemy."

I didn't want to be the enemy, yet realized it would take years of careful looking and listening to learn how not to be. In the meantime, I had to struggle on several fronts.

Almost everything that I planted needed constant attention. Various nematodes and bizarre fungi and secretive diseases plagued many of the avocado, mango, and orange trees I'd introduced. Leaf-cutting ants, also known as "parasol" ants, could strip a small fruit tree of its leaves in a single night and carry them hundreds of meters away to their colony deep underground, where the decaying leaves were used to cultivate a fungus that served as the ants' rice and beans. These super ants loved the tender leaves of the young orange and mango trees and would take great pains to get them.

Little black ants apparently enjoyed making holes in the branches and roots of the *guanabana* and orange trees and in the fruit, ruining them. Other kinds of ants favored the trunks and roots of other fruit trees. Swarms of sticky, black, stingerless leaf-cutting bees collected pollen and sap and ate the flowers of all the fruit trees, destroying the potential fruit. They also bored holes in the mango trees and guanabanas. Fruit flies filled countless fruits with their wiggling larvae. Wasps with elaborate ovipositors laid their eggs in many papayas, spoiling them. All kinds of insects and larvae – borers, suckers, cutters – wreaked havoc in almost everything we planted.

And there seemed no safe place to store fruit, vegetables, or grains. Fruit bats, opossums, and raccoons attacked stalks of ripening bananas inside the house. Cockroaches nibbled on everything. Moths and their larvae seemed to be able to sneak into anything and particularly into any place where grains were stored. Clothes, blankets, and canvas tarps were ravaged by voracious rats, cockroaches, and moths. Bright-green, buzzing wasps loved to make their hardened mud homes in any small fissure or hole, especially those found in radios, clocks, gun barrels, and tools.

Every two or three months, the weeds would grow higher and thicker than the crops, vines would start to strangle the crops, broad-leafed plants would block out the sun, tough grasses would commandeer root space. The *matapalo* (tree-killer) vine was dispersed to many of the fruit trees by innocent and beautiful birds who left the little seeds with some fertilizer on the branches. From there, this parasitic vine would sprout, dig roots into the host, and grow at an astonishing rate, stealing the sunlight and simultaneously strangling and sucking the life out of the tree. Skunks and opossums habitually raided the pineapples, eating the choicest, sweetest sections of the ripe ones ready for picking; monkeys would feast on the mangoes, knocking down and spoiling great quantities of unripe fruit; raccoons and coatimundis would mangle stalks of bananas and plantain.

Sometimes it all made me so angry that I felt like fighting back with DDT or flamethrowers; other times it made me just want to give up. Parasites and competitors were everywhere, all the time. I was losing and couldn't live in peace with the pests that were defeating me. I wished to eat the fruits that the creatures were eating before me, so for lack of alternatives, I did again what everyone else told me to do, what I had vowed I was no longer going to do: I threw poisons at them.

I hated to see the pastures fill with deep-rooted weeds, so, like the other ranchers, I sprayed herbicides on them. I hated to see the cattle infested by the disgusting screwworm fly larvae, which dug into their hides, and I hated to see the horses' manes and ears with ticks in them, so I did what my neighbors did: I doused them with pesticides. I wanted to prevent the cattle from dying from diseases, so I did what the veterinarians told me to do: I vaccinated.

I wanted to be a successful farmer, so I used the toxic chemicals prescribed by the experts. On one trip, I stopped by the University of Hawaii's Tropical Agriculture Department and was given the same advice: "If you want anything to work down there, you must use poisons." I spoke with an agronomist from the USDA and heard the same: "In the tropics, you *have* to go heavy on the pesticides."

I soon found that if I adopted the program of commercial fertilizers, fungicides, herbicides, pesticides, antibiotics, and vaccines, I had to keep using them or the plants and animals would be more susceptible to disease and parasitism than before. I didn't like depending on so many things from the outside, transportation being so costly in every way. Also I was instinctively afraid of using the noxious substances prescribed by people only interested in maximum production and profit, not the long-term health or well-being of the people, plants, animals, or soil.

I searched for ways to avoid the poisons, but I admitted failure after seeing the pests gobble up with even more appetite the plants I had sprayed with an "organic" concoction of crushed garlic, super-hot chilies, and caustic cashew shells. In vain I sought help among professionals in agriculture in Costa Rica and the United States, where the organic farming movement was still in its infancy. Most advisors agreed on one thing: in the tropics, the competition from the pests and other plants was simply too great for any farm operation to succeed commercially with organic methods of agriculture. Still, I decided to quit using the nauseating poisons on any plants that I was planning to consume. I also quit using commercial chemical fertilizers, because the highly acidic, eroded clay soil at my place needed the kind of enrichment only organic matter could provide. And I accepted the fact that the insects, fungi, diseases, and critters would take their share, hoping that they would leave something for us humans.

I still had to spray the cattle for screwworms and vaccinate them and inject them and the horses with poison to kill their internal parasites every few months. I still killed vampire bats whenever I could and gunned down snakes, skunks, and opossums that we caught eating our chickens and eggs. It was with pleasure that I watched the termites die as I soaked them in diesel fuel. I still poisoned the hives of the black congo bees. I still set poison traps for the beetles that ate the palms. Yet, unlike the neighbors, I would not shoot the hawks, otters, or ocelots who were also chicken eaters; or the monkeys, raccoons, coatimundis, and parrots who raided the cornfields; or the chachalacas who ate the beans; or the doves who ate the freshly sown rice.

To raise certain plants and animals, one had to defend them, but to what extent? Once again, who had more right to be there, the wild plants and animals or the ones man introduced? Who could judge impartially? Did man belong there at all on a permanent basis? Where nonindigenous people intruded, the trees fell, the topsoil washed away, the springs dried up, and the animals fled or were killed. Children learned to find pleasure in killing birds and other creatures with rocks and slingshots, and slashing trees with their machetes.

To some extent, more than I like to admit, I was following this path of destruction. From my beginnings there, I prohibited all hunting and unnecessary killing of any harmless creature, but there were an overwhelming number that were harmful. I felt I must kill some in self-defense, like the poisonous snakes. I even paid a day's wages for every poisonous snake brought to me. The first few years, about 30 were killed for bounty, then fewer and fewer. I was purposefully decreasing their population and would wipe them out altogether if I could. Did I have that right? Was it wise?

One day I stood staring at one of my favorite orange trees, which had just been stripped of half its leaves by parasol ants. Half-moon pieces of leaves littered their neat trail, which was clear of any other debris.

"That's odd they left so many cargoes behind," José said, kneeling down to inspect the bits of leaves.

I was too angry at the destruction to pay too much attention to José's curiosity. I sent him back to the house for some special ant poison and told him to meet me at their colony, which I hoped to discover by following their trail. The leaf pieces led me across the stream over the slippery fallen tree-bridge. On the far side, I discovered a large pile of cut leaves, also abandoned by the ants.

I then shared José's bewilderment. Why would they work so much for nothing? I continued through the forest and came across columns of army ants on the march. Then I understood. The parasol ants probably abandoned their cargoes to return and defend their colony.

When I arrived, the army ants had already penetrated the innermost chambers of the colony, had overtaken the guards, and were carrying away thousands of defenseless, white parasol-ant larvae. The battle was fierce; the combatants were locked together in a bristling ball of thousands of red and black ants wrestling and severing each others' body parts, producing a unique munching-crunching sound.

José arrived quietly with the poison, and we watched the spectacle together for quite some time, pointing out certain grim details and scenes to one another. I didn't want to disrupt the amazing sight, much less throw any poison around. Besides, the army ants were doing an excellent job of destroying our enemies, so I considered them our friends. If only I could count on more allies like that! Had the natural ecosystem not been so disrupted by human activities, I might have been able to. In the tropics, as in most parts of the globe, the natural balance had been altered so severely and unfortunately that the benign creatures were disappearing and the destructive ones were multiplying.

The leaf-cutting ant population soared, causing much damage to many of the plants people grew for food, because hunters and dogs decreased the anteater populations so much. I was told that there once had been a little animal like an opossum that fed mainly on the destructive congo bees. That invaluable little mammal became locally extinct around 1970, however, and the congo bees multiplied so successfully that they even displaced the wild honeybees. This displacement worked to everyone's great disadvantage, for instead of serving as pollinators, the black bees destroyed the flowers and fruits of the trees and defecated in their own honey, making it useless to humans.

The scarlet macaws, the red monkeys, the tapirs, the forest deer, the giant anteater, the peccaries, the jaguars – what other less-well known animals had man killed or scared away, and how did their disappearance affect the natural balance? Could man learn to live in the tropics without killing everything?

The answer, I found, lay in accepting these adversaries as an inseparable part of the environment, and in emulating those plants and animals that developed methods of coexistence with them. I noticed many plants generously giving away fruit and nectar to monkeys, bats, birds, and insects, apparently in exchange for the service of pollinating, germinating, and dispersing the seeds and pollen. These intricate relationships between highly adapted living creatures, though not obvious, seemed to hold together the conglomerate of tropical life in all its amazing variety.

Most of the apparent symbioses involved the social insects – ants, bees, termites, and wasps, which represented a surprisingly substantial chunk of the local biomass. The *cornizuelo* ant manifested a classic and easily observable example of symbiosis. Living exclusively in the small, sparsely foliated cornizuelo acacia tree in the understory of the forest, they repelled with ferocious biting and stinging any intruders, plant or animal, that posed a danger to their tree home. In return, they were rewarded with catered food in the form of nectar and safe lodging within the hard, bullhorn-shaped thorns. The local people knew to stay clear of this successful team of tree and ants, because the ants were notorious for their kamikaze attacks, jumping down on unsuspecting passersby, and attacking in small armies if anyone dared molest the tree.

One day while I was clearing weeds in an orchard, I came upon what appeared to be a termite nest, dark brown, about three times the size of a basketball, nestled in the main branches and trunk of an orange tree. There was nothing extraordinary about it, except that it had medium-sized black ants crawling all over it. Maybe it was an ant hive, I thought. When my companion, Antonio, at my request, tried to knock some oranges down with a pole, the nest immediately erupted with fountains of ants, in unbelievable numbers. I was quickly covered from head to foot with the biting ants. So many were jumping down on us from higher branches that they sounded like rain as they hit the leaves on the ground. After some frantic hopping and swatting and stamping, taking off and putting on clothes, I found myself laughing, since the bites were not painful.

I was unharmed but angry, and to show Antonio, the foreman (at that time), I wasn't going to be defeated so easily, I sliced into the crusty nest with my machete. And then there was another surprise. Along with hundreds of ant eggs and larvae that came pouring out like white rice, I saw thousands of small, soft, white-and-brown termites falling to the ground as well. A more professional biopsy proved that the ants and termites were living together, not only in the same apartment building but apparently sharing the same floors. Their living quarters were so similar that I didn't know which had built which. I did see that the new outer additions to the nest were being constructed by the termites.

On further inspection, we got another surprise: small honeybees were entering and exiting the nest through a small yellow wax tube between the swarming ants and strange blind termites. I stood spellbound, staring at three species, all of them excited, all ready to defend their home, all harmonious with each other.

Mysteries piqued my curiosity and constantly renewed my love for natural sciences. Why didn't the ants, which we believed to be omnivorous, devour the helpless termites? Did they taste bad? Or *were* they eating them, little by little? Or did they knowingly permit them to continue their convenient construction? Was it mere coincidence that the much larger ants could occupy the same living quarters as termites? Why didn't the ants attack the bees or eat their honey? Or would they do that eventually, perhaps after the bees had made an appreciable amount? Maybe the bee/termite relationship was more truly symbiotic than the ant/termite or ant/bee ones. Maybe symbiosis between species passed through different evolutionary stages, and could be permanent or temporary.

For more than a year I studied the details and pondered the significance of this three-species relationship occurring in a 15-year-old orange tree, a nonindigenous species introduced by another nonindigenous species, which introduced itself. In what ways were humans influencing nature's infinitely intricate dynamics?

I received another lesson in symbiosis one day when Pedro (one of Aurelio's sons) and I rode by a mango tree, picked some ripe fruit, and trotted on. I noticed some tiny holes in the shiny peel, the sign of fruit flies, whose white larvae could be found wiggling wormily in the fruit. Pedro was heartily devouring his mango when I told him that the mangos had worms. He laughed and replied, "That's protein, amigo, don't you know? That's good for you! Besides, riding a horse, you don't notice them!"

I laughed with him, examining my bouncing mango and trying to convince myself to adopt Pedro's very positive philosophy. I watched him smiling back at me, trotting along and chomping into his mango – enjoying both it and my consternation tremendously. I thought to myself that maybe this was one way of learning to get closer to nature, be willing to try something new.

While Pedro kept gazing and grinning at me, I bit into the delicious mango and avoided looking for any of the short little crawly guys, which luckily had no taste at all to them. Pedro lifted his half-eaten mango in salute, and though I still felt light years away from enjoying mutually beneficial symbiosis with anything, I realized that I could keep the mango pit and plant it somewhere, or simply pitch it in the dirt by the road. Either way, I would be carrying out my part of the arrangement by dispersing the tree's seeds.

After that day, my range of diet expanded to include all sorts of other fruits that the fruit flies may or may not have been fooling around with, and even if I did bite into something and discover a few grains of white rice wriggling around, I could bite around them or just eat them and refuse to be disgusted or alarmed. They were not welcome friends, but neither were they foes.

Just as I was beginning to think I was fitting into my niche in the local habitat, I was presented a great challenge to my new code of ethics. It happened when a hawk discovered the ease with which he could swoop down and carry off the farm community's young chickens.

He was a beautiful and graceful black raptor with a striking yellow beak and clean white band on his tail feathers. He lived in a giant dead ajo tree that stood in the treeline of the forest on the other side of the stream on the land I had purchased from Oscura, which I left untouched. I always told the farm people not to disturb the animals or plants in there. The towering, straight trees in that forest were a logger's dream, and I always said no, even though the wood would make first-class lumber and could easily be cut and transported. No.

When the hawk ran out of small chickens, he started on the hens. The finca's employees pleaded with me on behalf of their wives to kill the hawk, but I replied, "Who has more right to be here, the chickens or the hawk?" Their reply was, "Soon we will have no poultry or eggs to feed our families."

I hated to lose favor with these poor people because of a conflict between my rigid ideas on wildlife preservation and the value they placed on their poultry, so I did my best to see that everyone got more fish and conch to eat. But after awhile, during a rainy season when we caught few fish, the women became noticeably more irritable and frustrated with each pass of the hawk. The foreman confided in me that the people of the finca resented the way I favored the hawk over them.

There was no way I could explain my position to them in a satisfactory manner. The way they saw it, as long as I sided with the hawk, I was siding against the human community on the ranch. Having hawk friends and human foes was very poor politics, and the community – never as peaceful as I wished – grew restive.

Finally I decided it was best to subordinate my love of nature to cooperate with my own species, and I gave Manolo my .22 rifle. "Okay Manolo, here are ten bullets," I said. "If you can kill him from this side of the stream, it's all right with me."

He was an excellent shot and an experienced hunter whose wife took great pride in raising 60 new chicks that dry season, only to watch them be carried off one by one in the hawk's talons. After several days, Manolo had fired off his ten shots but reported he hit only feathers. The hawk's favorite perch was simply too far away and too high to waste bullets on. We tried blocking the hawk's favorite angles of attack with pieces of discarded fishing net, and this nearly caught him, but he escaped all the wiser.

Eventually the women could no longer conceal their sadness and anger over the dwindling number of poultry, and they announced to me they were going to sell their few remaining hens. When I heard rumors of disgruntled families planning to move away because of "the gringo's hawk," I knew the problem had to be solved once and for all.

This was a hard thing because I had known the hawk for several years. I enjoyed observing him while hour after hour he perched up in that giant old tree amidst the strongest winds and rains. I had great respect and love for him.

One day after fishing, as I was walking through intense heat up the sun baked pasture to the house, someone pointed out the hawk on his limb and said maybe it would be possible this time to finally hit him. Several people standing nearby seemed particularly anxious to hear my response. I was in a whimsical mood and said that if someone brought me my .22, I'd shoot a few rounds for the hell of it, even though the bird was a couple of hundred yards away and I wasn't the greatest marksman.

Someone ran and got the rifle. The strongly prochicken populace fixed their eyes with serious concentration on the black silhouette way up in the dead ajo tree across the stream in the forest I had sworn to protect. I steadied my gun on a tree branch, aimed, and fired. My friend the hawk dropped without a flutter straight down into the forest.

I was shocked. I really hadn't meant to hit him. The people cheered. Hypocrite that I was, I laughed with them, suddenly the hero, the nice boss, a friend of the people, sharing their triumph.

Miguel, a skilled woodsman, asked me if I wanted him to bring the bird back. I said yes. He searched for an hour but came back empty-handed and said it was a great mystery since everyone saw the hawk plummet in a deathfall straight down from its perch. I didn't care much for the mystery. Unless I knew the hawk truly escaped unharmed, there was no way to feel good about any part of this incident.

I would never quite recover from that one wild shot, which proved that I had become capable of destroying something I truly loved. Whenever I sat alone in my rocking chair at dusk, watching the ever-changing panorama of forest and coastline, I would sense deep loss as I would become aware of the dead branches of the hawk's tree, black against the pastel sky, where he used to accompany me. The silhouette of "the gringo's hawk" was no longer there to remind me of how I betrayed the bond we shared, a bond between two individuals, two species; and a sadness, remorse, and loneliness deeper than any I'd known would well up within me. For years, I would feel tremendous guilt – for myself, and for my species.

From then on, I decided to ditch the advice of the college psychologist in terms of making it a priority to "adapt" to local sociocultural "mores." The reason our planet and its inhabitants were taking such a beating was because all over the world people were listening too much on the outside and not enough on the inside. We were too often doing what we were expected or told to do. We were pulling the trigger too easily, not just aiming and firing at nature, but at our fellow humans. We weren't draft dodging enough. We stupidly accepted landmines, poisons, nukes, and the destruction of irreplaceable beauty, of irreplaceable habitats, of irreplaceable species, and irreplaceable peoples. We might send in a check to save the whales, the rainforest, or the children, but rarely did we actually go, see, or do. Rarely did our elected politicians become actively involved. We were mostly too lazy and complacent to mess with the darker realities, which was perfectly normal, but wrong.

Killing the hawk made me realize that my true identity in Costa Rica was no longer that of the participant-observer/follower I'd been, but perhaps more like that of a human "indicator organism," a more independent human who had perceived differently than most and was willing to try and act accordingly toward a greater good, an educated person who'd experienced tropical reality long enough to earn the right to talk about it and to be heard.

Mariposa azul (blue morpho butterfly)

Chapter Nine

On the dark side – are there really witches?

During the first several years of my life in Costa Rica, amid inner turmoil stirred up by such events as the killing of the black hawk, I experienced episodes when I was unsure, not only of what was right and wrong, but also of what was real and what was not. During these times I noticed myself listening more receptively to the people of the finca and the elders during their nightly talks, especially when they spoke of the spirit world, of omens, and of good and evil. To them, the natural and supernatural were closely linked, and events in one had a distinct impact on events in the other.

In the late 1970s, when people started killing each other in the Nicaraguan Revolution and when I was going through a series of local, personal crises with termite-infested buildings; employee problems; incurable diseases and misfortunes with my orchards, palm groves, cattle, and other seemingly doomed projects, an "Indian" curandero came to the finca one day and gave me a slip of paper with a message on it: "There is a lady neighbor of this place that curses the farms of others. Many farms are damaged by her. That woman is evil." Was this one more crisis for me to deal with, or nonsense?

Presuming he was a fake, I asked him to tell me who he was talking about, but he refused. When I asked if it was Oscura, he

smiled slightly and walked away. Oscura hadn't done me any harm
that I knew of, and in fact I felt mostly sorry for her – alone and poor
with two small children, trying to survive in such a rugged place. I
wondered why people still claimed she was a witch.

"If she's a bruja, then how come she is so poor?" I asked Santos's
mother, wrinkled old Doña Alejandra, one day. She replied, "They
say that all the bad things a witch does to others eventually come back
twice as strong on herself."

Oscura was the subject of many such tales and rumors in the
village. One day, Macedonio – the cowboy who became foreman –
had a need to talk about her. "Oscura is really and positively bad,"
he said as we slowly herded a group of cattle from one pasture to
another. "A few days ago she comes to my house late in the afternoon.
Marcos and I were playing guitar, and a few people were there passing
the time. Oscura went to the outhouse and I thought she must have
had stomach problems because she stayed there such a long time. It
started to rain a little bit and started getting dark, and Oscura was
still in there! Finally she came out and came to the house where
Marlene gave her some coffee. I was curious to know what she was
doing in there so long, so I just casually went to the outhouse like I
had to use it.

"There right next to the toilet seat were a few drops of blood and
a piece of bone or hoof or claw or something like the end of my tiny
finger. It had blood on it, too, and around the middle of it a little
string was wrapped and tied. You should have seen such a disgusting
thing! To me, it was pure pigshit-witchcraft!" He spat violently. "I was
afraid and repulsed to touch it, but I didn't want to leave it there,
either. So I picked it up by the little string and took it into the kitchen
and threw it in the fire without Oscura seeing me. Look, you've never
smelled anything so horrible in your life as the smell that came from
that little 'charm' burning in the fire! You know how bad burnt tooth
or hair or bone smells. Well, this was *much* worse, so bad that everyone
had to evacuate the house, go out in the rain, and get away." He spat
again with disgust. "The smoke poured out of the kitchen and filled
the whole coconut grove! It was quite some time before we could
return to the house."

One day when I was helping to plant pasture grass, I heard Miguel
say to Quillo, "I'm not afraid of any woman, but of her, yes. One night
I slept in her choza and she told me that sometimes a spirit came
around at night, so I slept very little but didn't see anything."

Quillo said, "That spirit they say is one of her past lovers or something like that. The person who claims he's seen that spirit was the schoolteacher who went away last year. He says that twice in the middle of the night a person who he thought was a woman put hands on his chest, but when he reached out there was nothing, and he got up to see if it was Oscura, but she was sleeping."

"That woman is bad-intentioned," Miguel said. "My mother and her are mortal enemies. They once fought with machetes and my mother almost cut Oscura's hand off. You can still see the scar across her knuckles."

Quillo said, "My mother and Oscura are also mortal enemies. I'm not sure why, but they haven't spoken half a word to each other in years. I don't think she's a real bruja. She has an old man up in the mountains do her evil works for her. She pays him to do it. Now that man *does* know witchcraft. He learned it from an old Indian from the Talamanca range who was the pure demon."

What was all this business about witches, spirits, and demons? During the nightly gatherings, all sorts of bizarre stories were told. I had discounted most as imaginative superstition, but the longer I lived in this tropical wilderness, the more I fell under the spell of its candlelit and moonlit nights. I became a connoisseur of my neighbors' tales of shady mystery, of legend, fantasy, religion; and I collected many of the popular stories as if they were valuable artifacts or historical relics.

Don Arturo: "The devil can appear in many forms. There are many demons, disciples of Lucifer, the king of the demons, just as God has many angels on his side, too. Men used to make contracts with the devil, signed in their own blood, they say, for women, riches, cattle, and material satisfaction . . . but as soon as these people died, they became the property of the devil. When these people are put in the coffin and lowered into the grave, they will disappear and go to Hell, or stay in the world working for the devil."

Don Dimas: "I do believe in life after death, and that's why it is a good idea to make sure to be good before you die. They say – I'm not sure if it's true or not, but I think it probably is – that it's bad to bury money, because if you die and it's still buried, you have to come back and beg someone to dig it up so that you can be at peace.

"One thing I do know: The dead are there and they'll come if you call them in the right way. I remember when I was a young man, about 16 years old I think, when I did a foolish thing. One night my mother and I were sitting outside the choza when, across the valley, by a trail that passed by there, I saw a small light moving along. I thought it was probably someone walking by with a flashlight. I asked my mother, 'Who knows who that would be?' All of a sudden the light floated down the hillside into the darkness of the stream where I thought it must have extinguished itself. I asked my mother what it could have been, and she looked at me strangely and said, 'What light? I didn't see any light.'

"'How could you have missed it?" I asked her. Then the light came up out of the stream, through the forest, getting bigger and bigger, until it came right in front of us, lighting up the whole hut and all around. I remember clearly seeing the green grass outside the choza just as if it were pure daytime. 'Mama, what is it?' I screamed, staring at the brilliant luminescence.

"'What, what?' she demanded.

"'The light! The light!' I yelled at her. The silent, luminous presence then disappeared and all was dark again. I realized that my mother hadn't even seen that light that gave me chills down my backbone. I hardly slept that night.

"The next day a neighbor came over early in the morning to tell my mother and me how she had seen a great white light pass by her choza the night before, lighting up the whole pasture, and that her husband saw nothing and thought she was crazy. My mother thought we were both crazy. I said to the woman carelessly, 'I wish I could have talked with that spirit or whatever it was.'

"Immediately I knew I had made a terrible mistake in saying that, and the woman scolded me: 'Don't be so foolish! You know that something could happen to you for saying that? That light might come back!'

"And, in truth, that is what happened. That night I was lying awake on my bed when the bright light appeared before me, lighting up the whole inside of the choza, the beams, the palm thatch, everything. The strangest thing was that the light passed right over the dog, which didn't even growl or bark, and he was a jealous dog for protecting at night! Out of the light the figure of a man appeared, with black pants and white shirt. His face was in a kind of blurry darkness, so I couldn't tell if it was someone I had known. His figure floated and wavered up in the air.

"'Mama! It's back! It's in my room!' I cried.

"She snapped back, 'You just quit thinking about those things, you hear?'

"'But mama, he's *here*! I'm looking right at him! Don't you see the light?' I yelled.

"She shouted back, 'I don't want to hear any more of that talk. Now shut up and go to sleep!'

"I lay there, stiff and cold from fear, my eyes fixed on that spirit that came to bother me, because I had been so stupid to say I wanted to talk with it. After a long while, the light went away and never came back again. For a week I had a hard time sleeping, and for a whole year we lived in another choza."

Don Arturo: "Once several years ago two men went deep into the Osa Peninsula to hunt and dry the meat and cure the skins. They were paddling their canoe up a river where the people told them not to go very far because many accidents had occurred up that river. But they wanted to go way up where they had heard was the best hunting in the whole country, which it was. There were herds of hundreds of mountain pig; tapirs were common; you could take as much meat as you could carry out, if you didn't run across an angry jaguar. The two men kept going until the river got so steep and swift that they couldn't go any farther.

"They made a clearing on the bank and built a little *ranchito* with two bunk beds. One man began to carve a small wooden San Geronimo, who is a good contra against evil. The other man laughed at him and said, 'You're crazy bothering yourself with that, unless you can get him to send you a good woman to keep us company while we're here. Now *that* would be worthwhile!' And so, while one was thinking about his saint and spiritual things, the other was wishing for a woman.

"Late that afternoon, they saw a beautiful blonde woman expertly maneuvering a canoe up the strong current. The one man remembered how difficult it had been for the both of them and so thought she must be a bruja or demon. The other man thought none of these things. He was overjoyed to see her, just what he hoped for, and helped the woman pull her canoe up the bank.

"The other man was humbly praying to Jesus Christ for help when night came. The woman agreed to stay with the one and slept with him in the upper bunk bed. The religious man took the lower one. Late in the night, the lone Christian heard a low growl, a grunt, and a groan. Then on one side of his bed he heard a dripping, which he thought must be the blood of his friend. Terrified, he jumped up, grabbed his machete and ran to his canoe. The woman's canoe was gone. In the night he set off down the river and in a couple days reached the village.

"After resting a few days he and a few others took the journey back upriver to see what had become of the other man. When they arrived at the campsite, everything was burned. The shelter was in ashes. The rifles were smashed. There was no sign of the man. . . . He must have been eaten by the beast that came as a beautiful woman. This was work of the devil.

"A lot of people believe in wooden idols and saints and devils and things like that, but the only thing I believe in is God. My Uncle Leonides used to worship an idol. One day he was traveling in his *bongo* [a dugout sailboat] with his wife, but when he was going to land, the sea was very rough, the waves breaking far out from shore. He waited for a calm spell, but there was none. So he had to catch a wave and ride it in, but as it got more shallow, the wave grew bigger, and when it broke, it turned the boat over. He made it to shore and his boat was washed up in shallow water, too, but a rip-current carried his wife out to sea.

"He righted his boat, bailed out the water, and set out through the breakers to save her. Again and again he failed as the boat filled with water. Again and again he bailed out the water and headed back into the waves. Finally he lay exhausted on the beach. He had a wooden saint in his boat that he believed in; I forget which saint, but he began to pray and plead to that saint to give him the energy to go and save his woman who was now far out beyond the breakers. He pleaded for a calm spell. Again he set out, and again he failed. Again on the beach, he got on his knees, crying, and prayed to God for help. That's when he swears the sea calmed and he was able to go and save his wife who was about to drown. When he got home, he took the wooden saint, chopped it up, and used it for firewood. It was God who helped him save his wife, not the wooden saint."

Don Aurelio: "I had a Jamaican friend, a black man, so black that at night all you could see of him were his eyes and teeth, which were very white. He spoke *bad* Spanish. He was heading out from shore in a well-built boat to go from Parrita to la Palma. In his suitcase he had all his money and clothes, everything he owned. Then a big wave came and turned his boat over. He barely made it alive to shore. His suitcase floated with the current out the mouth of the Savegre River. He was a Protestant and so didn't believe in anything, but he was in such bad condition, almost naked and with nothing, that he began to jump up in the air on the beach with his arms spread wide, yelling,

'God, I believe you, you bring back suitcase. I promise, I believe you. Please, please.' He lay down on the beach exhausted and after a while stood up and looked out to sea where his suitcase had been floating, but he couldn't see it any more. Then he found it there on the beach. From then on, he believed in God."

Despite having been raised in a society of people who, at least officially, accepted God, Jesus Christ, and other religious figures as part of their daily existence, I had never experienced the close relationship between the natural and supernatural accepted so casually by the people here. Gradually, living with these people, my perceptions changed.

Sometimes, after one of Anita's excellent meals, I would walk back from Carlos's home in the dark, often without a flashlight, and would feel fear when I entered my own cabin. Fear of what? Might Oscura have a surprise for me? Would a devil be there waiting for a grab at my soul? Might a spirit come and light up the old place? Often, alone in my cabin, which was far from any other dwelling on the farm, I stayed awake thinking about these things.

One night during a full moon – the kind of night when I often shared some of the animals' restlessness and anxiety – I woke to the sound of children singing a beautiful but eerie song down by the stream, the sort of song Debussy might have composed. I got out of bed and walked out to pay more attention to the fantastic phenomenon, which was the first of its kind I'd ever experienced. I thought, "If I am dreaming it or half-sleep imagining, it will go away," but it didn't go away. It still came to my ears, faint, but unique and unmistakable, from down in the stream. Mesmerized, I gazed out over the veranda. The intense moonlight lit up the new buds of the huge *higuerón* tree like candles and reflected off the rocks and grass, giving way to darkness under the shady trees lining the stream. I truly enjoyed that haunting music, for a few magic, Peter-Pan-like minutes, while at the same time wondering whether I should acknowledge it at all, whether I should let it seduce me.

The next day I asked Javier about it, because he lived closer to the stream than I. He said he also heard it that night and twice before in his life, but thought it, like the flickering lights he had also thought he'd seen, were creations of his imagination or unexplained occurrences related to the full moon. Smiling, he added, "Of course they might have been the *duendes* [forest elves], you know." He paused, grew serious, and said, "You are the one with the college education from the United States of America. Some day you will believe me when I say there are mysterious phenomena no professor can explain."

Later the same day, he gave me a demonstration of just such an "inexplicable" event. Grabbing two bananas from a stalk hanging on his porch, he kept one for himself and gave me the other. As I was about to peel it, he said, "Wait a moment. Let me show you a trick." He took out his machete and made three cutting motions in the air around my banana, and said, "Okay, go ahead and eat it." I didn't have a clue what his apparent joke was about and proceeded to peel my banana while Javier grinned at me. A two-inch piece fell into my hand, cut straight and clean on one end.

"How in the hell . . . " (I usually spoke in English when truly surprised or angry). The banana had been severed internally into two more pieces, without damage to the peel. Javier smiled so wide he showed the gold front tooth he was so proud of. "Okay, Javier," I said energetically, "how'd you do it?"

"Magic." He flashed his gold tooth again.

"Come on, damn it, tell me how you did it!" I laughed but felt embarrassed not to have the slightest idea how he'd done it.

"It can only be performed on ripe bananas, that's all I can tell you . . . oh, and sometimes it works for a whole 'hand,' even an entire stalk."

I was frustrated but didn't press him to explain, accepting it as just another one of those mysteries that violated my need to know facts. There were others: Don Arturo apparently *could* cure injured and bleeding cattle with just his "secret oration." An astrologer I met on a surfing trip in northern Costa Rica in 1974, *had* told me incredibly personal things no one else knew, even things that would happen to me later. We *did* have better luck fishing when we least expected it and when we were least equipped.

The list went on. Was it coincidence that the gringo who told me one day in San Andres how his worst fear was of drowning, did drown the following day in the same place where we'd talked? Was it coincidence that Elias, who frequently ridiculed one-eyed Maximo, lost an eye himself? Macedonio swore he witnessed an old *brujo* (a male witch) make an old rotting cow carcass get up and walk a few steps and fall back down.

What was real and what was not? Who was lying and who was not? What were the true connections between people and reality? How could reality be altered? What were "luck" and "fate" and "astrology" and "witchcraft" and "magic?"

Javier, the following day, did his machete cutting-in-the-air business all around the hanging stalk of bananas, grinned at me confidently, and said, "I'm not sure how well I may have performed this, but go ahead and try a banana – any one." I circled the stalk, trying to analyze the bananas scientifically from various distances and angles. There was absolutely no sign of tampering of any kind. The bananas adhered to the stalk, undisturbed, unhandled. My heart beat faster as I broke off a banana and examined it carefully. There was absolutely no apparent damage to the peel, and it felt like a perfectly normal, intact, banana. I really didn't want to believe in Javier's type of magic, so when I peeled the banana and discovered it neatly and precisely cut into three equal pieces, I was disappointed. I tried another banana from the opposite side of the stalk – the same. A few more from the innermost parts of the stalk – the same.

For days, I felt animosity toward my friend Javier for not explaining to me the whole truth about his "magic," but he kept insisting it would no longer be magic if he told his secret. Finally, my curiosity led me to offer him a moderate sum of money to divulge his secret, and reluctantly he did, on the condition I wouldn't tell anyone else.

Javier's banana magic showed me that many things we don't at first understand are mysterious but explainable, and that many things we take completely for granted, such as the beating of our hearts or the properties of water, are more truly in the realm of magic.

One dark night of a new moon and overcast starless sky, I left Carlos and Anita's after a late dinner and headed for my cabin about 200 yards away. I had stayed late and had again forgotten my flashlight. I could barely see the dirt path leading up the hill. In the distance ahead on the path I thought I could see a patch of darkness blacker than the night. But how could that be if the night was pitch black? I held my hand out in front of me and couldn't see it at all against the night. I continued on slowly, thinking it must be some phenomenon related to my vision, but as I approached the shadow, it became clearer. It appeared to be about ten yards away and the size and shape of a person.

Stopping to assess the situation, I thought, "Well, it could either be that Indian curandero, or some brujo or bruja, or Oscura, or maybe some soul-hungry demon or something along that line, because there are no animals in this pasture now, and there are no posts or plants or objects of any kind where that one is now."

The damn thing was right on my path. I had either to run back to Carlos's or keep going. "I'm going to see what it is, whatever it is,"

I said out loud to myself in a low voice. "I'm tired of this evil spirit-witches-duendes-magic bullshit." I walked slowly on toward the dark figure, and it didn't budge. I remembered the bad scare I received years before at Chinto's finca, that night in the hammock when something or someone approached me, how I was frozen with fear and foreboding. Now I was afraid but didn't feel any of those really bad vibes, and I wasn't going to run away.

I stretched my arms out in front of me for a little protection as I inched toward the black object. What if the thing grabbed my hands? "To hell with the devil!" I whispered like an incantation to ward off evil. I was only a yard away when the black figure rose high in the air with a tremendous jump, let out a terrifying snort and a fart and went galloping away. "A horse!" I shouted, laughing triumphantly. "You see?" I said to my heart, which seemed to want desperately to be elsewhere.

I didn't know he had gotten into that pasture, he wasn't supposed to be there, but it *was* a horse – a black stallion. I must have scared him badly the way I'd crept up on him like that. No wonder he jumped up and ran away! Lucky I didn't get kicked!

I wondered how many other times I feared something mysterious that was caused by benign, natural circumstances I simply was unaware of. Conversely, I wondered how many times I should have been terrified by something, yet remained totally oblivious to its dangers.

As "civilization" crept up on Morita, as the road construction advanced, the nightly talks became a thing of the past. Work and progress and profit and news were happening at an accelerated pace. The duendes retreated back into the forest along with the other night-roaming spirits. We discovered the dreaded river spirit, *la tuli,* to be a huge sort of owl that made incredible yet very explainable sounds. The dead stayed in their graves. And Oscura became just a poor, aging, husbandless woman who had to work at least as hard as any man just to live halfway decently.

I, too, changed, and eventually grew to miss the way it had been the first few years I spent in and around the rainforest on that primitive coast learning the basics of a different world, getting to know people who were so close to the powers of the earth. I missed the close relationship between the ancient and modern worlds, between the older and younger generations, between the natural world and the human world, between the fantastic and the mundane. I missed the nightly candlelit talks, the tales of great hunting adventures, of savage animals, of fearless pirates and wise Indians, of enchanted treasures, spirits, and witches. There was so little left in the modern world to take their place.

Chapter Ten

Being boss – and not much liking it

I was an unlikely figure as boss of a 400-acre ranch in a remote part of tropical Central America. Naïve, sometimes overly sensitive and temperamental, I was only 23 in 1975, and a gringo to boot, the only foreigner in the vicinity, and the only person with blond hair and blue eyes for many miles in any direction. I tried to keep a sporting attitude as I struggled to learn the ropes, and fortunately the rewards from working and living there were every bit as substantial as the punishments. Just being there was an adventure, like a bluewater sailing trip – it could get rough, but rarely was it boring.

There was one day of every week, however, that I truly dreaded: Saturday (*sábado*), which always seemed like an anti-sabbath. First, I had to review all the contract work and evaluate the merits and shortcomings in monetary terms. I put away the friendly smile of an interested student and replaced it with the stern business manner of el patrón. Or at least I tried. Actually, I would never be macho enough for the job.

"José, you forgot to cut all those spiny weeds down by the forest on the other side of the hill."

"They were full of wasps. You should see Victor's face – he got stung by a whole bunch of *chías* and had to quit early yesterday, one eye all closed, with fever and swollen glands."

"You cut all the weeds way too high, not like we agreed that they had to be chopped just a hand above ground level. Now it's going to make it hell on the next people who have to do this contract, you know, because all the trunks of the weeds will just grow thicker and sprout out. . . . The way you did it looks okay but isn't worth as much as I offered you for the lower-cut job."

"There were too many rocks, and we didn't want to break our machetes or have to sharpen every ten minutes. You know how much machetes cost now."

"We'll talk about it later this afternoon when I'm paying."

The contract machete-men would sometimes do a much better job in the areas they knew I would inspect first, by a gate or in the shade on a hilltop, and would do shabbier work in the less-accessible parts, counting on my laziness. Sometimes I would have to go myself the day before or send Carlos to walk it all over to make sure the contract had been completed.

The chainsaw men would have their lumber and posts all arranged when I reached them in the forest Saturday mornings. They tried to make sure I would see only the first-class lumber and not the wood with cracked, rotten, or disfigured parts. I paid one price for first-class lumber and 20 percent less for second-class. They often tried to put everything off as first-class and resented my pointing out to them the second-class pieces.

"Ah no, señor, don't penalize us so much. You know what it takes to cut those two-by-fours out of this whore of a tree on such a steep hillside?"

"What's wrong with the tree?"

"Look and see how it landed. We lost two days of work just accommodating the logs so they wouldn't roll down the hill! And half of it splintered inside when it fell. We took half a day readying the block, and for what? We knew you wouldn't receive splintered wood, so we junked it. Not only that, but this *manglillo* has parts in it so hard the chain throws sparks! It's taken us twice as long to get the same number of inches of lumber, and still we have to sharpen three times a day. This old log is going to wear out two brand new chains, and you know how much chain costs. Really, señor Jon, you ought to pay us better for the lumber, at least so we can break even. We were going to tell you that this afternoon. . . . ."

"Okay, we'll talk about it later." I had great difficulty granting raises. Even at a meager $2.50 a day (plus milk, fish, favors, and loans) for the day-wage workers, I was still paying better than any of the other local ranchers and farmers paid their workers. They made it clear to me from the beginning that I would be doing a disservice to all the employers in the area if I kept raising the daily wages and evaluations for contract work. The other ranchers said I was forcing them to pay their help more and complained that they were losing their workers to me. They would express this complaint directly to others, who would relay it on to me, but whenever we saw each other at the local bar, La Pichinga, or at a soccer game, they would, as custom dictated, refer to any such possibly conflicting issues in a very polite and nonspecific way.

These ranchers and farmers who ran herds in the hundreds and grew rice fields of hundreds of hectares, were hard-working, stern, competent, no-nonsense "real men" who drank and smoked a lot, boasted of their extramarital conquests or desires, and viewed nature mostly as an adversary or something to exploit from which to profit. Truly, we didn't have a whole lot to talk about when we did meet.

I saw their point, but I also entertained the possibility that I could help the laborers and their families rise above their bare subsistence level by paying them more generously. This may have been a worthy goal, but to most of the local people – even to my own employees – it was just another crazy gringo idea.

But, as I'd learned from the wrongful killing of the black hawk, sometimes it was best to disregard the status quo, so I honored my personal dissatisfaction with the long-standing cultural traditions of the patriarchal labor system. The assumption by elites of the leisure class, fortified by their fellow politicians, that the lower classes – especially the farmers and the fishermen – were hopelessly backward and incapable of making wise decisions for themselves or their country, seemed to be an excuse to maintain the dominators and dominated in their respective places.

Historically in Costa Rica, the naturally peaceful rural people that formed the country's stable majority were successful and content with feeding and caring for themselves and providing enough for the city folks as well. In my opinion, however, trouble began with the continued loss of fertile topsoil due to unsustainable agricultural practices. Along with the increasing reliance on expensive chemical fertilizers and pesticides that had to be imported from industrialized countries, and with the rapid increase in population due to a high birth rate and heavy immigration from poorer neighboring countries, the political class grew disproportionately large. Land tenure changed, and the once independent farmers who now wanted to provide their families with the imported things advertised on radio and TV, had to go to work for powerful bosses who were pressured to produce for profit and for export – local consumption and workers' welfare becoming secondary. Loss of culture, increased crime, and hunger became much more pronounced. This trend was well under way when I arrived in 1972, and it just got worse.

As in many other Latin American countries, a relatively small number of families of aggressive, agro-industrialist businessmen, lawyers, and politicians seemed to gobble up the best lands, forests, lumber rights, fishing rights, mining rights, export rights, and taxing rights. They seemed to establish preferential subsidies, laws, tariffs, contracts, and politics to make sure their group would maintain the privileges, they convinced themselves at cocktail parties, they deserved. Often, they treated public funds literally as their own and seemed to get away with it, whether the public knew of their wrongdoing or not. Of course, these opinions could be mistaken. I am not accusing anyone of anything, and I hope I have the freedom to speculate on this subject.

Human history has shown all sorts of social experiments, but it's always been more likely for a person to be born into slavery, servanthood, or the hardworking class than into the privileged class. Is our geo-socio-economic birth status a random lottery, or if not, what? The elite among ancient Egyptians, Romans, Hindus, Chinese, Incans, Mayans, and Aztecs believed they *deserved* their royalty (or "divinity") and enthusiastically encouraged strong and sometimes compassionless class systems. Jesus Christ was radically revolutionary in teaching equality, fraternity, loving our fellows as ourselves, loving even our enemies! Yet, despite so many noble declarations, constitutions, and verbiage about "democracy," "communism," or "Christianity," we are still far from adapting to Christ's way.

Revolutions in Latin America have been common for the same reason they've been common throughout history. Just as the Somoza family, corrupted by power, insanely attempted to prolong their dictatorial domination of Nicaragua even after 40 years, and had to be violently overthrown in the late 1970s, so the haves and the have-nots have always taken turns, unfortunately creating horror, death, and destruction in the process. Why couldn't we finally figure out the right way to ensure long-lasting peace and prosperity?

Since 1950, Costa Rica had enjoyed wonderful peace and stability created by its big, happy, healthy middle class. But the same sort of greed and corruption that makes fools and/or monsters out of men (like Somoza and Idi Amin and so many others) began to threaten idyllic Costa Rica. The rapid growth and power of the seemingly legally immune political class was a bad sign and often while at the farm, though apparently isolated from national and international events, I wondered whether or not someday I would end up having to make a forced evacuation, leaving my dreams and projects behind. Every few months, a United States military helicopter (or a few together like giant wasps in a 1960 sci-fi movie) would noisily pass overhead, coming from or heading toward the Panama Canal zone. I figured that if Costa Rica ever got as bad as it did in Nicaragua, Colombia, Honduras, Guatemala, El Salvador, or Haiti, then I would hopefully get a ride in one of those choppers.

The expanded ramifications of the issue of boss-to-employee relationships being so complex and potentially serious, I always felt somewhat uneasy when I made the rounds at the ranch. I knew that if I came across to my employees as too lenient, foolish, or gullible, then chaos, disrespect, and loss of productivity would immediately ensue. And if I was overly strict or critical, I would quickly find myself alone to do all the work.

As for paying a little more than other employers in the area for work that I knew was really worth a lot more, I decided that if my parents and I could afford it, why not try to help these people, at least temporarily, to improve their living standard a little? If we haves, who had been lucky socio-economically, could afford to share some of our luck, why not go ahead and try to help the local people, the school, the community projects, and the environment? Of course, I still had to learn that it wasn't nearly as easy as it seemed it should have been.

On Saturdays I would ask the foreman and cowboys to round up the cattle in the main corral to count them and to cure anything that might need attending to: wounds, internal and external parasites, problem hooves or horns, apparent weakness, udder infection.

"Twenty-one 2-year-old steers in that group, right?" I might ask so that I could check it in my notebook.

"Eighteen."

"What do you mean eighteen? Count 'em yourself, Manuel."

"I did. There are eighteen. Twenty-one with the three heifers."

"Oh, I see . . . what are they doing with the steers?"

"They got mixed up this morning."

"Why aren't they all marked with our brand?"

"They are, patrón, just that you can't see them all so well."

"Listen, Manuel, I want them all marked so that I or anybody can see the brand perfectly well. I thought I told you to make sure about this last week."

"If you want a better cowboy . . ."

"Oh, take it easy and don't be offended, just do me the favor of redoing some of the brands that didn't mark so well. How's your total count to date?"

"Carlos has it written down."

"Carlos?"

"Sixty-five . . . sixty-seven with the oxen."

"All of them? I thought there were sixty-nine with the oxen."

"No, remember the bull and the three cows we sold last month?"

"Yeah, but the new bull, and the five newborn calves?"

"Well, I've got it all down at the house."

"Carlos, when we see the cattle on Saturdays I want you to have all that stuff with you here at the corral. I'm sure there should be sixty-nine, and if any are missing, we'd better go looking for them. Do me a favor and bring me your records this afternoon to see if we're in trouble or not."

The carpenters working on the house or other buildings would usually pick a Saturday to inform me of problems with the lumber, which they blamed on the lumber cutters. When I saw where they had measured wrong, they would say that the wood was green and had shrunk or warped. When they ran out of the correct-size nails, they would keep working anyway, using smaller nails that wouldn't hold properly or larger ones that would split the wood. When I would ask why there were so many split planks, they would calmly say, "Because the larger nails split the wood." When I would ask them why they hadn't told me they needed more nails, they might say, "We didn't want to bother you" or "We didn't want to have to delay the construction by having to wait for more nails from San Cristobal."

The fence makers would sometimes take a different route than the one I'd shown them, and when I asked them why, they would say, "Tito told us to go this way"; and when I would find Tito and ask him why he changed the route of the fence, he would say, "Carlos said you wanted it that way"; and when I would find Carlos and ask him about it, he would say, "Tito thought it would be a better route to take." After the workers had dug a hundred post holes, hauled a hundred heavy posts, positioned them in the holes, and pounded in the dirt around them, I would also be inclined to agree that this, indeed, was the best route for the fence.

There were plenty of other problems that made their appearance on Saturdays. A new worker might have cut down a couple of perfectly healthy palm trees and left the dying ones standing. The 400-yard-long water system might have gotten clogged, or macheted by a careless worker, or dug up and severed by a playful cow or bull. I would discover the damage when I turned on the shower to rinse off the sweat, dirt, and cow-related material and got only a spit of dirty water followed by a dying gasp of air. All these inconveniences seemed to lie camouflaged all week, only to ambush me on Saturdays.

Saturday was also the day many of the workers spent a sizable portion of their pay at La Pichinga Saloon in Morita.

At first, I tried to discourage this by giving them a few drinks on Saturdays after pay time, so they would stick around. That seemed only to whet their thirst, so I stopped. Eventually, as the problem with drunken workers grew worse, I prohibited liquor on my land.

I especially grew tired of playing policeman on Saturday nights, when the problem workers who didn't stay overnight in Morita would return with a bottle in one hand and a machete in the other, anxious to share a drink or threaten harm, depending on whether you were friend or foe. It was always hard to tell which you were.

The best man with horses and cattle I ever had was also the biggest drinker I ever had. One Sunday morning his wife sent me a note in barely comprehensible Spanish: "Don Jon. If you can do me the favor and come quickly and don't tell him because he'll kill me even faster." I did my best to stay out of personal affairs, but I knew Chango and what guaro did to him, so I decided to go see if I could prevent a possible murder. Luckily, Chango was impressed with my visit and settled down when I confiscated his bottle.

That seemed to fix him for a while, but eventually I had to fire him and a few others like him who were always asking for raises and threatening to leave if I didn't give in, but who kept spending all their money on weekend binges, missing work on Mondays, and leaving their families poorly fed and poorly clothed.

Paydays were bad for the first few years, when the jungles were thick and the people were rough and I was green. That changed, fortunately, and paydays became increasingly uneventful. However, people-related problems persisted, and though they did not represent the norm, they still kept postponing my dream of creating a peaceful, prosperous, self-sufficient farming community nestled between the mountains and the sea.

Many of the problems were exacerbated by my inexperience and my unfamiliarity with local custom and local conditions. How different it all was from my home country, with its fantastic infrastructure; its hospitals, schools, and supermarkets; its plumbers, electricians, and carpenters who were only a phone call away. How unprepared I was, a product of all that access to convenience and the fruits of affluence, to jump into a place where nature had yet to be subjugated, where there was so much hard manual work to be done, and just us to do it.

I tried to do my part by joining the laborers to whom I was paying the equivalent of 35 cents an hour. Hauling cargo on my inexperienced shoulders; wielding ax and machete with my softer, book-reading hands; building things without the basic know-how under the indifferent sun and rain, I realized with a little horror that if I hadn't been relatively wealthy, I would have had difficulty even surviving there.

I remained uncomfortable with this class division between myself and the low-paid workers who made it possible for me to live out my tropical fantasy. I insisted on continuing to participate in the heavy labor, but all I proved, again and again, was that my back was simply not as suited for the heavy lumber all the other workers could carry with such apparent ease, that my hands were incapable of more than a few hours a day of chopping or shoveling or digging or sawing. Even 70-plus-year-old Don Dimas outdid me in all categories.

Everyone said it was just a matter of practice and time, but even though I reached the stage where my back, hands, arms, and legs could last until lunchtime, I never was able to keep up with the rest of the workers. This was quite humbling to me at first, since I took pride in my physical condition. I had been captain of my high school soccer team, a respectable competitor in swimming and track, and an active surfer and skin diver; but when it came to applying myself to practical hard labor, the kind many of us in the United States rely on someone else to do, I was unable to keep up.

It wasn't until years later that I discovered I perhaps wasn't as poor and weak a worker as I had thought. I had been ignorant of an unwritten law of Moritan social structure: a landowner and boss was expected to oversee his workers, not to work as much or as hard as they. It turned out that when I had gone to work with the others, I had unknowingly been setting the pace. No matter how hard I worked, they all felt they had to work even harder. When I put three boards to my shoulder to carry a hundred or so yards out of the forest to where the oxen were, everyone else would carry five boards. When we were chopping through jungle or weeds, I would need to rest at least once every half hour and would invite them to join me, but they seldom did.

It was disturbing to realize how hard I had been pushing the workers without intending to. When I finally did understand the rigidity of the unspoken Moritan social laws of labor, I restricted myself mainly to overseeing. When I did work, it was usually by myself or with just one or two others for just a few hours.

This was not the only cultural rule I violated. Every few months I would have a pig killed to distribute to the employees and families, and we would have a barbecue and drink rum. Other landowners later confided in me that this was not wise, that it was not advisable to be so familiar, friendly, or generous with one's employees, and that a patrón should never drink with them. This was hard for me to accept. I took pride in paying the best wages, housing the workers and their families adequately, and providing "my people" with fish and milk and even land if they wanted to grow something in their spare time. I enjoyed treating employees as friends and hoped for the same in return.

Yet I had to admit I had more problems with the employees than I thought I deserved. Often they seemed discontented or frustrated. They often told me they felt like moving on to seek work elsewhere. They seemed to enjoy putting me in a position where I had to try to convince them to stay.

Many workers spent a lot of their salaries on weekend binges. The underlying reason behind it all, according to my few fellow boss-friends, was that I treated my employees too well. I was too lenient and too reluctant to fire. If I wanted a superior, more stable, more contented work force, I was advised to adopt a certain aloofness, to be less sympathetic, never to admit incompetence or ignorance, to laugh less, to keep my mouth shut more, and to issue orders sometimes for the sake of discipline and obedience rather than for efficiency.

In effect, I was told to grow up, to treat my employees as another class of people, as uneducated laborers who knew no other way of life, desired no other way of life, were unsuited for any other way of life, and would probably never appreciate my treatment of them anyway. I stubbornly rejected these attitudes as far too harsh, unjust, pessimistic, counterproductive, and generally ridiculous.

However, after many years of sincere efforts to boost individuals' and the community's level of education and standard of living, I couldn't truthfully say that I helped very many raise their living standards permanently. It wasn't easy to help when the help wasn't wanted or taken advantage of. For example, I maintained a well-stocked library in Spanish and English for all levels of ability and interest, but was able to attract only a handful of young people to use it even though I offered them the books and magazines free of charge. Illiteracy was part of the problem, but I also had a lot of magazines like *National Geographic* that were full of fascinating pictures and didn't require reading ability.

After 12 years, I put all the books and magazines in storage. Once again, my efforts to help had run afoul of rules and cultural forces I didn't understand. For many of the people, particularly the older ones, reluctance to use the books and magazines had grown out of fear and embarrassment to see pictures of things in the outside world that completely mystified them. Some people weren't comfortable accepting such "gifts," which left them feeling indebted and awkward toward the giver.

Although they had many different cultural, social, and spiritual priorities, the "have-nots" of Morita shared some of the same desires for material wealth as the "haves" in my homeland. This was driven home to me when I discovered Carlos, my first "pirate" friend and partner, apparently appropriating farm supplies such as ropes, gasoline, and herbicide and selling them for his own profit as well as skimming proceeds from labor contracts and sales from the farm's small general store.

I wasn't so much angry as I was disappointed and confused. Here was the man who had sent me the fateful letter that lured me back to Costa Rica, who worked from dawn 'til dusk helping me manage the finca, who more than anyone helped me to become established, to purchase parcels of land, who served me well as foreman for six years, whose wife provided me with hundreds of wonderful meals. Friendly and cheerful and smart and hospitable, seemingly content and prospering – why would he start cheating me? Surely there must have been some mistake, but I couldn't help remembering Doña Miranda's warning to me about him years before, and wondering if I'd been a fool to have ignored her advice.

Afraid to lose him, I tried to persuade him to reform. He promised he would, and he did for a while. Eventually, however, he began to drink more heavily and got involved with another employee's wife. Mostly to protect Carlos's family, I fired that employee so he would take his wife and kids elsewhere. This time, I warned Carlos to quit drinking, "or else."

After a short visit to the United States, I returned to learn that Carlos had taken my .22 revolver, pulled it out while crazy-drunk in La Pichinga – where he'd been playing catch with a bag of money comprising the finca payroll – and fired three shots into the saloon's tin roof. The local Rural Guard, who was good friends with Carlos, confiscated the money and gun temporarily and released Carlos on the condition he go home.

Still hoping to salvage my friend, I gave him one last chance, which he used up one Easter weekend. After fishing that morning, Carlos and his 10-year-old son and I stopped for a visit at Conchal Beach, a beautiful half-moon stretch of sand a few miles south of the finca. While I was talking with some people on one end of the beach, Carlos found someone with local guaro, which he gulped down like water. Ready to return to the finca, I found Carlos intoxicated and told him it was time to go back. Walking back toward where our boat, Siete Vueltas, was anchored, I heard a sudden burst of commotion and shouting behind me. When I turned around, I saw him lying on his stomach in the sand, pinned down by a muscular stranger who was grasping Carlos's right hand with all his strength. In Carlos's fist was a large, shiny knife.

"He tried to kill you!" the sweat-drenched stranger shouted at me as he squeezed and shook the blade out of Carlos's grasp.

"No, no, it was a joke! I was just kidding!" Carlos laughed nervously, and with an expression of fear, embarrassment, and drunkenness – sand glued to his sweaty cheek. The other man released Carlos and told me clearly, "As soon as you turned your back and started walking away, this idiot grabbed the knife and went after you with it raised for stabbing."

I couldn't believe it. The accusation was so serious, so personal, that at first I tried to deny it. "Oh come on, he's my friend. He's drunk and was probably just kidding."

"You can believe what you want," the stranger said. "All I know is that he was attacking you, so I tackled him." He looked at me as if I were a hopeless fool.

Apologetically, I shook the man's hand with both of mine and thanked him sincerely for his providential intervention. Could my naïveté be so deep that it actually endangered my life? Once again I denied the frightening possibility. I was going to return alone in the Siete Vueltas, but Carlos's son was crying, and I feared Carlos would get into mortal trouble if I left him, so with the help of another employee, I got him and his son into the boat and back to the finca.

I wanted so badly to disbelieve all the charges against Carlos, to reject such a profound personal defeat, that when he pleaded with me to give him another "one last chance" I yielded. But when I caught him violating his promise not to drink again, I fired him and gave his job to the cowboy, Macedonio.

For years I wondered what had gone wrong, finally deciding that perhaps the other ranchers had been right – I got too close to Carlos; I empowered him with too much money and responsibility for his capacity; I was too tolerant of his shortcomings. He wanted so badly to have the power and authority, the possessions and leisure time that I enjoyed so casually, yet he had no idea how to obtain them. His sporadic fits of intoxication and petty theft were probably products of his mounting frustration and resentment.

When Carlos and his family left for a place near the Panamanian border, he took his parents, Don Arturo and Lucía, with him. The farm would never be the same. Nor would I.

My parents were also saddened by these events, especially since the relationship they had struck up with Carlos, Anita, and their two sons had been the most rewarding part of their only visit, which had been a bit rough, with airplane delays and bouncy flights, mud and biting gnats, and the discomfort of the hot, steamy jungle compared with the cool, dry climate of their home in New Mexico.

My parents, as always, were helpful to me in overcoming the setback of losing Carlos. This time they encouraged me to think beyond ranching and offered me the financial help I needed to explore the possibility of creating a small tourist development to tap into the infant "adventure travel" industry.

Before leaving, Anita had sent word to her tallish, brown-haired younger sister, Delfina, in her stead to come and cook for me and the wifeless workers.

Due to a tragic motorcycle accident, Delfina was already a widow at 25 years old, with two sons, three and five. It was not love at first sight, but I soon found myself more and more attracted to her. One day while walking alone with her on a forest trail, I tied a small rope around her hands, looked into her big olive-green eyes, and told her she was mine. She accepted, and we began living happily together.

In one month I lost my closest male companion and gained an even closer female companion. I sincerely hoped to have much better luck with Delfina than I had with Carlos.

Tortuga "lora" (Olive Ridley turtle)

Chapter Eleven

Tropical paradise – maybe someday

Delfina was such an excellent cook and able general helper, and we worked so well as a team, I thought that, not only could I survive in that place and be happy and comfortable, but also that we really had a good chance as inn-keepers.

In 1980, when the Coast Highway crew boldly traversed the existing horse trail and pounded an obstacle course of wooden stakes in the ground to remind the horses, oxen, and everyone else of their plans to build their highway, I hurried our lumber production and the construction of four rustic but comfortable wood cabins, built on posts to keep them away from termites, to keep them cooler, and to enhance their spectacular coastal views. At first, there was no running water at those hilltop sites, so we built the nicest outhouses possible (which still, being outhouses, weren't all that nice), and used portable water tanks for drinking and limited washing. The guests would have to take their showers three minutes' walk down the hill by the restaurant, kitchen, and our living quarters.

Delfina decided it was time to initiate in earnest the breeding of chickens and turkeys, and without thinking much about it, I agreed. The cackling and cawing of the free-roaming hens and roosters at precisely the wrong times of day and night quickly began to erode my initial enthusiasm for the feathered creatures, as did the fresh droppings they left everywhere. "Ah, yes, but you don't think of that when you're eating your roasted chicken or when your tourists insist on having eggs for breakfast," Delfina would tease me when I threatened to get rid of them all. She and every Costa Rican farm woman I had ever met loved to raise poultry, took great pride in it, and would defend them from any manner of man or beast, but all I knew was that waking up to a rooster's ungodly ruckus right outside our window at 3:00 a.m. was not good for me or people who had to deal with me that morning.

When living with Don Arturo and Lucía I had learned grudgingly to cope with domestic birds in close proximity, but when I moved alone into my own house I was happy to be able to banish them. Now, with Delfina, the best solution I could manage was a compromise – a chicken house.

"Chicken house?" she protested at first. "What are they going to eat?"

"Corn, chicken feed, whatever it is they eat," I said as if it were perfectly obvious.

"They need grass and little seeds and little creatures! They need to walk around and hunt for food! They'll get skinny and sick! These aren't *city* chickens!"

"Yeah, well then they'll have to learn." I wanted the chicken house far enough away so that the smell wouldn't reach the people house. Delfina wanted it close enough so that she could hear the alarmed birds when an intruder tried to make trouble at night.

"Delfina, the whole thing's going to be enclosed in chicken wire. There aren't going to be any intruders," I tried to assure her.

"They'll dig under and up," she replied, sure of herself.

"We'll put rocks."

"They'll move the rocks."

"We'll put *big* rocks."

"They'll get through it."

"Del . . ."

"Do you like to eat roast chicken on Sundays? Do you like eggs for breakfast? Do you want to please your tourists?"

We built the thing out of second-hand, termite-victimized wood. It took about five times as much chicken wire as we'd figured. We built it about 50 yards from our house down the hill in a palm grove, which turned out to be neither close enough nor far enough away. When the breeze shifted sometimes we could smell it quite well from our bedroom; at night, when we heard the screams of terrified birds being devoured, it took us too long to get our shoes on, grab flashlight and shotgun, and make it down the hill.

Opossums, skunks, ocelots, snakes, tolomucos – we had lots of customers for our chickens, and the predators devised a variety of ingenious ways to get through, under, or over the barriers. There were other problems as well: commercial feed had a way of getting humid and mildewy and full of cockroaches, mealy bugs, and fierce biting ants, and it was even worse when the Morita and Tortuga rivers were swollen with rain and the horses had to swim the cargo across. Don Dimas, my favorite employee, having provided faithful and willing service for eight years, reported humbly one day that he would have to quit if I sent him one more time to clean the chicken house. It was the only job he would not willingly do, and everyone else was quick to follow his example, leaving the chore exclusively for me.

At times, I went to great lengths to defend the chickens. One evening, after losing three birds to unseen poachers right at nightfall, I followed the enthusiastic advice of employees, wives, and neighbors and stationed myself on a rock by the chicken house. With a rum drink in one hand, a flashlight in the other, and a loaded 16-gauge by my side, I waited for the marauder to appear. Sure enough, the ca-ca-ca-caaaaaa alarm of a chicken began as soon as I'd finished my drink. Then I saw a familiar black shape with white stripes bob along the side of the building and slip into the hole that had already been dug under the wall and wire and rocks.

I waited for the chickens to become frantic, and then made my move, hopefully "not too soon, not too late" as my coaches emphasized. Trading my glass for the gun, I scrambled down to the chicken house, wondering about snakes lurking in the dark. The skunk was just about to sink his teeth into the chicken he had grabbed when I paralyzed him in the flashlight beam. His eyes glowed an unnatural green, and he dropped his surprised prey and made a panicky attempt to hide in the corner. I didn't hesitate – "Killing a skunk isn't like killing a beautiful hawk," I told myself. Holding the flashlight in one hand, I brought the gun up in the other, pinning it between my arm and my ribcage, and fired.

When the smoke and dust cleared, I saw the skunk still kicking a little, so, trembling, I reloaded and blasted him again ("Never underestimate the skunk's ability to withstand bullets or machete wounds," Manolo had warned). I didn't want to let this chicken-killer get away. It no longer moved, and I was sure that after two shotgun blasts, it had to be defunct. I remembered everyone's warning about never being too sure that a skunk was dead, but it stunk so bad and looked so shot-up and terminated, that I was sure.

I climbed the hill triumphantly. Delfina was happy and even seemed proud of me, a gringo mate who was capable of defending the family chickens, of killing the enemy rather than wanting to *preserve* it. Next morning the little varmint was gone, but the stink stayed for a month.

When Delfina wanted to let a hen keep its eggs for hatching, she would insist that the hen be allowed to set on them under the house where they could be protected better. She would also insist to the hen that it lay its eggs under the house. With some hens, it was a constant struggle to keep them from nesting in the forest or fields.

"Mommy, the red hen isn't in her place," one of Delfina's kids would yell, often while I was trying to read or do something else requiring concentration.

"Well, go and look for her and bring her back! And put your shoes on! And careful with snakes!" While the search was on, I would be unable to concentrate on anything else because Delfina would stand on the porch and loudly direct the children to likely hiding spots. Sometimes they would scream back excitedly, "Mommy, we found the painted black with eight eggs!" or "Mommy, Mommy! She's all torn to pieces and covered with ants!"

One time, Delfina made me go chasing after a ten-foot-long black snake she claimed had been swallowing up many eggs. I ran it down a hill by throwing rocks at it, while ready to take a swipe at it with my machete urged on by Delfina's "Get him! Kill it!" But the snake tired of that. Rearing up, it hissed so loud and struck out at me so convincingly that I didn't care that it wasn't poisonous and ran back up the hill, with Delfina laughing at me. Taking care of chickens made me wonder about the true costs of living in our tropical "paradise."

Besides raising poultry, cooking, raising kids, and tolerating me, Delfina was an expert at milking cows, catching prawns in the stream, gathering herbs, and getting fruit from high up in trees. I used to joke with her about her winning the lottery when she won me, but when she said "Who knows who got the better deal?" I had to admit she had a good point. We bickered a lot and had some problems, especially over her kids – they didn't want me to detour her affection, and I didn't want them to take her affection either, or to get in my way, or call me "Daddy," or misbehave, or cry, or wet their beds – but we mostly got along very well together and made each other much happier than we had been.

Trying out tourism as a viable business was as risky as anything else I'd attempted in Costa Rica. Cattle, coconuts, chickens, and just being there running a 400-acre farm with a dozen or more employees – I hadn't had any previous experience or training in anything that I was trying to do. Luckily, my financially tranquil parents and partners were willing to allow me to do some experimenting as the land appreciated in value. The place was so beautiful, nature was so exuberant, I loved just being there, but I really wanted to find the right activity that would pay the bills and salaries, for my parent-sponsors' sakes as well as my own.

Our first official guest, a friend of a friend in the United States (we still mostly advertised by word of mouth), was a tall young Iranian bachelor, an ex-prince turned insurance salesman (or something like that) who worked in Texas and had buddies with rhino-horn daggers. He seemed more fascinated by my relationship with Delfina than by the fishing or snorkeling or horseback riding or rainforest exploration. He expressed his personal approval of those activities, but he kept returning to our personal matters as if they were by far the most amazing thing happening at the finca.

"Surely you will return some day to America?" he asked me. "Yes? . . . I know. . .You love it here, don't you? Yes, you love it here." I didn't need to answer since he did both the questioning and the answering, all the time grinning as if he were confiding to me some coveted secret or profound truth. For $40 a night, including cabin and meals, I would listen and smile back. That was part of my job, and I wanted my job to last. He loved Delfina's food, especially the ways she prepared her chicken, but said to me in a whisper, "You know, in my country we could enjoy lower classes" (chuckle, chuckle), "but we would not consider living with them! Your girlfriend is very nice," he said in an accent like Count Dracula's, "but you wouldn't consider marrying her, would you? She's not even beautiful, you know! You know what I mean? Yes, you know, don't you? Of course you know." He grinned and moved his face closer to mine, but failed to get from me anything more than an ambiguous smile. Meanwhile I was wondering silently whether this was the typical sort of tourist I could expect. Was this an "adventure" tourist? And would he marry a beautiful aristocrat who would make him miserable?

I soon learned there was no "typical" tourist. Our guests usually came in couples, and they were always so very different. There was the elderly Audubon Society couple who got into trouble before we even made it from the pasture runway in Morita to my farm five kilometers away. I stayed close with them on horseback the whole way, but just as we neared the farm's entrance, the woman helplessly let her horse carry her into an empty clothesline, which caught the woman right across the neck and nearly yanked her out of the saddle. When I suggested that next time she pull back on the reins more forcefully, she looked at me disapprovingly and replied, "I don't believe in mistreating animals." I wondered what these "adventure travelers" had in mind when they chose to visit such a remote destination.

Two paunchy fishermen and their thin spouses from France and Italy, respectively, made our lives very uncomfortable around Christmas one year. Besides constantly complaining about Delfina's chicken (they would have much preferred the muscleless hormone and antibiotic saturated caged ones) and "unimaginative" meals, one of the women insisted on biting into the sticky, sappy peel of an unripe banana despite my warning that she could burn her lips (which she did). When we took the boat out to go fishing, the Italian had great success while the round, red Frenchman caught nothing. I had them change sides, change fishing rods, lures, everything, and still the Frenchman caught nothing while the Italian kept catching fish. The Frenchman grew even redder and more angry, blaming me as guide and accusing me of favoring the Italian by positioning his side of the boat where the fish were. I translated that for Fingo, the first mate, so that we could both have a good laugh.

The Frenchman's lack of success was especially amusing since he had been bragging about winning some fishing tournament with a big tuna somewhere and had sworn that if there were fish, he would be the first to catch them. The Frenchman finally got a strike, and it *was* a big fish. The line zipped out and the rod bent impressively, but it quickly popped back straight again as the line went slack. His euphoria turned to sourness when he reeled in and we all saw how the knot he had insisted on tying himself had slipped out. At the end of their visit, they refused to pay for their own special charter flight, so I had to, losing five days of profits.

A great couple from California kept returning year after year, and our friendship grew. Bob was an avid fisherman who always had exceptionally good luck in the area. The employees and their families living on the finca would comment when Bob was arriving, "Well, get ready to eat fish all week." I never knew what he would catch, since he caught species no one else had. His wife, Carol, was extraordinarily lucky in locating and viewing birds that I hadn't even seen in my years of living there. She was like a godmother to all the local children, and she always seemed to have gifts in her suitcase to make everyone happy.

Tourism was as highly rewarding as it was exasperating. When we opened to paying guests, we called the place *Aveoro* (gold bird) alluding to the exquisite gold eagle artifacts that occasionally turned up in excavations of ancient Indian sites. In one sense, Aveoro was just like a gold bird – so heavy it couldn't get off the ground. Just the frustration of the consistently delayed and gut-wrenching plane ride to and from Morita, coupled with a butt-bouncing horseback ride, were enough to prevent many tourists from returning. But poor transportation was only one of many unpleasant factors jeopardizing successful tourism or even happy habitation in Morita.

In a color brochure, we advertised the paradisiacal qualities of Aveoro, but they represented only half the story. Soon, in order to appease my own conscience, I changed the name of Aveoro to *Cantarana* (frog-sing) – which Chontales, the ex-hacienda's old cowboy, had humorously suggested years before. Delfina and most others disliked it because it was slightly derogatory, with slimy or swampy connotations. To me, however, it seemed to reflect the local tropical reality more accurately and honestly. Actually, I happened to be sort of a frog lover, and Cantarana harbored spectacular, day-glow, green-and-black poison-dart frogs, which impressed even the most blasé people. Frogs were becoming extinct all over the world, and I was happy that Cantarana still had plenty of them singing their hearts out.

Other aspects of that ultra-tropical environment did bother me and everyone else. We were most wise when we accepted them as normal, healthy, integral parts and parcels of tropical reality, which indeed was often at odds with human well-being.

If I had to choose a winner among the most overpowering of Cantarana's drawbacks, I would call it a tie between the heat and humidity, a tag-team that would have no problem at all bringing Hulk Hogan and Mr. T. to their knees. Sometimes I could not work hard for even an hour without becoming soaked in sweat and red in the face. Sometimes it was so steamy around midday I didn't have to work to sweat.

The hot, damp environment was ideal, of course, for a wide variety of bacteria and fungi that prospered and reproduced with exceptional success on and in humans. Sometimes the nights were intolerable, especially around full moons, when the sea breeze failed; the thick, clammy vapors rose from the wet earth; the gnats were out for blood; and the cicadas, beetles and crickets were buzzing and sawing and scraping and screeching at high-decibel levels. Though it was too hot even for a sheet, if you didn't cover up, bugs would bite you or lick you or land and crawl on you.

There were a million biting insects, and it was a mystery how people managed to avoid the vast majority of them. After a few years, I became so learned about insects, pestiferous and not, that I could have written volumes on their relationships with humans. Probably the worst one, though this was endlessly debatable, was the barely visible orange-red chigger-mite known as the *coloradilla*. They waited in the grasses like camouflaged armies, waiting patiently days or months for some unknowing tourist or child to sit down and enjoy the view for a while. In no time, the tiny assailants would climb up the victim's clothes and head for the waistline, armpits, and other nooks and crannies. They *ran* to get there. Within hours the itching began. Scratching did no good. Alcohol helped more when taken internally than when applied topically.

It seemed unfair to me that the coloradillas stole their minuscule meal and caused such discomfort, too. Vampire bats took quite a bit of blood without the host even noticing. But these little nasties defied one to scratch until bleeding, and this, I speculated, they did on purpose – one of those evolutionary biological maneuvers to exploit others no matter by what horrendous means.

Paradise for the coloradillas was soft, white skin imported from northern latitudes. Once they'd grown cozy, killing them posed a problem. I'd tried drowning them in the ocean, but they must have had gills. California Carol, who kept advancing her experimentation on the little demons, discovered that fingernail polish sometimes worked well, and sometimes didn't. The only sure way to get rid of them was to bring out the big guns and poison them or sabotage their air supply. Eventually we discovered the proper measure to avoid the chiggers in the first place: smearing Vicks or sulfur or diesel or regular insect repellent on shoes and lower legs worked wonderfully to repel the original invasion.

Quisquinas did not afflict human victims as often, so they had to settle for second place in the pest derby. The tiny yellowish ants, which could drive you crazy with a cruel mixture of itching and burning, lurked on branches and rubbed off or dropped down on passersby. The locals said it was their urine that burned and itched so badly, like an acid that couldn't be neutralized by water, oil, ammonia, or even the best anti-inflammatory ointments from American pharmacies.

Another nuisance was the *chincha,* or stinkbug. When one of the bottlecap-sized bugs with the distinctive triangular head landed on you and you instinctively brushed it off, it might spray its smelly acid on you. If you just left the acid on your skin, it would very slowly start to burn and produce an inflamed and perhaps blistered area, much like a chemical burn. The most proven remedy was to immediately irrigate the area with urine, the ammonia content being the key. This was one of those valuable things worth learning at Cantarana, but I was glad I never had to tell a tourist to put it to use (please, madam, allow me).

There must have been a billion ants for each person at Cantarana. How many army ants were there in a marching mass 2 meters across by 400 meters long? About ten to a square inch by 78 inches wide by 400 meters (10 x 78 x 39 x 400) was 12,168,000. These millions of fierce biting and stinging ants built an ingenious ant and stick bridge across the running Quebrada Chica stream and attacked and killed our two experimental European honeybee colonies. Uninterested in the abundant honey, the ants carried away the bees and then attacked our house and cleaned it out of every spider, cockroach, scorpion, and carpenter ant, which in many cases they drove out alive, like herding cattle.

After several hours of being evicted from our house, we returned to find no trace of any arthropods, and it wasn't long before we hoped the ants, which we first considered foes, would return.

Quita-calzon (take off underwear) wasps attacked so relentlessly and thoroughly that human victims often ran hundreds of yards displaying the peculiar behavior referred to by the species' popular name.

It was ironic how Bob, my best client and friend, drew the worst attacks, for he had a phobia for bugs. He would jump up and shake his head and hands wildly when a harmless beetle got caught in his hair. When a stingerless black bee assumed a surveillance pattern around him at lunchtime, he would shove back his chair, swear, and swat at the bee energetically. He would find ants in his bed, spiders on his clothes, bees in his drink.

There were worse things than chiggers, and once Bob managed to take a couple of tropical parasites back with him to sunny Southern California, where he couldn't help noticing a growing itching and swelling in his calf. After medicating himself with a few different topical shotgun blasts from his pharmacy and getting nowhere, he began to worry.

"There's something *growing* in me, *eating* me!" he realized in horror when he felt the distinct internal biting. He went to his doctor, who cut a small incision by the little hole in the center of the swelling and looked in with a magnifying glass. He turned pale, told Bob that indeed there was something moving inside, and urged Bob to accompany him to a specialist in tropical parasitology.

The parasitologist also turned pale when he probed the wound with forceps and struggled to pull an inch-long, tough, hairy, white-gray worm from Bob's leg. The doctor probed the hole again, found another worm, and pulled it out, too.

Apparently, a botfly, a familiar denizen of the tropics, had bitten Bob's leg and laid some eggs in the bite, or a mosquito had served as a vector for the eggs or larvae. When the eggs hatched, the larvae ate and grew happily and healthily. Had he let nature take its course, the larvae would have eaten a small chunk of his leg as they metamorphosed and grew and then would have crawled out of their meaty cave and flown away, to mate and enable others to enjoy the same kind of life. They much preferred cattle, never bothering horses and rarely people, and so Bob was really quite a celebrity to have been chosen for such a distinction, especially in California, where I doubted many botflies had the chance to visit. Bob kept his evicted guests in alcohol in a little glass jar, souvenirs from our tropical paradise.

When I heard his story, I laughed and said "gross!" like everyone else, but then was sad because Bob was a good friend and I figured we would never see him again in Costa Rica, where he was my favorite companion in exploring the remote Osa Peninsula and Faro Island. Apparently, however, his experience cured him almost completely of his insect phobia. Maybe he figured he'd gone through the worst possible insect-related experience, and as a result, the flying and biting critters of the world held no special terrors for him any longer.

Bob continued to visit us, and I swear the eight-inch locusts no longer flew in his face, the black bees kept their distance, and he somehow achieved near-immunity to the itching of the chiggers and the gnats.

Although many bothersome insects inhabited Cantarana, they were not nearly as plentiful as the harmless, beneficial, and beautiful ones, and I felt immense gratitude that mosquitoes and houseflies were quite rare.

Various poisonous serpents inhabited Cantarana – coral snakes, bushmasters, and several members of the pit-viper family, but they had not been able to sink their fangs into anyone on the finca – thank God. I lost my best horse and a couple of cows and calves and probably my dog to snakes, but no people or parts of people.

Having seen the effects of venomous snakebites – people in the hospital, suffering agony as an arm or leg rotted away to the bone, even with the best medical treatment then available – I harbored no affection for the creatures and sought to eliminate them from the ranch, paying out more than $300 in bounties in ten years at about a dollar per dead poisonous snake. Luckily, we had no snakebite victims at Cantarana, but just in case, I was prepared to combat the threat of death or tissue necrosis with low-voltage shocks using our cattleprod, an alternative treatment that proved promising.

Coral snakes, with their small mouths and docility, did not pose any real danger and so were not on our hit list. Nor did I have any quarrel with the boas or the other nonpoisonous snakes, which were obviously valuable assets in keeping the rodent population down.

Stingrays presented a hazard for the unlucky bather who happened to step on one. It rarely happened, but as with the snakebite, it *had* happened in the area and could happen again at any time. I'd only seen one case – the first visit I'd made to Costa Rica when I had to rescue my fellow student friend, Mark, after a big ray punched a hole all the way through the back of his ankle. Since then, I heard of two others. All cases were frightening; the wound inflicted by the barbed tail was extremely painful and required medical attention. Another evolutionary innovation, the stingray's barb was a defense mechanism to teach hungry predators such as sharks a memorable lesson, but soft-skinned human bathers paid a dear price for the education designed for the tough-skinned sharks.

Another of the major problems at Cantarana was the time and effort required to reach civilization – doctors, vets, dentists, a hospital, medicines, schools, tools, parts, groceries, telephones, and new paying customers were all far, far away. A 20-mile dirt-and-gravel road led from San Cristobal to Puerto Nuevo on the coast north of Morita, but the link between Puerto Nuevo and Morita remained a horse trail crossing scores of bridgeless rivers and streams, sandy beaches, and steep rocky hills. In 1985, the closest year-round roads remained 10 miles to the north and 15 to the south.

With all the potential hazards and inconveniences at Cantarana, it eventually dawned on my brother Kevin, who'd been helping me with the tourist business from the United States side, that Cantarana wasn't the most ideal setting for tourism. What's more, he believed the various risks for visitors left us vulnerable to being sued for everything we had. Litigation was fast becoming North America's favorite pastime, and we were guiding potential plaintiffs on real live horses, over slippery rocks, out in the unpredictable ocean, through authentic rainforests. . . . We were crazy!

Although we made a sincere and tedious effort to assess our obligations and rights according to international law, we learned that anyone could sue for anything anywhere. Our assets in the United States and our Costa Rican property were both fair game; waivers of liability were weak or useless instruments in the case of proven negligence. Adequate safety precautions were never considered adequate enough; the cost of insurance coverage would exceed our profits. Americans were suing innocent people for apparently ridiculous reasons and were being rewarded with absurdly large sums of money.

Now what to do? It was such a pleasure to have Delfina close by to tell my troubles to, especially because she regarded my sort of troubles, such as worrying about possibly devastating lawsuits, as mere fantasies unworthy of serious concern. But what helped me most of all was her deeply calm, unmolested look. When she focused it on me, I suddenly felt mostly ridiculous for worrying, as if I'd claimed to have seen a monster and she knew it was just my paranoid imagination.

In her mind, this was probably the case. After all, how could anyone possibly win a million-dollar prize by falling off someone else's horse?

I wished life really did make sense.

Flor de bejuco (rare flower from a rainforest vine)

Chapter Twelve

Big ideas – doing something

No longer were we dealing with just the heat, humidity, and potentially painful encounters with bugs, snakes, and stingrays. We had to begin dealing also with international lawyers and insurance companies, trying to transcend the possible liability problem, so we could continue the tourism business without fear of losing our shirts. Despite the many natural sources of discomfort and risk present in our venture, we were mostly encouraged to persevere by our first guests, especially Bob and Carol, who kept returning year after year. Although these were the kinds of adventure travelers or "eco-tourists" we wished to attract, we realized that it wasn't smart or fair not to offer our guests all possible amenities.

We hooked our water system to a spring higher up in the mountains of Cantarana and so provided gravity-fed showers and toilets to three of the four cabins. Then we began toying with the idea of electricity, another one of those magical luxuries most of us take for granted.

La Pichinga, Don Ramón's saloon/general store, sported an ancient diesel generator that rivaled a helicopter in noise and smoke output. Don Ramón fired it up a few times a week to recharge the battery in the antique, cockroach-infested radio – which was for

Morita the only communication with the outside world – to light up four light bulbs, and on Saturdays to activate the ailing jukebox, which could barely compete with the noise of the generator.

From the hilltop cabin at Cantarana, we could see Don Ramón's 100-watt outdoor light bulb 5 kilometers distant, although we couldn't hear the slightest hint of the Saturday night pandemonium. The entire rest of the coastline, visible for about 100 kilometers in both directions, was dark except for the very faint glow of Manuelito, some 70 kilometers north, and La Palma, about the same distance south. Shrimp trawlers produced a few lonely points of light in the ocean outside the mouth of the Terranal River, 20 kilometers south of us.

With few artificial sources of illumination, the moon was a very prominent character in peoples' lives, the queen of nighttime luminosity and mistress of the all-important tides. In Morita, and along much of the southern Pacific coast of Costa Rica, beaches were used as highways because inland there were no roads, just mountains, rivers, and jungle. Tidal differences were so great that at low tide, the receding ocean exposed 200 meters of sand, whereas a strong high tide would cover the beach all the way up into the thick vegetation and generate waves that kept anyone from passing. Being caught by a quickly rising tide in the middle of a 3-kilometer-long beach was not a laughing matter.

The moon governed other activities as well. Pruning and transplanting were done during the waning moon, when the plants would "bleed" less. Also, animals were castrated or operated on at this time. Trees were felled for lumber during the waning moon, so they would be more resistant to rot and wood-boring insects. Field clearing and weed chopping were done during the waxing moon, so the undesired growth would die instead of resprout. Water-vines and vaco trees would produce plenty of drinkable water and "milk" during incoming tides but be mostly dry on outgoing ones.

It seemed to rain less often on nights of the full moon, even in the rainy season. I noticed also that there seemed to be more fighting at La Pichinga and more problems in families during those times, and not just among people but among the animals as well. Although the full and new moon phases were often full of surprises and chaos, they were also good times, when cows and mares gave birth, and when near-term pregnant women also expected to deliver their babies and prepared accordingly.

Surfers claimed the best swells were generated around full moons, while fishermen much preferred the new moon, when light-shy pelagic plankton and squid and their tasty predators conveniently rose from deeper water. During our fish-drying days, Delfina and I learned something that we had been told by local elders but did not at first believe: the light from a full or near-full moon seemed to spoil salted fish hung to dry. After losing a couple of well-prepared catches, we had to learn to hang the drying fish where the moon's rays didn't penetrate during the night. The new moon was best for drying.

When to plant, when to harvest, when to travel, when to fish, when and where to hang drying fish at night, when to haul cargo, when to marry, when to party – the moon was consulted for everything. Everyone "knew the moon" and sought it out for orientation. "How's the moon?" was a more common a question than "What time is it?"

Although the idea of competing with the moon by installing electric lights seemed slightly sacrilegious to me, after ten years I'd grown tired of having poor light to read by, of relying on smoky candles and lamps, and of dodging the legions of reckless flying creatures these feeble light sources attracted.

I never considered a noisy, smoking, diesel-sucking generator. But a smooth, silent, efficient water-powered one? Don Umberto, 81 years old and quite eccentric, said it could be done. In his unique uniform of suspendered overalls and train engineer's cap, he created inventions of all sorts in the paraphernalia-filled workshop on his farm near San Cristobal, his tools and equipment powered by a hydroelectric plant he had designed and built himself. Visiting him there, I believed that if it could be done, he was the one to do it.

Quebrada Chica barely flowed in the dry season; in the wet season it gushed ten times as voluminously and swept massive tree trunks along after the hardest rains. The thought of damming it taxed my peace of mind heavily. Could it really be accomplished? And if it could, would I really want to divert all the stream's water in the dry season? What about the otters, prawns, fish, and birds that depended on the water downstream? Don Umberto assured me the project was mechanically feasible, and that he would build a dam that would allow the tree trunks to go over it at flood times and would allow enough water to pass in the dry season to preserve the flora and fauna downstream. After three days of sloshing up and down the stream and climbing over slippery boulders, closely examining the gravel and sand in his knobby, calloused hands, this man apparently learned more about "my" stream than I had learned in a decade.

Don Umberto didn't tolerate complaints or excuses. He didn't care whether a worker needed to rest. According to Don Umberto, since he could still wield the sledgehammer at his age, his young workers should be able to last twice as long. Don Umberto didn't care how difficult it was to procure tons of cement and hand-filtered sand, transporting it by boat, oxcart, horse, and finally by humans; he simply demanded that he never run out of these materials. When he did, there was hell to pay for everyone.

No one in the world had ever pushed me like that old ironman. Every Saturday, the workers would tell me they refused to spend another day carrying out his orders, even though I was paying them double. I had to scour the neighboring farms and ranches for new help, and they, too, lasted only a short time. I didn't blame anybody for quitting on Don Umberto. I contemplated doing the same myself, but at the same time I saw the method in his madness. He needed only the most fanatic of workers around him, only those who refused to quit, only those who had complete faith in him. He required this to be able to achieve his goal, and mine.

He began building the dam in the dry season, diverting the low flow of the Quebrada Chica through four-inch PVC pipes. Choosing a site between rock-solid banks seven meters apart, he began the tedious work of inspecting, selecting, and placing every rock that was to form the bulk of the controversial dam. In the meantime, he had delegated to me the equally arduous job of digging a 200-meter ditch through forest and field, which would divert the captured water to a cement tank. From there it would drop a steep 40 meters in 8-inch high-pressure PVC tubing to the Pelton wheel, which would spin the generator turbine.

I complained to Don Umberto that the course he marked out for the ditch was too level and went right through tree trunks and large boulders – surely it could be routed more favorably.

"Believe me, the water will flow. You will have to remove the trees and the boulders." He was always so sure of himself and expected so much of everyone. It made me angry, but also it made me more confident in him on the chances of our eventual success.

Don Umberto ate too little, rested too little, and worked himself way too hard. When he returned to San Cristobal to weld up the Pelton wheel and adapt it to an old, used, 300-pound German generator, he fell ill and stayed away more than a month before returning.

Meanwhile, I was still sweating and straining over my homework assignment, waiting for the dynamite he promised to send to help remove the most daunting of the obstacles to my ditch – two humongous boulders laying side by side, directly in the planned path of the ditch. Rerouting would have thrown off the level for the entire rest of the waterway; we had no choice but to blast through the rocks.

"Live" basalt boulders spelled bad news for the sledge-hammerers and chiselers. Once the "dead" outer layers had been knocked off, the rock just got harder and harder until sparks were all that one could get out of them. In this case, however, a not-so-minor miracle occurred: The vertical crack between the two monsters reached all the way to the level required for the ditch, and the rock on either side of the crack turned out to be breakable with sledgehammer and chisel for at least four inches. Excited, we began pounding and in a day succeeded in sculpting a perfect meter-long, 10-inch-wide canal through the rocks exactly where it had to be.

When Don Umberto returned, he beamed with satisfaction at our work and admitted he secretly feared for weeks that even dynamite might not have done the job had the rock been "alive," since it would have been so difficult just drilling the holes to insert the sticks of explosive. The natural canal between the two giant boulders symbolized to me a super-coincidental "sportiness" on the part of nature and/or God that I could not explain in any less fantastic terms.

After the usual delays and technical complications, the thick, squat dam was completed. It held back the dry-season stream flow with a few leaks, but no structural problems, sending enough water to the ditch to fill half of it. After all the root holes were discovered and filled, and after the earthen sides and bottom of the ditch no longer soaked up all the water, the flow hitting the metal cups welded around the two-inch axle was sufficient to spin Don Umberto's Pelton wheel at the required 1,800 rpm. That energy, transferred by a belted flywheel to the generator, was enough to crank out the needed voltage and amperage at more or less the correct number of cycles to convince the mysterious electric charges to behave in an appropriate AC way, speeding lightning quick through the cables up the hill to our house.

When that first bare light bulb lit up in 1980, we all applauded and shouted praise for Don Umberto's invention and our own considerable efforts. To this first artificial light, we added a couple dozen more to serve the employees' houses and the rental cabins. We put in a couple of electric fans in our house and adapted our house and our Swedish kerosene-run freezer to electricity. Except for minor adjustments, greasing, changing bearings, and repairs to the generator and the ditch, the hydroelectric system functioned incredibly well, putting out power almost nonstop for many years.

When I eventually sat down to judge the impact of electricity and all that went with it at Cantarana, I decided it had been good, very good. It made us more comfortable, it made life easier, and although the moon yielded some of its influence to the world of TV and electric radio, that trend was already under way thanks to wristwatches and small transistor radios. This was only normal and inevitable. Morita couldn't remain hidden forever. In fact, maybe I should have bought TVs for all my employees and encouraged them to watch for a couple hours a day. Maybe this would have been the best way to help them adjust to the encroaching realities of the "outside" world, which would eventually engulf Morita and belittle knowledge of the phases of the moon, the tides, water, vines, and all that other old-folks' talk.

It didn't matter that during the driest time of the year, which was peak tourist season, Quebrada Chica failed to produce enough electricity for everyone. Before that problem could become a problem, by 1982, when Delfina's chickens, turkeys, ducks, and geese were thriving, we'd given up on tourism anyway.

For two years we tried to devise an adequate way of insuring ourselves and our guests, spending thousands of dollars on lawyers' fees in an unsuccessful search for protection from possible lawsuits. But that wasn't the only problem we faced. Construction of the Coast Highway, which was to solve our transportation problems, hadn't even commenced yet, the Nicaraguans just over Costa Rica's northern border were killing each other in an increasingly bloody revolution, and the rest of Central America floundered in similar political, economic, and spiritual degradation. Oasis or not, Costa Rica was stricken from most foreigners' lists of travel alternatives. And with Alcoa pulling out all its interest in Costa Rica by 1980, and losing millions of dollars in the process, the country no longer seemed attractive to foreign investors.

In the early 1980s, with inheritance money I received after the deaths of all my grandparents, I was able to buy out my family's share in Cantarana and became the sole owner, to the great relief of my parents. I put employees' families in three of the tourist cabins, sold half the cattle, and concentrated on making some money with *cacao* (chocolate) production, which seemed ideal at first. There was no environmentally negative impact, the plants thrived, the profit margin was surprisingly high, and experts swore that the market would continue to increase.

Like everything else I'd attempted, however, the positive appearance of this new venture faded after just a couple of years.

World cacao production outpaced demand and the price plummeted. A fungal disease required extra care and poison, which I wasn't willing to apply. Finally, the monkeys and squirrels that had been eating a small portion of the crop, began gobbling up so much that I had to kill them, cure their addiction, or forget about making any money. I was getting tired of fighting and wasn't going to kill them, so, against my neighbors' advice, which I heeded less and less, especially after the black hawk episode, I simply abandoned the cacao project and deemed it another of my failures, and kept relying on the inherited stocks and bonds I hadn't sold. These produced enough interest to live on and maintain Cantarana as long as we didn't squander any of the principal. With wages around $3.00 a day per worker, no state taxes, no Costa Rican income taxes, property taxes of a couple hundred dollars a year, no utility bills, no vehicle to maintain except a skiff with a 25 hp motor, and being about 70 percent self-sufficient foodwise, we could take a vacation trip every year and still not be strapped for cash.

I turned then to the project I'd been wanting to get involved in for years: planting fine indigenous hardwoods and semihardwoods for the sake of reforestation and also to provide quality lumber for a future furniture business. I initially lost some respect and some rapport among the local people with this decision, which to them was especially strange because the profits from my "crops" would not be available for 15-20 years. They also felt that by selling half my herd, I caused my finca – the source of so many jobs and so much food – to deteriorate. I kept a couple dozen animals to provide milk and take advantage of the few small pastures that were unsuitable for reforestation or offered such beautiful views that I didn't plan to plant trees on them.

Reforestation, however, was *my* project, what I really wanted to do, what I was going to do, with or without everyone else's approval. Fortunately, instead of dismissing me as a rich gringo with another crazy scheme, the local people soon adapted pleasantly to my idea and in fact seemed to feel proud that they had a neighbor who was planting trees instead of cutting them down. It was something new in the area, as nobody was reforesting at that time, and few people had ever even heard of it being done. In 1979, lumber was cheap and plentiful, apparently an unlimited resource from the local perspective, so why take so much trouble and expense and time to grow it?

It was wonderful, and at the same time unsettling, to have the freedom to make radical decisions. I could afford to abandon the cacao and therefore avoid having to kill the fanatic chocolate-loving monkeys. I could afford to leave tracts of forest intact. I could afford to abandon hard-earned pastures and reforest them. I could afford to plant crops that would not be harvestable for 15 years. I could afford to make amends to the environment for what I had taken from it. I could afford to pay higher wages and offer better working conditions and benefits.

It was dismaying to realize the extent to which conservation and exploitation were tied to money, the money of distant strangers. Those who could most afford to consume the bananas and lobsters and mahi-mahi and hardwoods lived thousands of miles away and were unaware of or uncaring about the often disastrous consequences of their uncontrolled consumption. How many imagined or worried about their complicity in the destruction of pristine environments and the extinction of species? Likewise, most of those who could afford to make a difference, who could most afford to help protect habitats and species, also lived far away and seemed not to care about environmental degradation, not even in their own countries. I wanted to be among those who did.

Though the engineers from the Ministry of Agriculture offered to help me if I would plant the Honduran pine, Australian eucalyptus, Asian teak, and African gmelina they recommended, I thought they were insane to promote exclusively exotic species, and so instead I planted indigenous varieties I knew were valuable and naturally resistant to pests and diseases.

My insistence on planting native species caused me to lose out later on lucrative foreign-financed incentives available for monoculture plantations of non-native species. I saw others cash in with their lawyers on the money of foreign taxpayers, but I felt much better doing things the way I knew was right, which, fortunately, I could also afford. Once again, I found myself embarking on a project I knew little about and would have to learn about in the process of doing it. Once again, it was a small-scale venture, not requiring much capital, and so I could afford to risk making some mistakes while experimenting with different species and different techniques.

I had one very big advantage going for me – Manolo. Though we'd had our differences, Manolo, being one of those people like Santos who loved to roam and hunt in the forest, had a deep knowledge of and feeling for local nature. Walking in the forest with Manolo, preferably behind him, one was guaranteed to see wildlife, and often it was wildlife one had never seen before. I would never forget exploring with him on the Osa Peninsula after leaving Siete Vueltas beached in San Pedrillo (population: 4). We camped in Llorona and walked deep into Corcovado National Park where, among other things, we saw four species of monkeys, scarlet macaws, curassow birds, and a *danta*, or tapir. I'd never seen Manolo so happy and invigorated. He seemed very comfortable in the rainforest and was able to identify hundreds of different trees, plants, and animals, often explaining what relationship they had to ancient and modern people and to each other.

When I placed him in charge of the first 40-acre reforestation project, he already knew where to find the seeds or seedlings of the desired species. As we gathered fallen seeds from the *maría* tree, he pointed out that those chewed by bats had higher germination rates than the others. He showed me how to sprout the large, round, paper-like *manglillo* seeds by simply laying them on the surface of the loose dirt, how the *alazán* and *amarillón* seedlings could be pulled out with all the roots exposed and transplanted directly, without any losses.

At first, we used none of the plastic bags or poisons or fertilizers recommended by the government agronomists, because these *ingenieros* had consistently misguided us whenever we'd taken their advice. After a couple of years, however, we realized that the plastic bags were great for preparing and sprouting seedlings in dry season and made it easier to transport them to the planting sites. But stubbornly and self-righteously, we avoided chemical pesticides, fungicides, and fertilizers, despite the array of enemies we faced: insects, strangler vines, fast-growing weeds, chomping rodents, careless machete men, drought, deluge, fire.

Considering the great variety of dangers to the young trees, most did surprisingly well. After several years, people from the Peace Corps and Forestry Department saw our apparent success, and they expressed interest in our primitive methods. The impressive form and size of our indigenous species, which the professionals, too, knew were of high lumber value, helped change Ministry of Agriculture policy from encouraging foreign exotics to promoting native species instead.

I was very happy to think I'd played a small part in this vital change of policy, not just because promoting local tree species made good economic sense, but because it helped the local ecology prosper as well. Of course, there would still be huge plantings of African gmelina and Asian teak, but those who wished to favor indigenous trees and encourage biodiversity as well as make money would have the blessing and technical assistance of the government, and if they were lucky (or tricky), they might also receive financial incentives from other governments.

As the seedlings took hold, pushing confidently up toward the sun, adding inches of diameter and meters in height, local wildlife could be seen thriving in the shady reforested areas that had once been sun-blasted, weed-infested pastures. I realized I'd finally found the right project, and I knew my plans for a small furniture and finished wood business were perfectly feasible.

Disengaging from tourism, cattle, and cacao, and focusing on growing trees, proved to be a wonderful relief. Trees didn't complain or sue, didn't try to kick you or run you down, couldn't be stolen very easily and weren't hurt by monkeys or squirrels or hawks or weevils. The planet needed trees to trap carbon and release oxygen. The price of wood products was skyrocketing. Finally, I thought, I'd found a project that was successful not just for me but for everybody and everything – locally and globally, in the present and in the future.

I loved to walk through the shady groves of 20-meter-tall trees, remembering them as seedlings, thinking not of the lumber profits we would finally make but of encouraging nature, of replacing what had already been taken. These trees produced flowers and fruit from which local creatures benefited, enhancing biodiversity and the environment for me and my children and my children's children, and many, many other people and creatures I would never know.

Rana venenosa (poison arrow frog)

Chapter Thirteen

Becoming many – no man is an island

In 1980, during this period of personal calm, when I felt content about finally having discovered a good, lasting project, Delfina and I decided to have a child. It seemed she became pregnant about five minutes later.

Sensing (correctly) that it would bring about the end of my life as I'd known it, I departed with Delfina's permission and blessing for what I figured would be my last solo trip. I had an idea of the domesticating changes that affected married people with children, and there were some places I wanted to visit in case I never got around to it later. For three months, I visited some of the spectacular living wonders of the world that I'd dreamed of ever since I was a little boy.

Scuba diving the gloriously healthy Great Barrier Reef, which biologists and astronauts agree to be Earth's largest organic structure; appreciating the ancient legends, art, and wisdom of the Ramayana that still lived vividly in the Hindu people of Bali; loving the Buddhist culture and friendliness and the beauty of Sri Lanka, especially how the people smiled so contagiously and tilted their heads amusingly as they spoke; blissfully free diving in the ultra-clear and shark-filled waters of the Maldive Islands and being introduced to the powerful Moslem world there; meeting the proud and beautiful Masai and shooting dozens of rolls of film of the spectacular Serengeti migration, which is believed to hold the planet's largest concentration of wildlife; being deeply impressed with the scenic excellence of the southern tip of Africa, but being shocked in Capetown to witness my nonwhite waiter in a restaurant being kicked in the shins and verbally debased by his white boss; feeling uncomfortable taking the nontourist route in Rio de Janeiro, where the dirtiness, smelliness, and masses of desperately poor, hungry people were too disturbing for me. . . . By that time, with no more oceans to cross, I felt acutely anxious to return home to Costa Rica and to Delfina.

If I'd learned something about our world from that circumnavigation, it was that it was an incredibly diverse, beautiful, fascinating, and big world with so many different mountains, plains, rivers, seas, islands, plants, animals, peoples, languages, and cultures. In my opinion, the best places were those that had been the least industrialized, poisoned, exploited, or tampered with. I returned to Costa Rica more a conservationist than ever.

Back at the finca with bulging Delfina, I fell more in love with her than ever; as happy as we were, we feared spoiling it by getting married. As she got bigger and had a harder time getting on and off her horse, and as the rainy season sent the rivers into flood, washed out the trails, and made access to the outside world generally more difficult, I decided I didn't want to chance a farm birth. So I purchased a lot in San Cristobal, 30 miles inland, and contracted for construction of a mediocre cinder-block-and-wood house.

It had become increasingly frowned upon to take your horse or machete inside the saloons of San Cristobal, and the blacksmith who shoed horses felt out of place in the center of town and moved. Modern civilization crept in, bringing more cars than horses, and the place became more "decent" – which was fine for us because that's what we were looking for there. Decent postal service, telephone service, doctors, schools, grocery stores – these were necessities for families, and I had become, I kept realizing, a family man.

Our house sat in a pasture four blocks from the central park and main cathedral, and since we had no neighbors, no one complained about Delfina's chickens and turkeys, which she imported from Cantarana ("No city chickens for *my* family!" she insisted).

I never had imagined the variety and intensity of the emotions I would experience with Delfina's pregnancy, our daughter Molly's birth in 1980, and her first few years of life. Such paranoia, compassion, love, wonder, anger, frustration, joy! Molly brought a whole new dimension into my existence, such that I could truly say I was a participating member of the human family. When she was seriously ill with a mysterious stomach ailment, I felt like tearing the arms off the incompetent doctor who misdiagnosed and misprescribed for her and even allowed her to be mistreated in the hospital. I felt so grateful to the doctor who fixed her (with a short and simple treatment for giardia, a common intestinal parasite), and was elated when she became healthy and happy again. It was up and down, down and up.

Fortunately, by the time my second precious daughter, Tina, arrived in 1983, I'd become much steadier, and when my third precious daughter, Cloe, came in 1988, I considered myself a competent father and person. Between Tina and Cloe, Delfina and I got legally married, in part to appease the pesty Costa Rican and United States bureaucrats, but mostly to please my dear mother who had pleaded with us long enough.

"Three daughters!" everyone would say, unable to conceal their amusement. "And the son?" I had no answer for that, since I was a devout believer in population control and had already passed my two-child limit, leaving me with no plans to try again. I was profoundly content and busy with our daughters, and deeply grateful for their good physical conditions. Many Costa Ricans believed a man who had only daughters lacked the proper sexual vigor, know-how, or equipment, but I really didn't mind the blows to my ego, since generally I felt very content.

Delfina proudly proved to be a super-mom in every way as she had with her sons, and our children turned out beautiful, charming, intelligent, and loving, despite the usual bouts of brattiness. They traveled well, though our daughters had more difficulty than Delfina's sons in overcoming the disadvantages of their Northern genetic heritage when faced with the excessive heat, humidity, and bugs of Cantarana. Like all the other kids in Morita and San Cristobal, they occasionally succumbed to respiratory afflictions, and I frequently had to administer vitamins and syrups and pills. In the tropical environment, pathogens thrived, especially in children. Our kids got chicken pox, whooping cough, strep throat, intestinal parasites, skin fungus, ear infections, scabies, lice. . . .

Nicaraguan refugees pouring into Costa Rica, before and after the revolution, brought with them new strains of measles, meningitis, malaria, hepatitis, and finally dengue and cholera, and I wondered how healthy it was to raise children in Morita or San Cristobal.

Having children multiplied my vulnerabilities. When Tina met the quisquina ants, which left her burning and itching and made her writhe and scream, I felt the attack just as much as she. When Molly had to spend two horrifying nights in the hospital, I too felt tortured, but because of my serious protesting against the hospital's existing visitation rights policy, from then on, mothers or fathers were permitted to accompany their small interned children at all hours. It was no longer just a question of adapting myself to the world. It was now a question of establishing a comfortable niche for my entire family, which forced major changes in my priorities and, in some cases, required my efforts in acknowledging problems that affected everybody and acting diplomatically to achieve obviously needed institutional changes in Costa Rica. With luck, effort, friends, and sometimes but not necessarily a little money, one could make a positive difference and stretch the status quo a little.

We stayed as much at Cantarana as we could, but usually we didn't last more than a month before one of us needed medicine or doctor's advice from San Cristobal. Local families had their own health problems, too, but were poorer and braver and more willing to hold out. Sometimes they would be able to cure something with local plants, sometimes not. During rainy season, we had to ford rivers so deep that our horses had to swim across. Sometimes we had to walk several miles. There were dangers and minor accidents, and although we usually thought it was a lot of fun, little by little we found ourselves spending less time at the finca. When Molly started going to kindergarten in San Cristobal, there being no school anywhere near Cantarana, my family stayed mostly in town while I traveled back and forth to the ranch alone, by horse or four-wheel-drive taxi, then on horseback or on foot.

The busy household in San Cristobal was a magnet for our employees, neighbors, and friends from the coast and for Delfina's relatives from all over southern Costa Rica. Often when they visited, they brought sick or injured family members, and we offered them meals and lodging, since that was normal hospitality in the Costa Rican countryside. Farmers with machete cuts, cowboys with broken bones, pregnant women, people with mysterious maladies, people needing good doctors and humane hospital treatment – these campesinos were nearly all humble and shy. No matter how much I coached them on the need to moan and scream and faint when they got to the hospital, I would find them hours later in the Emergency Department, still waiting quietly and unattended.

This growing reliance on Delfina and our household as medical service and recuperation center led me to befriend the local hospital director and several doctors. I became a fair diagnostician and prescriber, serving as interpreter and middleman between doctors, pharmacists, and patients. I learned by experience, in the nonlitigious environment of Costa Rica, how to administer injections, not just to cows but to people, too. When our guests couldn't pay for the medicine or the services of a private doctor, I found myself stepping in to pay the bills and became one of the local medical establishment's best customers, rating special wholesale discounts from specialists and pharmacies.

Whereas in the United States an average diagnosis and prescription cost around $100, in San Cristobal it seldom ran over $20. I was thus able to help people suffering maladies ranging from stomach ulcers to anemia-causing parasites, from diet deficiencies to circulation problems, without incurring great personal expense. Being able to afford it, how could I turn these people away when all they needed was the access to modern medical magic I could so easily purchase? And with Delfina being so willing to do the cooking, why let these visitors go hungry?

This sort of philanthropy, however, could very easily get out of hand, and I found myself wondering what my true responsibilities were. I pictured in my mind a hypothetical warm, dry, wealthy man with an umbrella on a rainy monsoon day, standing next to a poor, distant relative who's shivering and getting wet. An umbrella vendor walks by and the cold man looks at the warm man and smiles. The warm man's conscience is pricked and he pulls out the five bucks to buy the fellow an umbrella, which both feel very good about. Then the poor man calls his wife and many children to get underneath the umbrella, but they don't all fit. The wealthy man buys another umbrella for the grateful family and he feels even better. But then bystanders who observed his generosity come to him with little purple-lipped children, people without shoes, some without sight, some mute, some without jobs, some without education, some without homes, some without anyone to love them or talk to them, some who are drunk, some who are chronically lazy. They all know the man can afford to help them if he wants to, and he knows it, too.

I found myself having to resort to covert guerrilla philanthropy, helping the public anonymously to keep the demands for help from becoming too great for my resources. Still, there were times I just couldn't say no, and it was probably fortunate for me that my blood wasn't so good for donating.

Elias was a relative of my favorite neighbors around Cantarana. One day, he and his brother were beating beans out of their dry pods on a big tarp with a green branch when one karmically charged swat sent a bean shooting into his right eye. The impact turned his life into a hellish ordeal.

Elias went to the hospital and they administered some eyedrops, which he claimed burned and blinded him, and then gave him some aspirin and told him to return in a month. His eye, however, remained sightless, painful, and so sensitive to sunlight that he could no longer work. He continued to receive ineffectual medical treatment, while I supported him and gave him a pair of sunglasses. I sent him to San José to see one of the country's best specialists, who told me by telephone, "Unfortunately, it's too late to do anything for the eye. If he'd only come in sooner. . . ."

I offered him work whenever he wanted, but he developed a serious drinking problem and was bitter because his unattractive eye made it unlikely anyone would marry him, though he tried hard to find a wife. What more could be done for him?

Doña Flora, a bright, cheerful old woman, was walking one day near her farm in the mountains around San Cristobal when a car hit her and the driver sped away. The Social Security doctors failed to correct her dislocated shoulder and later said it was irremediable. The resulting arthritis in her still dislocated shoulder caused her intense pain, and she also developed stomach cancer as well. Whenever she required the services of the SS hospital, she would stop by to stay with us a couple of nights.

Despite her torments, she remained cheerful and untiringly upbeat. Our children loved her, and we all considered her presence a blessing. Flora's good cheer was especially amazing in light of the indignities wrought upon her by the SS bureaucracy: she had to get in lines before dawn and wait for hours to get an appointment, was given stomach-irritating aspirin and the wrong medicines, underwent a botched stomach operation, and suffered terribly as doctors repaired her stitches without administering anesthetic.

When they knew she had terminal cancer, they refused to keep her in the hospital, even though her pain was too much for the cheap outpatient analgesics they prescribed. I protested to the hospital director, who by now was familiar with my reputation as a troublemaker, and he made it possible for us to get stronger pain medication that had to be injected every four hours.

For awhile, she stayed at our house and I injected the painkiller in her needle-bruised, emaciated hip. But although the needle always seemed too long, her flesh too thin, and the liquid too damned viscous, she shined gratitude on me. After several days, when her pain became more severe and the SS people refused to give us morphine, Flora decided she wanted to go back to her farm and die. A week later she did, in much pain, with much bravery, with much grace.

Don Arturo, my old storyteller friend who'd sold me that first and most valuable parcel of land in 1972, visited us in 1987 in San Cristobal with his white-haired, but still buxom wife, Lucía. He'd just been released from the hospital with the diagnosis of terminal liver cancer, and he wanted to know if we didn't mind giving him a place to die.

We'd been close friends, so I had the confidence to try to get a laugh out of the obviously suffering 80-year-old.

"Well, Don Arturo," I said, "as long as you don't mind me burying you by that mango tree over there – you can see it needs some fertilizing."

He burst out in a joyous, yet painful, laugh that I thought would surely kill him. Out of breath, trying to keep from laughing, he whispered to me, "You sure you won't mind eating the mangoes?"

As with Flora, we had some difficulty getting him strong enough pain medication, and also like Flora, Don Arturo was all skin and bones. Injecting him was an ordeal.

When Lucía came out of our little guest cabin crying one morning, I took my daughters (Molly, 7 and Tina, 5) to see and touch and not fear the dead body Don Arturo left behind.

I was already intimately involved in the local medical establishment through my informal activities on behalf of friends and family, so when local residents nominated me for membership in the Pro-Hospital Committee of San Cristobal, it seemed logical to accept. This drew me even deeper into the complicated and frustrating business of the Social Security system and the Ministry of Health. Since progress was made mainly by persistent agitation and complaint, I was a valuable member because of my experience getting disgruntled patients and doctors to ask for improvements. However, I began to feel like one of those big trees at Cantarana, slowly weakened by strangling parasitic vines.

How could I not get involved when some of the solutions seemed so maddeningly simple? Often I saw glaringly evident needs that, because of stupid bureaucratic reasons, were not met. Some I learned first-hand, as when I dislocated my ankle and went to the hospital for rehabilitation therapy.

The hospital had no whirlpool for treating injured extremities; instead, they put my foot in a small plastic baby bath and handed me a hose that barely squirted lukewarm water. The next time I was in the United States I purchased a $2,000 stainless-steel whirlpool for arms and legs and had it shipped from Florida to the hospital in San Cristobal, thinking of all those people in rehab who really needed it.

Six months later, it still hadn't arrived. The head of the orthopedic department and the hospital director said they knew nothing of it. I telephoned the suppliers, and they gave me the name of the airline that had taken it to Costa Rica months ago. Further detective work revealed that the airline people had personally, by phone, notified the head of the orthopedic department three times that the whirlpool was sitting in their warehouse. I contacted the regional director of Social Security and he promised to give personal attention to the matter.

A month later, I called the hospital director to inquire about the whirlpool. It was still in Customs because the hospital had been unable to pay the 100 percent ($2,000) duty. It took three more months of increasingly angry phone work to find the right individual in the SS maze in San José and convince him that the whirlpool was a donated piece of medical equipment, not something being imported for resale, freeing it from Customs and allowing it to be installed in the San Cristobal Hospital. There, it received rave reviews from nurses and patients.

Lack of initiative was sometimes as great a hurdle as mindless bureaucracy. Another doctor showed me a catalog from an American hospital equipment supplier that pictured a kind of roller for children with cerebral paralysis. It allowed them to lay on their stomachs and roll around to exercise and stretch their spinal columns. He said several local children needed this therapy and asked me if I could acquire one or two of these devices in the United States just as I had the whirlpool. The mechanism had no motor, no moving parts – I asked him why they hadn't fabricated a couple themselves, saving a thousand bucks and avoiding a million bureaucrats?

All we needed was tin cylinders the right size, upholstered with 2-inch thick foam and tough vinyl cloth. I found the materials, had a local furniture maker put them together, and within a couple of weeks kids were rolling around on them, exercising and having fun as they should have been doing for years. Grateful mothers thanked me, and I tried not to be bitter about the frighteningly unimaginative and complacent doctors and administrators.

I wanted to help more, but it all got too complicated. Playing the role of whistleblower got too tiring sometimes. I had so little to offer the people who came to me with leukemia or diabetes or Down's syndrome, and my attempts to intervene on their behalf to obtain more government assistance were seldom successful in overcoming the terrible obstacles. I also found it necessary to draw the line between compassion and healthy selfishness. I wouldn't let people in my house with possible tuberculosis, hepatitis, bronchitis, measles, lice, or scabies, and I instructed my kids to avoid them and any other suspiciously contagious people. When our house became too crowded, we simply said we were sorry and turned away even those with less dangerous maladies. As the years passed, better roads were built and buses provided more service, so we had fewer people spend the night. This was a relief for us as the kids got bigger, and we all preferred more privacy and fewer sad stories in our kitchen.

San Cristobal changed in other ways, too, exploding into a small city and bringing more homes, a soccer stadium, schools, a discotheque, crime, and a steady flow of people to our neighborhood. Feeling a growing need for security, for a refuge where my family could be protected from some of the darker sides of human reality, adapting "successfully" to the evolving urban environment, I followed the example of some of the neighbors and erected an ugly chain-link fence around our house.

I also put a portable shield around my heart, as I learned to be more careful whom I let in.

Monos congos (howler monkeys)

Chapter Fourteen

Melodrama – dealing with humans

Even though, by 1985, I finally learned to live fairly well with the limitations imposed by the tropical environment and had gotten somewhat better at coexisting with members of my own species, the task of living harmoniously in that little corner of the Earth at times became too draining for my limited physical, intellectual, and spiritual resources. I often feared that at Cantarana my cherished dream of creating a peaceful, prosperous, solid agricultural community might be doomed by the darker side of human nature. I wondered whether the infrequent and unreliable news received concerning Reagan's "star wars" and "Irangate" were just very inflated manifestations of the same sort of human bentness that I was having to deal with on a rather different level.

When the monkeys raided our favorite fruit trees, Delfina and I forgave them without any conscious effort. Monkeys were monkeys. We had more trouble accepting it when people raided the very same trees, or stole ripening pineapples or watermelon or mangoes or stalks of plantain or bananas, but we learned to let it go. Many of the local people, after all, did not share our values or sense of property rights.

But when people continually trespassed on our land to hunt and kill wild animals we had been protecting for years, the patience I worked so diligently to develop disintegrated. And the circumstances worsened in 1982 when squatters from the north invaded the former hacienda of Morita and were given title by the government that had purchased the land in order to sell it to Alcoa. Once Alcoa abandoned plans to mine bauxite and ship it from the deepwater port to have been built on Punta Morita, the apparently lethargic Costa Rican government irresponsibly released control of the flat, fertile 2,000 hectares. For obscure political reasons or favors, seemingly inconsiderate or possibly corrupt officials facilitated the invading strangers and rejected the requests of the nonaggressive, landless Moritans who legally and peacefully had signed up for the property in the government land office in San Cristobal months before. Those of us living in the area were shocked by the injustice and dreaded arrival of these unwelcome newcomers. Our fears quickly proved all too warranted.

Eighty parcel-grabbing families scrambled to cut down the forest on "their" properties in order to prove ownership – felling trees constituted legal land improvement. The wild animals that survived fled to nearby forests, only to be hunted down and eaten. When there were no more convenient tepezcuintles, some squatters settled for iguanas, but others took their dogs to hunt in neighboring forests like ours, which we had been mostly successfully protecting from hunters for a long time. The intensity of my suddenly inflamed sense of territoriality disturbed me deeply.

Most of the squatters had little or nothing to lose. Armed with hunger, poverty, and lack of respect for the rights of others, they cheerfully trespassed through our farms and ranches to kill the wild animals. The law was such that in order to bring legal action we needed two willing witnesses to catch them in the act. Even then, they faced an insignificant fine, while the accusers could expect vengeful retaliation against their persons, properties, fences, water systems, and domestic animals. These thorough agents of environmental destruction fought over the last tepezcuintles, the curassow birds, the stream prawns, the beach clams, the rock oysters, the estuary fish, the turtle eggs. Within a short time, the Moritans who had been consuming these foods on a sustainable basis for decades rarely ate or saw them again.

Maybe from having dabbled a bit in cultural anthropology, I pondered why, throughout history, it seemed the nice guys almost always ended up getting lionized. Perhaps the theory that the most aggressive and exploitive peoples dominate in history explained why more pacific tribes or ethnic groups and entire sub-species of humans, like the cranially well-endowed Neanderthals, were displaced by ruder, more hostile genotypes of humans – more like us.

It astonished me how in a fleeting decade – from 1985 to 1995 – I witnessed the nearly total displacement of the Moritans and their culture that I had so much admired and loved. The devastating highway construction that began in 1985, 15 miles north of Morita, fragmented farms and ecosystems and, as it made its way south, played a major part in destroying local livelihoods and culture and in attracting undesirable, noncultural immigrants.

The newcomers seemed to us indignant local residents to be of an inferior sort with little evidence of formal education or a sense for hygiene and having a knack for perpetuating conflict among themselves and their neighbors. The strangers showed very little knowledge of or respect for local flora and fauna and had no interest in the natural knowledge or culture the native Moritans might have shared with them. Yet, with their aggressive and occasionally criminal acquisitiveness, and the secret solidarity that they relied on when requiring the political pressure of their group as a unity, like tough, invasive weeds in a garden, the *precaristas* (squatters) from the north became the most populous and dominant human element in Morita. This was just one more of those things that life had a habit of producing that I would have never imagined happening, could never have prepared for adequately, and would have to learn to accept.

What I could least tolerate about some of the precaristas was their apparent contempt for all living things – not just forests and wild animals, but also domestic animals and even their own neighbors. I was never able to forgive and forget the "Panamenio" incident.

I had a horse called Panamenio because he was from Panama. He was an average horse, rather small and unimpressive, a dirty-white animal with good, tough hooves, whose outstanding characteristic was that he never shirked any job. He was just as willing to chase down a cow over rough terrain as he was to haul a couple hundred pounds of tourist or cargo up a steep hill. He was always the easiest horse to catch and saddle and was the most considerate to children, women, tourists, and inexperienced riders. Naturally he was a favorite, with us and our guests, and he didn't seem to mind being worked hard.

After ten years with us, Panamenio was showing signs of age. We could no longer rightfully load him with a full cargo or rope a cow with him. He was still the favorite for transporting children and older people, however, and when a teacher with a bum leg came to teach one year in Cachelote, members of the community asked me to sell Panamenio to them for the teacher's exclusive use. I sold him for $100, about half what he was worth, on the strict condition that if the teacher went away they must sell him back to me. After a year, the teacher left her position in Cachelote, but I was in the United States at the time and Panamenio was sold to one of the poorest, laziest, most heartless squatters that had moved to Morita.

When I heard a year later that Panamenio had been severely abused and abandoned to die in the public roadway that crossed my land, I immediately put on my boots and grabbed my machete to go see for myself. I'd never seen an animal in such pitiful condition. So lame he couldn't even walk to the stream to drink, Panamenio's skull and skeleton jutted through his skin. His ears were full of ticks, and his back was covered by lumps and sores testifying to the heavy cargoes he'd been forced to carry without enough padding. He didn't recognize me.

I was tempted to get my gun and put him out of his misery. But I couldn't let him die after suffering so much, not if there was the least chance of helping him. To do that, however, I would have to continue his torment. There in the roadway he was vulnerable to people who would laugh at him and torment him, and I knew I had to drive him home. But getting him to move would not be easy. I pulled my machete from its sheath and whacked Panamenio hard on his flank with the flat of the blade, yelling at the same time. He winced, took one step, snorted in pain and shuddered. Again I whacked him. "You have to go home with me you stupid horse!" He couldn't run to get away and I wouldn't leave him alone. When he finally realized that, he accepted the excruciating pain of walking and did exactly as I told him, with the incentive of a whack and a shout now and then.

The foreman was shocked to see Panamenio's condition. I told him to "fix" the animal and get him in riding condition as soon as possible. He laughed sarcastically. "The beast is about dead," he said. "I doubt he'll ever be ridable again."

"Then do what you can," I said irritably. "I want the best treatment, the best pasture, the easiest water, ripe bananas, corn and salt . . . 20 cc's of oxytetracycline every day for three days, 5 cc's of vitamin, kill the ticks, deparasite him twice. But first, fix his hoof."

The next day Miguel brought me a sharp walnut-sized rock. "We dug this out of Panamenio. What brutes to abandon a horse with a rock in his hoof!" he said with disgust. "We filled the hole with hot tar but it looks like he's going to lose a good chunk of his hoof. It'll take months for him to recover, if he ever does, if he's not too sick, too."

In two weeks Panamenio could at least get his own water, and his appetite was good, but he didn't seem to eat enough to cover up his bones. One day, one of the squatters came riding up to my house on a little skinny horse that looked nearly as bad as Panamenio.

"Good afternoon," I said. "Can I help you?"

"I heard you have my brother's horse and I've come to get him. My brother couldn't come down because he's got a job up the coast." He spoke without respect or courtesy.

I hesitated and tried to control my temper. "Yeah, well that's fine . . . I have the horse, but he was abandoned and I found him in the public road where they say he was for over a week. I brought him back so he wouldn't die."

"That's all right, but don't think just because you've got lots of money that you can take something that belongs to a poor person," he said scoldingly, looking down at me from his horse, fondling his machete.

"You think I wanted the horse because I thought he was *worth* something? You're crazy if you think that. That horse is good for nothing and might never recover from the mistreatment it's been given." I was aware of the rising volume and intensity of my voice and the deepening frowns on my face, but I didn't care.

"You can say that, or whatever you like, that makes no difference to me. I don't know or care about the day I was born or the day I die. To me it's the same to cut the damn horse's head off with my machete, which I'd rather do than leave him here. But that's all right – if you don't want to turn him over to me I can just go get the policeman to make you give him to me. Of course, you have an alternative: you can buy him." He smiled sickeningly, showing rotting teeth.

"Buy him?" I shouted in disbelief. "He's worth nothing! I just wanted to let him alone. I'm not going to use him for anything. He's not worth anything."

My friend Felo called me aside and tried to reason with me. "Look, he's got you. You don't need to hassle with a policeman, and you don't need to make an enemy out of this barbarian. Ask him how much he is charging for the horse."

That was hard for me to swallow. I preferred the idea of pulling the snickering low-life off his horse and throwing him to the ground.

But I still had some self-control and had great confidence in Felo, who had always provided me with sound advice in the past.

"How much for the 'quarter-miler'?" I asked him derisively.

"Three thousand colones," he replied, which was about $80 at that time.

"Give it to him and get it over with," Felo told me in front of everyone. "You're not going to turn Panamenio over to someone who you know is going to keep mistreating him, and you've got the money." This was Felo's manner of publicly reproaching the squatter. "Just pay him, you have no choice. Don't expect justice."

Felo was right, but I resented it. Luckily I was able to control my indignation and went into the house, brought out the money, and handed it over.

"Deal made," I said in the formal way, forcing the words. "Great pleasure doing business with you, goodbye," I said in a way that made everyone but the squatter chuckle.

I couldn't look at him. I feared the depths of his poverty and my almost total lack of compassion for this unfortunate fellow human being. I remembered my friend, Humo, the bull I'd sold to a merciless comerciante who'd made the animal suffer unnecessarily before slaughter. I remembered Lolo the monkey everyone harassed. I remembered the black hawk I killed myself. What made people so wrongfully inconsiderate and cruel to our fellow creatures? The contempt and disgust of years pounded inside, wanting out, wanting trouble, against my best interest.

It disturbed me profoundly to wonder how many people, given the same environmental conditions, the same lack of nurturing, education, and opportunity, would have become like the man in front of me whom I wished to harm in some stupid way. How would *I* have turned out? Or was it more a question of heredity? Or astrology? Fate? Luck? Karma?

Little by little, Panamenio improved. Six months later his hoof had healed and he put on a new form. In six more months, he was a "real" horse again, cheerful and ridable over easy terrain for a couple of years before he died of old age.

Soon after my near-violent episode with the precarista who'd maliciously made me buy a half-dead horse, the same man's neighbor was murdered and the first thing I thought was that it could have been me. Squabbling over a tiny strip of public land near the beach, a usually good-natured guitarist named Chacón jumped from the bushes to attack Gerardo in front of Gerardo's pretty wife, Tanya, their two small children, and two other men.

Chacón whacked Gerardo's arm nearly off with his machete, while Gerardo screamed, "Don't kill me!" Chacón yelled back, "I *am* going to kill you. I told you I would!" and then finished him, whacking into his skull many times as if he were killing a snake. Tanya tried to fend off Chacón's final attack with a piece of driftwood but fell exhausted with terror in the sand, where she saw her blood-covered husband breathe his last.

A motley group of people came to Cantarana to tell me the story two days later and to ask me to transport the corpse to Puerto Nuevo in Siete Vueltas, which in 1986 was still the only boat for miles seaworthy enough for the job. It was a very rainy October, with the rivers flooded and the only road washed out, and because I had the only suitable boat, I felt compelled to say okay to these people – but on the condition that they first wrap up the corpse and put him in a box. They invited me to accompany them to see the bloody victim where he still lay untouched on the beach, but I decided I had other things to do.

The local policeman explained to me that he couldn't allow the body to be moved sooner because the federal police hadn't seen it yet. But since the roads were out and the rivers were raging, and the corpulent federal officers weren't going to walk the 15 miles from Puerto Nuevo, he would give permission to move it for inspection and autopsy in San Cristobal. Gerardo's body had lain in the sand in the sun and rain for two days already, guarded by sleepless Tanya, children, and friends who had to scare the buzzards away.

"You know how many machete cuts I counted?" the grinning Rural Guard in his ragged uniform said to me. "Twenty-seven!" T-w-e-n-t-y- s-e-v-e-n," he beamed with a sort of pride at his discovery. "As policeman here, it was my job to examine the victim's body." I wasn't very good at listening to all this. I felt the same stupid impulse that made others grin idiotically and chuckle foolishly amidst such horror. "This isn't a TV, you idiot!" I kept saying to myself. "This isn't a psycho-thriller!" But what, really, was it? One more piece of reality I hadn't seen before and still didn't want to see. I shuddered when I imagined the fear in the open dead eyes, the blood-soaked sand, and probably hermit crabs, indifferently scavenging. I didn't want to expose myself to the indifference to that perverse negation of human meaning, which others went to stare at and later told me they were sorry they had.

I took the foreman of the finca, Cacho, of Jamaican ancestry, to accompany me on my errand. We picked up the coffin on the beach and got a powerful send-off from a hundred enthusiastic helpers. I'd never had such a strong shove into the sea, nor had I ever seen so many people on that beach.

The ocean was rough and gray, a dark wall of rain approaching ominously from the seaward side. Even with the breeze, the smell from the decaying body was powerful. When we were well under way, Cacho smiled dubiously and gestured to see if I wanted him to put out the trolling lines as usual. I smiled back, then frowned and shook my head no, and called him closer to whisper, "I'd be afraid of catching something weird."

We delivered the seasick policeman, the exhausted widow, and her dead husband into the waiting hands of the pot-bellied police in Puerto Nuevo and headed back into the choppy seas to brave the menacing storm for the two-hour return voyage.

A week later, the widow asked me how much I wanted for transporting the corpse. There she was, thin from grief, with puffy, sleep-deprived eyes, mother to two fatherless children, her pretty face and attractive figure soon to be exploited by men who were already contemplating it. I told her she owed me nothing and walked away, proud not to join the buzzards.

Months later, after returning from a trip with my family to visit my parents in the United States, I learned from my other employees that Cacho, who was married, had been frequently seeing Tanya in secret. The staff also said Cacho had taken up drinking like his father, who finally died of it, and that he sometimes wouldn't even appear in the morning to direct the day's work. Other times he couldn't last even a couple of hours and would leave the other workers offended and leaderless as he returned to the hammock in his house. Sometimes he would take one of my horses and come back a day later drunk and incapacitated. He sacrificed care of his own family while he bought food and gifts for Tanya and her children. Twice, another man who was also "in love" with the widow, attempted to murder him.

I often walked into trouble when returning from vacation, but generally it was something minor. This time it was flashing blades on a moonlit beach, broken families and fatherless children, a good bunch of workers abused by an incompetent foreman, poverty, despair, hate, vengeance, lust. This sort of thing was relatively rare among Costa Ricans. But with all the recent machete violence, I couldn't help questioning my perception of Costa Ricans as sweet, calm, and peaceful souls. Should I start wearing a machete wherever I went? I would have much preferred a different kind of bad news.

Within a few days of Cacho's deterioration, one of my favorite helpers, Manuel, who'd been with me for six years, lost his patience with Cacho and with me – for not firing Cacho immediately – and left with his wife and child for his father's farm. Although I feared similar reactions by the other workers, still I hesitated to fire Cacho. He was my friend, and I was afraid that firing him might drive him deeper into alcoholism. His wife and children deserved the chance of his recovery.

Cacho and I talked, and I tried to make it clear – as a friend, but also as an employer – that his job, family, and life were on the line. Strangely, like so many of the people I'd employed, he seemed unworried about losing his security. His pride was strong, and he said he thought it might be better for him to just leave with his family. I was surprised, as always, by how very little thought or concern he showed for his family's future.

His rival for Tanya, a married man named Baudilio, was a Panamanian with no legal identification who had lived in Morita for many years. Stocky and mottled, with frizzy hair and mustache, he was fond of guaro and his machete and was a close friend of Marcos the sheriff, the one who had told me about the 27 machete wounds he'd counted on poor Gerardo. This meant that Baudilio was immune to the law, since Marcos *was* the law in Morita.

The ramifications of this alliance were demonstrated during one of the dry-season fiestas, which always included horse races, bull riding, a beauty contest, and cold beer and booze – with ice from San Cristobal. Marcos always picked Baudilio among his deputies to help him keep order, and when an Indian from out of the area got involved in a skirmish during one of the festivals, Marcos and Baudilio decided to make an example of the man.

Although he'd done nothing to start the fight, they grabbed him and threw him roughly in the *Boca Negra* (Black Mouth) jail. He somehow managed to escape and instead of running away, casually rejoined the festivities. After a while, the sheriff and deputies rediscovered him and tied him to a tree. Baudilio was an experienced cowboy who knew ropes and knots, and when he said the man was tied, he was tied. In less than an hour, however, the Indian was loose again, and this time he wisely disappeared.

People thought this was hilarious and ridiculed Baudilio for his tying job. His ego injured, Baudilio dreamed of revenge, and he finally got it the next year when the Indian returned for the summer fiesta. Calm and unarmed, sober and inoffensive, he approached Baudilio to make peace with him and apologize for the previous year's mischief. Baudilio's long-awaited reply was to reach into his boot and pull out a double-edged blade, which he thrust into the other man's stomach. Blood splashed, and Baudilio thrust deeper and twisted his grip. The Indian gasped and collapsed, yet Baudilio, insanely murderous, had to be pulled away.

The road was in fair condition and so a Jeep driver was able to get the blood-soaked unconscious man to the hospital in three hours. Miraculously the man lived. Baudilio was not punished. Sheriff Marcos testified that the knife used was not Baudilio's, that the Indian had provoked him, and anyway that Baudilio had been an official deputy at the time.

I didn't relish being caught in a conflict between Cacho and Baudilio. But when Cacho reported that Baudilio attacked him twice with a machete during fights over Tanya, I agreed to have my lawyer investigate and see if suit could be brought.

What we learned did not offer much hope for success. Cacho and his witnesses swore he'd been attacked by Baudilio, barely escaping with his life, but Baudilio had Marcos swear that the two of them had been together in a different place each time. Then there was the judge at La Palma, who was said to be capable of anything, especially when a little money was passed the right way. But Cacho and the lawyer wanted to push on with their suit against Baudilio, and I grudgingly agreed to help however I could. A surprising number of Moritans also wanted the suit to come to trial because they hoped it would expose their much-disliked Rural Guard's injustices once and for all.

Nothing went as planned. Although Marcos was responsible for notifying Cacho of the court date, he told him nothing. The day before the trial was to begin, Cacho's brother stumbled across the notice in the sheriff's office while Marcos wasn't there, and Cacho frantically rode all around Morita begging witnesses to accompany him to La Palma that night. Two of his four witnesses had received threats from the accused and refused to go. But two did accompany him, riding all night to court, which was about 30 miles away. There was no time to notify me or the lawyer, whose preparation was thus in vain.

Baudilio was freed with the equivalent of a thirty-five dollar fine and warned that if he misbehaved again, he would be sent back to Panama. Annoyed, but not very surprised, the lawyer remarked simply, "That's La Palma for you."

Even though Cacho had been a poor example as foreman and had upset the peace of Cantarana, there was no other qualified employee to replace him. With me, he was almost always cheerful and ready for anything, and I didn't want to lose him. But I kept hearing rumors – that Tanya was pregnant by him, that she was having problems with her pregnancy because of nutritional deficiencies, that Cacho wasn't helping her with her problems, that she was going to have *twins*. When she did give birth, Cacho went to see the dark-skinned twin boys, thereby dispelling anyone's doubts as to who the father was.

Cacho's wife, devastated, confided in me that she wanted to go away with her children, but I convinced her to stay and hope for the situation to change for the better. "Maybe Baudilio will escape with Tanya!" I laughed, making her laugh too.

Eventually, much as I hated to do it, I had to fire Cacho. He subsequently quit seeing Tanya so often and learned to pay more attention to the needs of his own family. While this was a positive development, it also left Tanya to figure out how she was going to fare with four children and no breadwinner.

On and on it went, the characters and the props changing regularly, but the human drama was always in play. I tried to stay behind the scenes, but now and then I found myself being dragged to center stage. More often than not my performance there seemed entirely unconvincing – at least to me.

In the mid-1980s, around the same time The Standard Fruit Company – after decades of growing and shipping bananas from southern Costa Rica—finally gave up trying to communicate and negotiate successfully with the Costa Rican people and left the country, I seriously asked myself why I put up with the whole frustrating human drama that accompanied ownership of the ranch. When the farm community was entangled in conflict over a missing hen or a leaking toilet or a cow that ate someone's laundry, or over someone's husband who smiled at someone else's daughter, or over two wives who shunned a third, or over one employee who refused to speak with another, I asked myself why I didn't just give up and sell the place. Why did I insist on sticking around and enduring the conflicts and gossip and rumors?

The answer was simple: it was a trade-off, and I got the better deal by staying. Truly serious problems were rare. There were no kidnappings or rapes or tortures or child sexual molestation as far as we knew. There were no cases of psycho-serial killers or spaced-out drug addicts on the loose that I ever heard about. Nobody opened fire on innocent people, there were no rioters or looters, no terrorists, no war, no military, nobody dumping toxic wastes in our backyards or experimenting with nuclear or biological or chemical warfare. Comparatively speaking, I considered Morita and San Cristobal safer for my family than most places in the United States. The human drama in which we participated was rather bizarre at times, but that was an inevitable part of life anywhere.

In the United States, where a lot of people were constantly moving and often didn't know their next-door neighbors well or at all, maybe the human problems were basically made of the same stuff. If I were ever going to adapt satisfactorily to living among my own species, *where* I was going to be didn't matter so much as *how* I was going to be. Maybe that was what the college psychologist had been trying to tell me so long ago when she insisted that I was the one who needed an attitude change. Maybe I owed her an apology for my defensiveness, but she owed me a bigger apology for trying to convince me that misfits are usually at fault while society is not. Often, it was the other way around . . . or so it seemed to me.

Besides, for all my self-absorbed complaining, the positive aspects of living at Cantarana far transcended the negative parts. The people were mostly wonderful. Though they wouldn't feel much compassion for anyone with a simple cold or a minor injury, they would not hesitate to run five miles to get help for you if you really needed it. If you needed a horse or a place to sleep, or a meal to eat, they would provide it free even if you were a stranger. If you got your vehicle stuck, they'd be glad to help you free it. They were the most hard-working and least complaining people I'd ever known – calm, humble, courteous, and respectful, not resentful or jealous of wealthy foreigners. Their community soccer games, tamale-making reunions, and outdoor dances were almost always good fun for everyone, like the beach picnics I remember as a child in California. What had happened to such family events in the United States? What happened to the families?

Cola de ballena jorobada (fluke of humpback whale)

Chapter Fifteen

Staying and fighting – was it worth it?

One of the reasons I was attracted to Morita in the first place, besides the people, was its pristine tropical wildness. The tropical awesomeness was real, and, after that blissful experience at Playa del Tunel when I was 20, just me and my horse on that hidden, totally pristine beach, surrounded by beautiful, warm ocean, huge trees and fragrant flowers, and tolomucos and butterflies advertising the wonders of that life-filled place, I knew I wanted to stay and explore the magic I sensed, learn the lessons that life taught there. Maybe it was this promissory crossroads event that jolted me with a sense of place strong enough to make me stay in spite of the drawbacks.

College dropout or not, I never quit being an enthusiastic student of biological wonders. Year after year, I kept running into new species, not just new insects, which I discovered almost daily, but fish, amphibians, reptiles, birds, and even mammals. And the local people spoke of many more creatures that I had yet to see for myself. Knowing there was always some new creature to see kept me continually open to pleasant surprises. Besides new species, I kept witnessing new and unexpected forms of behavior, incredible relationships between individuals or groups of the same and different species.

Now and then I recorded my observations and speculations on unique and fascinating things, like the large community of ants, termites, and bees I found living harmoniously together; or the way several adult yellow, blue, and black euphonia birds cared for a single pair of new flyers; or the way a tolomuco, which looked like a little black panther, hid a stalk of green bananas under leaves and urinated over them to ward off others from the bananas that he would return to eat as they ripened; or the way the golden-brown howler monkeys and owl-like laughing falcons and nighthawks publicly forecast the weather by making their calls at certain times in particular ways.

This was great stuff for me! This was what I had dreamed of somehow researching for a living before I quit college, having gotten only as far in academia as killing and dissecting frogs. Cantarana was the perfect place to watch and wait and record, without killing, without tagging or tranquilizing or capturing. Besides ecological material, my notes got fat with anthropological information, not just about the current inhabitants, but those of the past as well.

Past and present seemed so intertwined. While Manuel was digging a hole for a fence post, he uncovered a one-piece hand-knife with handle, sculpted from stone thousands of years ago, which fit perfectly in the closed right hand. He casually offered it to me, and then just as casually, he cut a wide leaf by the stream and quickly fashioned it into a watertight cup, which he handed me for a cool drink. Both past and present were so alive!

The opportunity to learn was a priceless treasure. I enjoyed thousands of magical hours just sitting in a chair or on a rock or sand beach, appreciating the changing views of forest, coastline, ocean, sky, animals, and people. Screeching flocks of lime-green parakeets would fly erratically by, then a swift hawk would swoop down and catch something, then I would hear the howler monkeys, then the strong perfume of a flowering *ilán* tree would envelop me, and a cloud would shade the sun and a fresh breeze cool me. It was never the same from hour to hour, and my thoughts and insights changed accordingly.

Exploring Cantarana, a process I would never complete, kept turning up such intensely beautiful, perfectly pristine little places among the streams, gigantic trees, black-boulder coast, and sand beaches.

Perhaps what had me really hooked to Cantarana, the thing that I just loved too much to leave for long, was the ocean that blessed the property. Some of my favorite times in the United States had been in or by the oceans of southern California and southern Florida, in spite of the sticky-gooey tar; the itchy, smelly seaweed; the frequent stinging jellyfish; the garbage and boats and high-rises. There was none of that anywhere in Morita. The mangrove estuaries, the coral reefs, the bird-covered islands, and the long sand beaches, were all pristine and loaded with life.

From my earliest days in Morita, I'd established a respectable reputation as a skin diver and seafood provider. It was a role I was proud of, not just because I learned to get fish, lobster, and conch, but because I could give my catch away or trade it for meals, groceries, favors; it enabled me to occupy a useful place in the local society.

I was particularly proud of my integrity as a spear fisherman. Since I hated to have injured fish escape, I forced myself each time to take the time to be sure of my shot, and after a while I averaged four caught fish out of every five shots, which was good by any spear fisherman's standards. I enjoyed returning after half a day in Siete Vueltas to Cantarana with plenty of seafood for the families living there and maybe for the neighbors, too.

The truly great thing about Morita was that you could enjoy its clean and bountiful warm ocean without a million other people trying to enjoy it next to you. The coastal waters of southern Costa Rica were wilder and more prolific with life than any I'd ever seen. Healthy coral reefs and shallow shoals harbored thousands of spiny lobster and reef fish of many kinds, the massive coral heads shading big cubeira, red and rock snapper, and an occasional grouper. Large schools of silver jacks, cobalt jacks, barracudas, parrotfish, and sometimes corvina, passed by frequently. Curious Pacific hawksbill turtles swam just out of reach. Often when I dove down to peer under a coral head or into a rock cave, I would see several large lobsters and a couple of 20- to 30-pound fish among everything else. Sometimes, with my small speargun in hand, I would see so many fish all around me that even though they were all big and good eating, I was too awed to fire at any of them.

For the first few years, I was one of only a handful of people who dove in the area, so the fish were relatively tame as well as plentiful. I took only what I needed for the people of Cantarana and no more. I tried to instill this in those I taught how to dive. I also emphasized that they should leave the female lobsters carrying eggs, and anything that was too small.

Every dry season, December through March, huge schools of sierra mackerel, black tuna, roosterfish, and yellow jack followed the schools of the sardines to the area, and then we took enough to dry and give away or trade. During the same time, humpback whales and bottlenose dolphins also frequented the calm, protected bay. In the rainy season, June through November, hundreds of Olive Ridley turtles flippered up the Morita beaches to lay their eggs. Some mornings I would be the first person to ride along the beach and would pass five or six paths where turtles had crawled up from the water to lay their eggs the night before. Sometimes I would dig up one of the nests and take half the eggs (40 or 50), cover the rest, and then go by each of the other nests and disguise them by brushing the turtle tracks away with a palm frond or by digging another hole close by to fool those who came along later. Turtle eggs were excellent eating, and the locals would empty all of the nests if not dissuaded.

Some 30 miles away lay Faro Island, which harbored more and bigger of everything, a place where incredible experiences and fantastic adventures were the norm. From Cantarana we could see Faro perfectly, a small, raised plateau on the horizon off the coast of the Osa Peninsula, itself the home of jaguars, tapirs, and scarlet macaws. Faro Island was one of those extraspecial reasons I stayed in Costa Rica. I enjoyed just sitting and looking out across the ocean, savoring thoughts of how and when I would next venture out to it.

In Siete Vueltas, with a 25 horsepower outboard and a full load – four people, 50 gallons of gasoline, extra motor, diving and fishing gear, food, five gallons of water, sheets, three oars – it took us five hours to get there. Approaching an island like Faro in the open ocean seemed to me one of the finest experiences available on this water planet. Deep-green forest surrounded by white coral and black lava sand beaches, incredibly clear warm water, whites, greens, and blues – Faro was a haven for the exploring spirit.

In the middle of its forested plateau, several hundred acres at about 40 meters above sea level, lay an ancient "Indian" burial ground. Hundreds of shards and large pieces of stoneware littered the sites where previous *huaqueros* (tomb diggers) purposefully broke and scattered the less valuable items to throw off later treasure hunters from the tombs they wished to return to. Exquisite jade and golden artifacts by the kilo made rich men and then drunks out of most of the huaqueros. The very first to raid the site were probably pirates (like Morgan and Drake), but there was still plenty left for modern treasure seekers, though it was difficult to locate due to the extensive tampering.

From the plateau flowed springs of cool, fresh water, which formed small streams and waterfalls on all sides of the island. The lush vegetation was conveniently free of poisonous snakes, which were so abundant a mere 15 miles away on the Osa Peninsula. Only the northeast lee side of the island was easily accessible, with sand beaches and favorable passages through the lava pinnacles and reef.

On one of these small semiprotected beaches sat the only building on the island, a little house that was used to shelter a huaquero/pig farmer/part-time employee of a banana company that apparently had wanted to lay claim to the island, using the employee to establish squatter's rights. After several visits to the island in 1977, I discovered another man, known as "Crazy Chicken," apparently doing his best to cut down the forest (luckily with just an ax) and claim the island for himself and his behind-the-scenes backers, and I became determined to raise a fuss. Faro was too beautiful to allow it to be destroyed or turned into an international casino resort as planned.

The way to get things done in the entangling bureaucratic "system" seemed to be by shouting, stamping, threatening, and accusing, and by getting the mess published in the newspapers. I did that and managed to generate a midday news bulletin alerting the populace to the impending "total devastation" of Costa Rica's most precious island. What counted was that a "North American ecologist and conservationist" had locked horns with the complacent officials of the Ministry of Agriculture and its National Parks Department and was being rudely shoved aside "while trying to protect one of Costa Rica's most valuable assets."

I joined efforts with the University of Costa Rica's biology department, which fought hard to protect the island – some brave students even blocked the bulldozing of a runway on Faro – and after several months of continued pressure in 1978, Isla del Faro was officially declared a National Biological Reserve. This meant it was legally protected from any kind of exploitation – no more huaqueros, no more casino developers, no more felling trees. Crazy Chicken, expelled from his island, sent word to me that if he ever saw me in that area again, he'd sink my boat and kill me. I was glad we'd never met face to face.

I continued to visit Faro a couple of times every dry season, when the ocean was usually most calm and clear and squalls rarely threatened. Wahoo, sailfish, rainbow runner, whales, big schools of yellowfin tuna, sharks, manta rays, dolphins – diving off Faro was like jumping into the big tank at Sea World, only much, much better.

Having pursued my favorite activity in various spots around the world, I could judge Faro with some authority. The Great Barrier Reef of the Coral Sea, the Tuamotu atolls, the Maldive atolls, the reefs of Belize and Bonaire, all easily beat Faro as far as reefs and corals and colors were concerned, but none of these famous places could compete with Faro's consistently huge schools of fish, or its variety and abundance of big pelagic species.

Once in the water with mask, snorkel, and fins, even experienced divers hesitated to venture among the 50-pound dog-toothed snappers, the massive schools of 20-pound barracudas, or among the 300-pound bull sharks. I spear fished there once just to get a tasty lunch, but I did it in fear, always on the lookout for the big tiger sharks I had seen from the surface. The story of a Frenchman who disappeared close to shore while spearfishing kept my own underwater ambition there to a strict minimum. Besides, over the years I preferred more the role of observer to that of hunter. And when the exploitation by commercial as well as sport diving and fishing became noticeable underwater, I preferred not to be an accomplice.

Around 1980, when the foreign demand for local seafood doubled, and around 1985 doubled again, and northern Costa Rica became mostly fished out, another chapter in my life began, as I adopted a cause I believed in enough to fight for on a long-term basis. People thousands of miles away were hungry for lobster and shrimp and were ready and willing to pay top dollar for them. The shrimp trawlers from the north invaded Moritan waters in greater numbers and dragged their devastatingly effective nets on the ocean floor day and night, scraping up tons of creatures of all sorts. The shrimpers had no interest in most of the life forms they caught willy-nilly and killed, and they threw back all but the largest shrimp and fish; they did this for years until they were destroying the reproductive cycles of many of the species with which I was well-acquainted. And since the area, with its mangrove estuaries and shallow bay waters, was a breeding ground for many species, this destruction affected many species in a very large area. Because I was one who had witnessed over two decades the changes over-fishing caused, I felt a responsibility to tell the world what was happening. All over the world lonely observers are put in the same situation, while the vast majority remains largely ignorant of the destruction and its effects.

A canary in a coalmine communicated that something was very wrong (no air!) by dropping dead in its cage. Amphibians, hawks, and big cats just disappeared from places. As a human indicator organism of sorts, I figured my job was not to die or disappear, but to try to stay and keep adapting, communicating, protesting ecological abuses, and trying generally to improve the local situation.

When I discovered the crew of a rotting little wooden shark fishing boat trying to harpoon dolphins playing in their bow wake, intending to use them for shark bait, I felt like blowing them out of the water. Instead, I traveled to San José to see what could be done in a less satisfying but more conventional way. I learned some interesting things on that trip. Costa Rica had no laws prohibiting the slaughter of marine mammals. There was no enforced regulation protecting anything in the ocean. The National Parks Service and the Fisheries Department were parts of the Ministry of Agriculture and Livestock(!). The Fisheries Department dealt exclusively with issuing licenses for the exploitation of marine resources. No one dealt with their management or conservation.

Professional lobster divers with generators and compressors pumping air down to them through hoses spent hours at a time scouring the bottom for lobsters of all sizes, including females with eggs. There were no laws prohibiting them from doing this. And I was just a lone gringo who had no business suggesting anything to them anyway. After several teams of divers wiped out the lobster down to 80 feet, they decided to start on the conchs.

A gringo in Quepos who came to Costa Rica as a surfer with $100 in his pocket, but had a real knack for no-holds-barred capitalism, eventually equipped himself with a small fleet of vessels and vast refrigeration space. He was paid well for everything he could get out of the sea, which he exported twice weekly to Miami, and without any qualms whatsoever he targeted the rich Morita area. His buyers in Miami urged him to obtain more and more, as seafood became more popular among North American consumers. They didn't know where it came from or what the real costs were in terms of local ecological damage. Maybe they didn't care. I loved seafood, too, and so didn't blame them for their healthy appetites, but obviously this kind of exploitation wasn't going to last long.

Sardine boats came by to chase down and net the small fish, but they were so proficient at it that after only a couple of years there weren't enough sardines to make it worthwhile.

The local human population increased so fast that when the turtles went up the beach to lay their eggs, people with flashlights had heated discussions over who had rights to the eggs. Some individuals even macheted the turtles coming out of the ocean and cut out their eggs so they wouldn't have to wait until the eggs were laid.

The oysters no longer had a chance to grow to a nice eating size. A price was put on clams, and so they too became scarce. Delfina, years before, had joked to me that someday people would even go after the tidal red crabs, which prospered in great numbers on the beaches. I remember laughing, but their days seemed numbered, too.

Commercial fishermen who had grown tired of their own depleted coastal fishing areas began to spend the extra diesel and time to fish Faro Island. Although the island was protected, the waters around it were not, and more fishermen were lured there by stories of incredible one-night catches that filled a boat's entire hold and of fishermen striking it rich by catching large numbers of red snapper for export. Lobster divers made small fortunes in a matter of days. Shrimp were plentiful year-round.

It was time for another round of shouting and stomping and letter writing. Simultaneously, the Costa Rica University biology department was exerting a lot of pressure to protect the waters around Faro, and the director of the National Parks Service was personally enthusiastic about our proposal – to assure legal protection of the reefs and shallow areas around the island and to preserve an ecosystem containing some of the best underwater wildlife scenery in the world.

I don't know how it finally happened or who accomplished it, but, in 1983, after more than a year, our proposal was accepted and imposed by legal decree. Of course, there were many such conservation laws, only a fraction of which were enforced, but it was a start for marine conservation in Costa Rica.

Bob (my friend from California who visited us every year) and I helped Faro's guardians acquire a small fiberglass boat, two outboard motors, a small generator, and a shortwave radio in order to patrol and report. It wasn't easy to convince fishermen who were accustomed to making big catches within 3 kilometers of the island that it was now a restricted Biological Reserve, but it was the only way. Otherwise, Faro soon would have been fished out like so many other places in the world. There was no avoiding the unfortunate hard feelings between the parks people and the fishermen, and I knew that if I ever again had engine trouble in the area, I'd better depend on my own mechanical skills instead of a passing fishing boat.

All around Morita, however, the exploitation continued. Catching seafood was no longer so easy, and when I dove down to look in the same caves that had for years guaranteed lobster and good-sized table fish, I found a few squirrel fish, sergeant-majors, surgeon fish, puffers, and triggerfish that were too bony, small, or distasteful to take. The most beautiful reef fish, including my favorite, the elegant yellow, black, white, and gold Moorish idols were gone, taken by the latest exploiters – divers supplying the foreign market for salt-water aquarium fish.

I put away my speargun for good and concentrated my efforts on doing something for the exploited area around Cantarana, where I thought I might have some influence. I felt I owed it to the place, having enjoyed so much of its former abundance.

Our house in San Cristobal proved to be a wonderful place to work. Unlike at Cantarana, my desk didn't provide a breeding center for cockroaches, wasps, scorpions, and geckos. With my typewriter free of the rusting sea breeze, I could write letters and send them from the post office four blocks away. When I consistently didn't receive any replies, I got a telephone. Refusing to pay the 400 percent tax on automobiles, I rode the bus to and from meetings in San José. Soon, the government office people would know me as the outraged and outrageous gringo who always insisted on seeing *el Jefe* (the Chief). I'd always been bull-headed, and I felt satisfaction directing my orneriness toward a cause I believed in. Sometimes, I actually enjoyed the role of watchdog!

My friend Bob and I financed a preliminary ecological study by two graduates from the marine department of the University of Costa Rica, which backed the theory that the Moritan mangrove-estuarine zones, combined with the protected bay, coral reefs, shoals, and shore, created a breeding and development area for many resident and migratory species. Among them were the Pacific hawksbill turtle, and from December to May, small groups of humpback whales, both of which were on the International List of Endangered Species and were the kind of charismatic creatures that drew a lot of fans. The two areas of coral reef were the most pristine on the Pacific coast of Costa Rica.

Even though all these characteristics were officially confirmed, and despite the signed support of the leaders of the community and hundreds of their supporters, the National Parks Director still wanted little to do with our coastal marine preservation plan.

"Costa Rica has a wonderful system of national parks protecting humid tropical rainforest, dry forest, special areas – I just don't see how a marine park would fit in," he said.

I could tolerate a terrestrial bias in most people but did not understand how such an apparently well-educated individual could harbor such a pitifully limited conception of the mother of life on Earth, the very thing that made the "water planet" different from any other visible object in the universe.

"Biodiversity," at that time, was a relatively new concept, but I took it upon myself to impress the director of National Parks with the fact that, taxonomically speaking, terrestrial habitats harbored 11 phyla (chordates, or back-boned organisms being one of them) whereas marine ecosystems included 23 phyla (at least).

I became used to the long bus ride to San José and learned to purchase two seats next to each other to avoid being made miserable by children throwing up around me or adults sneezing or coughing on me or nudging me into a nervous wreck. I learned to drink the cold sugary coffee they always offered at the meetings with government bureaucrats, to not raise my voice or whine, to offer possible incentives in the right way at the right time. Not only did I learn to function effectively within the inefficient morés of Costa Rican bureaucracy, but I was even put on a government-appointed committee and officially declared an honorary member of The National Parks Service.

I did feel honored during the two years I volunteered my participation with the newly created "Marine Parks and Reserves System," and I thoroughly appreciated the chance to be a part of the beginning marine conservation efforts in Costa Rica. Our first task was to firmly establish Cocos Island as a national park. It was a truly oceanic island 350 miles offshore, which I already had visited a few times in various live-aboard dive boats and knew was one of the highest-voltage scuba-diving destinations in the world. I also knew that increasing numbers of commercial fishermen, responding to Asian markets, were cruelly and disgustingly decimating the huge schools of the magnificent, harmless sharks around Cocos. They were catching them just to cut off their fins (to dry and sell for sharkfin soup) and tossing back the mutilated but still-live animals to sink to the ocean floor and slowly die.

Our committee, with the invaluable professional help of Mario Boza and Alvaro Ugalde, generally considered as the founders of Costa Rica's National Parks Service, succeeded in freeing Cocos Island from the jurisdiction of the Ministry of Security (whose representatives occasionally used Cocos' resident bottlenosed dolphins for rifle target practice), providing a preliminary management plan and short-term protection (with Parks' employees patrolling and reporting poachers) of the spectacular marine life of Cocos from the very disgruntled long-time commercial divers and fishermen.

One day in 1989, my family went to the beach at Playa del Tunel and had the pleasure of meeting President Oscar Arias and his gracious wife, Doña Margarita. It was rare to find anyone else at all on that beach, much less el Presidente de la República and the First Lady, in their bathing attire. They'd flown in the previous day, landing on Don Oscar's cousin Eduardo's private runway, and were staying at Eduardo's big thatched rancho on the finca south of Cantarana. They seemed extremely friendly and modest, especially for heads of state.

We talked about how beautiful and undeveloped the forest coast was, and I expressed my desire to see it legally protected. Don Oscar at first seemed mostly interested in building a house by the pristine beach, but Doña Margarita and I discussed the possibilities of creating a marine-terrestrial park, including the bay, coral reefs, Piedra Cachelote, and Playa del Tunel. I offered to donate 20 acres of climax forest on my end of the beach if Eduardo would do the same. Fearing to further disturb their vacation away from affairs of state, I then changed the subject, satisfied to see the environmental interest in possibly the two most influential people in the country.

Months later, Don Oscar was drinking coffee in the humble house of one of my employees when he received the news from Oslo that he'd received the Nobel Peace Prize. When I next took Don Oscar and his family snorkeling in my lowly boat, I felt much more concerned for his safety. He loved the snorkeling and was very good at it, and though I feared taking him to the deeper, rougher spots where there was more marine life, he enthusiastically insisted on my doing so, even if his wife and two children had to stay in the boat.

I swam beside him to guide him to the giant school of silver jacks, a turtle, two large palometa, red snapper, all sorts of small colorful reef fish, in fortunately clear conditions. He loved it so much that he didn't want to get back to the boat. When he did get out, I noticed that awed look in his eyes that I hoped signified good prospects for establishing a protected marine area. Over lunch, he admitted thinking the coral heads I had pointed out to him were "just rocks" and said that in his opinion there was so much marine life there it could never disappear. Even so, he and Doña Margarita seemed genuinely interested in the idea of a marine park for Costa Rica, which had none, and in stimulating the economy of the local area, which they wished to help in some way. When I was finally able to convince them that humpback whales visited the area, giving the close offshore island and the local community their names, they showed special enthusiasm.

Since Don Oscar expressed that the yearly presence of whales was crucial to the creation of the marine park, I did some serious research into humpback whale migrations, but even the most recent scientific studies done by specialists in marine mammals cast doubt on whether the Cachelote whales were humpbacks at all, and if they were, whether they were southern- or northern-hemisphere whales. The time they arrived, between December and May, indicated that they were wintering northern-hemisphere whales, but according to the latest literature, those animals supposedly traveled south from Alaska only as far as the Revillagigedo Islands off Mexico, 1,500 miles to the north of us.

I spoke of this question while meeting with Jean-Michel Cousteau, son of the late Jacques Yves Cousteau, in San José, and he gave me the names of Mark and Debbie Glockner Ferrari of the Center for Whale Studies in Maui, who he said might be able to set me straight. I visited them that winter in Lahaina and offered them photos of some Costa Rican humpback tail flukes for identification purposes. Sally Mizroch of the National Marine Mammal Laboratory in Seattle eventually discovered a match with a whale photographed off California, proving that at least some of Costa Rica's humpbacks were from the northern hemisphere. This meant that these animals were migrating 3,000 miles farther a year than expected. Migratory patterns would have to be remapped.

In 1989, with Mark and Debbie, I enjoyed one of the most memorable days of my life, joining them in the water next to the colossal subjects of their research. I will never forget the 40-foot female "Kilauea," so tranquil, docile, mysterious, huge, so motherly in caring for her small (a couple thousand pounds), playful, curious, and cute calf; and with Kilauea's submarine-like suitor singing directly beneath us, filling us with such powerful, blissful vibrations that I could hardly restrain my joy. I returned to Costa Rica more fanatical than ever to protect these superlative beings with whom we shared the planet.

It took more signatures, more support from different sectors, more bus and taxi trips to San José for meetings, more letters, more promises for financial support, more politics, more headaches, and more time, but eventually Cachelote Marine National Park was established by the Ministry of Natural Resources and by presidential decree. We "Friends of the Pacific Islands of Costa Rica," a small, loosely organized group of Costa Rican and United States ocean lovers and marine conservationists, shouted "Victory!" And it was, for a while. It seemed nothing lasted for very long.

Some of the lobster divers and gill netters, who came from northern Costa Rica to join the squatters on the beaches of Morita, paid little attention to the decree or the first official park guards. As was obvious all over Costa Rica, environmental laws, even within national parks, were only respected by the "nice" people, since the renegades had little chance of being caught or prosecuted for illegal logging or poaching and faced only an insignificant fine if they were. The temptation to join the poachers was great; even members of my family, who loved lobster and hadn't eaten any in two years, were split on whether I should resume bringing them to table.

The laws were complicated and contradictory, seemingly designed only for lawyers who spent incalculable time and other people's money to decipher, twist, and avoid them. With the change of government administration, Arias' successors abolished the forestry law upon which many national parks, including Cachelote Marine National Park, were founded, and once again a presidential decree had to be won restoring their protected status. After a normal bureaucratic lapse of a year, it was. Then the new National Parks Director threatened to nullify the park, despite it already having been supported by two ministers and two presidents, reasoning that a marine park with no land was "ridiculous" and lacked a "decent image."

In other administrations, this important figure had championed the evolution of the National Parks System. However, he had a phobia about the ocean and had never put on a facemask to see what was in it. He simply wasn't interested. The only way he would cooperate was if we amplified the park to include the 50-meter zone of the coast above the high-tide mark, a particularly controversial and legally questionable zone occupied by poor subsistence fishermen with nowhere else to go and nothing to lose by violating the park's management efforts. A sociological study and land-tenure study had to be completed, and the new draft was redone and resubmitted, reaccepted, and rerejected.

Working toward conservation at first satisfied a personal need of mine to accomplish something meaningful, but I was beginning to be worn down by years of working with ineffectual committees, dealing with the implacable swarms of opposing interests, enduring the rumors and bickering, and being tossed around by a contradictory legislation and incompetent government officials. I did my best to make a positive difference, but I increasingly came to regard my efforts as representing more a nice gesture than meaningful change.

Faro Island Biological Reserve and Cocos Island National Park were in the same mess as Cachelote Marine National Park, where the legal protections were so weak that Parks Service employees found themselves unable to carry out their mandate. Government regulation was marked by infighting between the old Ministry of Agriculture and Livestock's Fishing Department – which issued all fishing licenses and received their proceeds and was vulnerable to pressure from strong commercial fishing interests – and the new Ministry of Natural Resources, whose job supposedly was to protect natural resources.

It made little sense to those of us working in the conservation movement that the same government would have one large ministry using old laws and old alliances to exploit the country's natural resources, while at the same time directing a small new ministry, without any empowering new legislation or alliances, to protect those resources. It was especially annoying when, despite this official contradiction, Costa Rica heralded itself in slick travel-agent propaganda as the hemisphere's initiator of "eco-tourism" and "one of the most advanced countries in conservation," attracting international praise.

The gulf between full-page, glossy color advertising and reality might have been comical, but wasn't. The forests, the reefs, and the terrestrial and marine wildlife were being destroyed with incredible speed. That Costa Rica was considered a positive example in Latin America only emphasized how bad the situation was elsewhere.

Jureles ojones (big-eye jacks)

Ballena jorobada (Humpback whale)

Chapter Sixteen

Inevitable invasion – like Dad said

The stakes kept getting higher, and I kept wondering whether I should keep throwing more of myself into the pot or fold and leave. If Alcoa had to retreat after 20 years and millions of dollars lost; if the even earlier-established Standard Fruit Company had to pull out of southern Costa Rica in 1982 after not being able to withstand the continued multimillion dollar losses from labor syndicates that convinced hundreds of workers to let the bananas rot; if even my favorite neighbors were selling out and moving, why didn't I do the same?

There was nothing in the world better than Cantarana on those special days when the clear ocean shone ultramarine blue, the sky bright azure, the clouds light-gray bursting with brilliant white plumes, the vegetation a vibrant green; when the crystalline stream came dashing down with recent rain from the mountains; when a slight, steady breeze caused branches to sway and bore the perfume of flowers floating invisibly by; when plentiful and colorful wildlife was easy to see and hear; and when there were good diving and fishing, fun exploring, neighbors coming for visits and bringing gifts and good will, beach picnicking, people happy and friendly, projects progressing, trees growing. The powerful and enduring magic of the place helped me cope with the gathering forces of change and decay.

I knew that the construction of the Pan-American Coast Highway, slated to bisect Cantarana, would inevitably be a stressful experience, but I did not expect such a long, drawn-out string of nightmares. Like the swamps of Darien in Panama, which were still the lone remaining obstacle for the PanAm highway route between Alaska and the tip of South America, Cantarana was part of the major obstacle to the coast route – "The Stopper," otherwise known as "The Cork," – a 20-kilometer stretch of mountains, valleys, rivers, streams, beaches, and swamps that consistently defied permanent road construction. Determined to make way for the vital route, which would save motorists some 60 kilometers of driving and allow them to avoid the treacherous passage over the *Cerro de la Muerte* (Ridge of Death) between southern Costa Rica and San José, engineers had for 20 years blundered their way through the rough terrain, traversing jungle and forest, corn fields and pastures, chopping and surveying and plotting different plausible routes.

Since I first arrived there in 1972, every couple of years, a "Chief Engineer" would come to scare me to death by proposing a route that would run through our bedroom or, worse, would run so close to the ocean that it would destroy the coast and the pristine forests bordering it. They wanted a straight and level highway, which was impossible through "The Stopper." Since for years – with the change in command of different government administrations – the final verdict remained undecided, I was very hospitable to these *jefes* and their entourages; I kept my mouth shut on antigrowth, antiprogress, and antipolitical themes, and they loved to stay in the hilltop cabin as honored guests.

When they eventually settled on an inland route that spared most of my most valuable property, I was never quite sure whether it was out of deference to my wishes and hospitality, or whether it was to spare my neighbor Eduardo's runway. The neighbors told me Eduardo had unknowingly saved me, since he had valid influence in the appropriate political party and did not want the highway cutting his runway in half, especially since there was no other stretch of flat ground where he could build another. And without the runway, how could he fly his beautiful girlfriends and Dobermans in and out?

One day as I returned to Cantarana from San Cristobal, my heart leapt into my throat when I saw a stranger with a smoking chainsaw busily felling one of my favorite trees right by the Quebrada Chica stream. Another stranger waited nearby with a bulldozer, and another had a big flatbed truck ready to take a load of logs over the dry-season road, which they'd fixed up for their own purposes. It was as if I were being raped or violently assaulted, or was witnessing such a crime against a loved one.

When I then saw their filthy camp on the stream, on my land, where they were depositing garbage and excrement with equal abandon, I nearly ran to get my shotgun. The leader, anticipating my reaction, yelled down to me from his perch on his deafening dozer, which he didn't bother to turn off.

"*Tranquilo* [take it easy]. We paid 11,000 colones [$90] for the permission to take this wood. This is the Coast Highway right-of-way, and we have a permit from the Forestry Department and Ministry of Public Works." I just scowled at him and went to look for Antonio, my foreman, to vent a little bit of my rage for not sending me word of this before.

"But they said they had permission," he responded.

"Did you see it?"

"No, but they offered to show it to me," he said, disarming me since I hadn't demanded to see the permit either.

I returned immediately to San Cristobal in the same four-wheel drive taxi I'd come in on, and went straight to the Forestry Department office. There, I learned for myself that the loggers, led by the infamous Trino – *Ameba* (nicknamed after a regional parasite of the worst kind) – *had* been issued permission and was apparently partners with a high official in the Ministry of Public Works and the director of the Forestry Department.

"But no one can give permission to cut trees right by streams! Or to trespass on private property! And they don't even know for sure where the highway is going to be!" I protested to the regional forestry director with the unforgettable name German Coffin.

"I'm sorry," he said calmly, like the Muzak in a dentist's office, "but I have no vehicle to make an inspection."

"I'll take you in a taxi, if you like. We can go right now. I'll pay," I said enthusiastically. "Look, these guys are in my forests cutting down my trees. You've got to stop them!"

"I'm sorry," he said, smiling as if amused by my outburst, "but I really don't have the time today. Why don't you go to the office of the Rural Guard for help?"

I went to the Rural Guard office and they said, "Well, you know that's really a Forestry Department problem, especially since they issued the permit." I agreed.

Irate phone calls and telegrams to San José, demanding justice from a variety of government offices, accomplished nothing. The loggers moved on to Eduardo's property and I indulged visions of Rambo-style revenge, because surely Eduardo with all his power and influence and lawyers would squash "the Ameba." Incredibly, he did not, and I considered the startling possibility that maybe he *could* not. After that, I understood why people had given the Ameba that name – certain types of amoebae were extremely difficult to get rid of, even with the most powerful anti-parasite medicines.

While Señor Ameba had taken a few dozen trees locally, large tracts of forests were being destroyed regionally, some by people like him, but mostly by the rapidly growing number of small-scale farmers who cut the trees down to plant their plantain, rice, beans, and corn, and to create pasture, to help stake out legal property claims. In the 1980s, it was popular in the United States to blame the hemisphere's rapid destruction of rainforests on the "cattle barons" and fast-food "hamburger giants," but the multinational banana companies were, at least in Costa Rica, much, much worse than the meatmen, and, in the 1990s, the wealthy, politically favored Costa Rican loggers with government permits were worse than everyone else combined.

It would have been a lot easier to pin the majority of deforestation on a small number of bad guys, but the very unsatisfactory truth was that at least 50 percent of the finest hardwood timber in Costa Rica was burned or left to rot, along with the accompanying forest, before 1980, to make way for subsistence crops. Halting the grotesque environmental deterioration required changes too radical for any government ministry to attempt alone because it would cause the government to lose favor with too many people. Losing favor of the people was bad politics, and the country was run by politicians.

With the forest went the creatures of the forest. One of the saddest experiences at Cantarana was to note the progressive local extinction of terrestrial and marine species. In just a couple of decades, less than a third of the life span of a human, I observed the disappearance of several spectacular species. How many of the less-spectacular or nocturnal ones were dying without anyone's knowledge? And this was happening in a small agricultural country of only three million human inhabitants, with a relatively high level of education and an internationally acclaimed "environmental awareness." If this is what was happening in a nation enjoying a relatively high standard of living, with a stable economy, no army, no revolution, and no war, what must be happening in all those countries around the globe with none of these advantages?

The local people, too, were disappearing. With the highway construction finally proceeding in earnest and hungry land speculators making offers hard to turn down, I began to lose precious friends and neighbors. Manolo, my favorite woodsman and reforester, sold the little farm I'd loaned him the money to buy and moved south with his wonderful wife, María, and two children. Don José, my closest and favorite neighbor, sold out to a German-American absentee couple and also moved south with his large extended family. The closest school to Cantarana closed for lack of children. The one in Cachelote operated only half the time. The informal afternoon and weekend soccer games died out, and the community fiestas, the neighborhood trading, the fishing trips, and the meetings all became history.

Old friends were replaced by strangers, hunters, land speculators, tourists, developers, garbage-strewers, smugglers, plant-collector thieves, bird catchers, and careless bulldozer operators. Even the landscape changed. Hills were leveled, valleys were filled. Incredible volumes of orange clay earth and huge basalt boulders were taken from one place and deposited in another. Don Arturo's choza, for years the meeting place for the nightly candlelit talks, lay buried under thirty feet of dirt and rock. The Quebrada Chica, completely silted up, became a mudhole, its water diverted and channeled through a tunnel 50 meters long under 15 meters of fill; landmark giant trees were no longer standing; trails no longer crossed in the same places or at the same levels. For months, my family and I felt lost and uprooted, as did the neighbors.

The hidden beach, Playa del Tunel, was damaged by dirt and rock falling from above, but even before that, Eduardo, who I knew had good intentions, violated its pristine state by breaking our longtime verbal agreement to do nothing with that beach or its surrounding forests. His employees chopped down most of the beautiful natural vegetation, the wild fruit trees and fragrant flowering plants, between the sand and the steep forested hills. They burned the cleared area and planted foreign crabgrass and palm trees as if catering to tourists in South Florida. He built a rustic tin-roof house within the maritime zone, possibly to deter squatters, and had a concrete-and-rebar bathing tub built at the base of the waterfall where we all used to drink and play. Unfortunately, his tub quickly filled to the rim with rocks and mud, becoming so ugly and dangerous that neither he nor anyone else benefited in the least from the addition.

Playa del Tunel had been an extremely rare beach with its intact rainforest, plenty of animals, and no lasting signs of humans, and it was where many years before I felt my roots so timidly extending, where I felt welcomed and filled with the possibility that there I might thrive and grow. I felt deep identification with this place, and now I felt pain, loss, and sorrow, as parts of myself were being severed, trampled, and ridiculed. Once pristine places like that were violated, once places that formed vital inner parts of people were rudely invaded, was there any way of restoring what had been lost? It had been so therapeutic, so transcendent, so fun; it had been my special place! And then it wasn't anymore.

I was not so unaware as to think I was alone in losing "my special place." I wasn't losing a source of food or water or an ancient culture. What must it have been like for entire indigenous tribes to be displaced by invaders with bullets and dogs and bulldozers and dams and religions and diseases? Where did they go? How strange to know that this very same thing was still going on, in fact was common, in many parts of the tropical world. I had become close to the departing jaguars, tapirs, peccaries, scarlet macaws, red monkeys, ocelots, and harpy eagles. Was I part of the blighting invasion, or was I a victim of it, or both?

As the natural habitat disappeared all around, animals sought refuge in the forests and reforested fields of Cantarana. One day a wandering or hunted cougar walked casually by my house and spooked the oxen, which had probably never before seen such an animal but still retained the instinct to fear it. As Cantarana became a refuge, it also became a popular hunting destination, and I became the game warden to be evaded. It seemed too much to ask of the foreman and employees, who openly admitted fearing the consequences of confronting the hunters and who warned me that "nowadays hunters of an animal would rather shoot you than give up their kill." Just how responsible a steward was I willing to be on my little piece of the planet?

I loved the idea of Cantarana as refuge and wasn't going to give up without a fight. My reputation spread after several incidents: I cut the tail off a hunting dog (I meant to just crease him with my machete, but I guess my adrenaline got carried away) that was attacking a pretty, spotted tepezcuintle; I caught another dog and made the owner come and get him, preventing him from leaving until he received my sermon; I put another lost, sick old hunting dog out of its misery with a little fast-acting poison. Word got around that I was a mean old dog-killer, and that helped wonderfully to keep local hunters away.

However, with the advancing highway construction, outsiders, who knew little and cared less about my anti-hunting sentiments and the No Hunting/Private Property/No Trespassing signs we put up around the periphery of Cantarana, brought more valuable hunting dogs and made it clear to a few neighbors that they would defend their dogs with guns. Were they bluffing?

One day, frustrated and angry and hot on the trail of some hunters who'd been active in and around Cantarana for two days, I finally got close to one of their dogs. Ready to tie him and take him to the Rural Guard, I felt around my waist for the yellow rope I brought, and surprise – no rope. I backtracked and looked all over but couldn't find it.

It dawned on me that maybe my guardian angel or somebody was taking care of me, that if I *had* taken the dog as hostage, I would have been in serious danger with the hunters.

"What are you doing anyway?" I asked myself, standing in a tangle of arm-thick vines. "Risking your life trying to save *tepezcuintles*? While tigers and leopards and panda bears and rhinos and bongos and gorillas and orangutans are going down, you're trying to save a large *rodent*? What are you – *crazy*?" I thanked my lucky stars and my guardian angel for saving my hide.

I never did find that yellow rope, and I considered its mysterious disappearance a sign. I decided never to go alone again after hunters or their dogs. I was too inexperienced, too unarmed, too vulnerable, and had too many loved ones who depended on me to get into such avoidable life-threatening situations. I had to keep remembering that the human forces of destruction were dangerous to defy, at Cantarana or anywhere in the world. One had to be properly armed, in the bush or in the courthouse.

As the forests were felled, the wildlife fled, the topsoil washed away, the harvests decreased, and the indigenous culture vanished, the local people no longer felt much intimacy with the environment. Young people with suddenly threatened identities, no longer secure in the knowledge they would inherit their parents' farms, had trouble focusing their energies. They only knew that they wanted to sell their lumber or land or cattle and leave with the cash if they could. Money had been something to buy cloth to make clothes with, to pay for medicine, soap, matches, salt, sugar, coffee, a few farm supplies – the list wasn't long. But now, desire for cash and store-bought things replaced the old reliance on household planting and harvesting and local trading. Money, however, did not bring the same pride in self-reliance as the traditional ways.

Government economists aided this transformation by encouraging farmers to grow nontraditional crops for export, and agents were sent all over the country advising people to grow vanilla or black pepper or cacao or achiote (for red food coloring), or pretty flowers. Guaranteed rising global demand, guaranteed increasing profits! It had sounded great to me, too, and had convinced me to get involved with cacao in 1978. Over the portable radios, which blasted most of the day in many households, and in the newspapers and on television, the march of materialism had already softened the will of most of the populace. There was a wonderful and exciting world of bargains out there! Toothpaste that guaranteed sex, clothes that guaranteed all the boyfriends or girlfriends you wanted, snack food that made tortillas taste like dirt in comparison, cigarettes and whisky to make your life worth living – all you needed to enjoy these blissful luxuries was money. With money and things you were somebody; without, you were not.

People no longer remarked approvingly of a neighbor that he was a skilled carpenter or ox driver or cowboy or rice grower; a standard phrase of admiration became, "that guy's got a motorcycle." The farmers around me, seeing the money-god's domain encroach so rapidly with the highway, all of a sudden felt lost, lowly, and unlucky. They had been happily isolated, but now that they were not, they wanted the money and things available in the civilization absorbing them. And so, following the economists' advice, they gave up on the cheap staple crops and dedicated their efforts to growing cash crops.

In our area, the agronomists focused primarily on cacao, which was a good choice because it thrived there, was environmentally benign, and supposedly offered an attractive long-term profit margin. A large cooperative was formed, technical assistance offered free of charge, and special hybrid seeds sold at a dear price to the growing number of interested farmers. It didn't really surprise anyone that after years of intensive labor, and even with the best soil, fertilizer, and pruning, the special hybrid plants failed to produce a third of what they were supposed to. The price of cacao then plummeted to let-the-monkeys-have-it levels, and most of the cooperative's assets vanished mysteriously, leaving the poor farmers much worse off than before.

When President Oscar Arias asked me sincerely what I thought the people of the area could do to prosper, I was in a sporting mood and couldn't help myself from joking, "it seems the only way for someone to prosper around here is by becoming a politician." Everyone laughed with me but him, and I immediately regretted my foolish jest, which could put me in the indelible ink on his persona non grata list. I'd judged him to be a man who could laugh at an ignorant gringo's joke, but the truth was, I had unknowingly touched him in a sensitive area. The truth was, politicians were prospering, showered with favors, inflated salaries, and exorbitant pensions, while the country's hardworking majority was floundering. Don Oscar knew this and didn't like it.

In the little town of Morita, where La Pichinga had been joined by two other bars and a tiny restaurant by 1990, the subsistence fishermen and tourists gave at least the bar owners steady profits. The beach was fouled with fish guts and trash, watched over by fat vultures, but the enthusiastic bathers didn't seem to mind. On special weekends, a *Disco-movil* sound system with a gasoline-powered generator came to blast the sense out of the dancers, which I guessed was precisely the effect they wanted. Unlike La Pichinga's obsolete jukebox, the boom-boom-boom bass beat of the new system could be heard for miles throughout the countryside, including across the bay at Cantarana.

Out of the apparent local chaos surged a small but impressive environmental movement, which I liked to think I played a role in forming. For years, I'd been trying to convince people that by protecting the breeding and development of commercially valuable species within Cachelote Marine National Park, they would be protecting a guaranteed long-term source of livelihood for the local fishermen who plied their trade outside park boundaries. Prohibiting gill nets within the park, while allowing families to fish from shore for consumption only, would not only offer further protection for the area's fisheries, but would enable the local people to count on a consistent diet rich in fish.

People actually came to believe these ideas and put them into practice. Soon, tourists began to rent fishing boats and guides to take them sightseeing and snorkeling. They purchased food and drink and lodging. The community cleaned the beach of guts and garbage. Businessmen became interested in starting up ecologically sound development.

Progress was not unobstructed. There were setbacks when the government cut its budget, and untrained park guards abused their authority and alienated the community, and greedy real estate salesmen and fishermen looking for quick profits put up obstacles to the park's management. This bothered me but didn't surprise me, as everything in Morita and Costa Rica oscillated like that.

Meanwhile, local reforestation was getting a strong shove in the right direction, thanks to a couple of particularly energetic Peace Corps workers: Scott, a lanky, good-natured silviculturist, and Megan, a pretty blonde cell biologist from Yale. These two gringos made me feel proud to be a gringo, too, and made me think maybe the Third World was better off with us than without us. By motorcycle, horse, and on foot, with enough language skills to do their jobs, they visited local farmers and ranchers to help them reforest. Even when the Ministry of Agriculture people were regarded with much suspicion, following the fiasco of the cacao cooperative, an inspiring number of landowners welcomed Scott and Megan wholeheartedly.

They recommended species and techniques calculated to protect watersheds, streams, and springs, or to produce pulpwood for quick harvest or fine furniture hardwoods for long-term investment. To a great extent, their recommendations were based on successes and failures they observed in my oldest reforestations. They encouraged planting indigenous species as much as possible, except where the soil was so degraded that only certain exotics could grow well in it. Through these reforestry pioneers and a few enthusiastic Moritans, a large local nursery industry sprouted and thrived, selling tens of thousands of bagged seedlings locally and regionally. Fifteen Moritans gained steady employment at the nursery, and the successful example of their activity offered great encouragement for conservation activities in the region.

I kept riding up and down on this wild roller coaster of emotion, which took me from optimism and motivation to desperation and apathy. Often, I got off in the middle of the Moritan ride to rejoin my family in San Cristobal, where I was living half or two-thirds of the time. There, a slightly different kind of ride awaited.

Destruction/construction of the Costanera Highway

Chapter Seventeen

Getting comfortable – finally, for awhile

Until around 1987, it seemed San Cristobal was exactly what Delfina and I wanted – a rural town with gravel roads and no traffic lights only three hours away from the farm (when the coast road wasn't washed out or the rivers full), with relatively well-stocked hardware stores, veterinary supplies, doctors, and schools. When Delfina and I walked around doing errands, it seemed we knew about half the people and they knew us, and I spent much of the time shaking hands, waving, having a beer, and talking with the wonderfully friendly people.

I wasn't satisfied, though, with the quality of the public elementary schools, and neither was one of my friends, a former Peace Corp member named Linda, from Kansas, who had some teaching experience, so we decided to create our own school.

A great thing about Costa Rica was that if you *really* wanted a national park or an elementary school, you had a good chance of creating one and making it work – as long as you were willing to make the necessary sacrifices of work, time, patience, frustration, and more patience. Together, with some seed money from my folks, two brothers, and me, Linda and I founded San Cristobal's first nonprofit private school. In five years, our bilingual program swelled from eight students to well over 100, using imported textbooks and emphasizing individual attention in small classrooms.

Living only a few blocks away, Delfina and I walked the kids to school or I rode them on my imported Schwinn – a "chopper' with a banana seat – one by one. We lived close enough to the center of town that I was able to do most of the errands by bicycle or on foot. Not owning an automobile was actually a money-saving blessing – no maintenance, no insurance, no danger of getting it stuck in some mudhole or soft sandy beach or river or jungle, no worry about it breaking down and having to get towed by a bulldozer or something. Taxis were clean, cheap, and dependable, and the drivers were, like most Costa Ricans, wonderful people.

Another thing about not owning a car – it helped maintain a low profile, which I considered desirable in a place where 50 percent of the people could barely pay their subsistence bills. Not being singled out as a rich or decadent gringo was high priority for me (especially for my family's sake), particularly when the cocaine trafficking that came from Colombia after the mid-1980s brought some uniquely disgusting foreign criminals to Costa Rica. I wanted to be liked and accepted in San Cristobal; I wanted to set myself apart from other foreigners who had no respect for local ways. Conforming to a locally respectable image was important enough to me that instead of doing my errands in sandals and shorts, as I had been doing, I adopted long pants, black leather shoes and socks, and tucked my shirt in, unless it was a Panamanian *guayabera*, which was worn out. Riding my bicycle, I might almost have been mistaken for a Mormon missionary if it weren't for my bike being a "Stingray," my longer hair, beard, sunglasses, visor, and of course my lack of a tie and an umbrella.

Tennis kept my body in the shape required of me at Cantarana, though the game sometimes put me into conflict with the handful of other players in San Cristobal, who like me learned not by doing right, but just by doing it any way at all. Even on our laughable level, we imitated some of the pros, cussing loudly, throwing rackets, trying to hit the balls to the moon. It was often preferable to lose, since it could be more embarrassing to win, witnessing the occasionally poor sportsmanship of the loser. A real tennis player from San José took up residence in San Cristobal and charged me $5 an hour to play with him. After a couple years, he improved my game so much that I entered national level tournaments in San José and won a surprising number of games, even with my "grenade-toss" serve.

At first, my tennis buddies invited me to parties where they would try out their latest gringo jokes on me, and to bars where they would talk of sports, cars, and women's abdomens. Drinking and eating so much gave me a headache. I didn't dance merengue, or rancheros, or salsa; I wisely and responsibly feared getting involved with the attractive women – I would go home too early, a partypooper – and so, though we were still friends, I fell from their favor, which was okay with me and Delfina.

I had no group, was an expat everywhere, inside and out, in limbo socially and culturally, without really close friends (had I ever really had any?). I always had trouble that way. It was nothing new for me. When night came, I loved to sleep, and to get up with the first songbirds at first light.

In the rainy season, I fooled around with acrylics and oils on canvas. Again, I had no formal guidance, but like tennis and guitar and children and a couple of other fun things, I enjoyed painting a lot and maybe once a year finished something I knew was mediocre, but pleasing to the eye and appreciated by the benignly uncritical general public. San Cristobal was wonderful in that I had a lot of leisure time to experiment and play with, and almost zero peer pressure.

When our home became temporary home or pit-stop for too many other people who had no other place to go while in San Cristobal, we purchased another piece of pasture next door and, after growing beautiful delicious sweet corn on it for a few years, built another house, and a one-room guest cabin, and another little cabin for Delfina's tall, mustached 80-something-year-old father (her mother had died). We were an active little depot with our doors opening and closing, people moving in and out, telephone ringing, messages passing in, loud voices, hands shaking, children playing. I liked that. Most of the people were extraordinarily humble, polite, respectful, friendly – a joy to be around.

I no longer had to do so many errands, usually being able to get someone else to do them or to do them by telephone (marvelous invention! I was glad we'd finally gotten one). I resisted the mounting pressure to get another phone or a fax or a car, fearing the machine proliferation that raced on with the washing and drying machines my mother gave us, and the Betamax, which of course had to be replaced by a VHS, and a new and larger television, then a water heater and a lawnmower. I felt I had to draw a line somewhere, but my wife, my two stepsons, and my three daughters kept ganging up on me and making me stretch that line.

Cantarana became a very vital place for me to retreat to, and eventually I came to accept the notion that I was antiquated, anti-technological, anti-growth, and most unfortunately, becoming obsolete. I failed to adapt to or keep up with modern Western civilization, and that was fine with me. I merely wanted my family to accept that in me. In some things and at some times they did, in other things and times they did not. I didn't expect any different, neither did I think I deserved any better. I was generally so happy and in love with my family that I thought I would accept most personal inconveniences for their benefit.

When our neighbor, who worked in the Ministry of Agriculture and Livestock (and whose starving cows used to break through our fence to eat our corn, decorate the sidewalk with manure, and attract flies to the neighborhood), started growing tomatoes and spraying all kinds of bad stuff on them, my sense of father-as-protector/defender got riled. Some of these toxic chemicals from foreign companies like Dow, DuPont, Bayer, and Monsanto had been banned in the United States for their health hazards, yet were still being produced there and exported. Now they were being carried by the innocent and usually welcomed breeze into our bedrooms, giving us headaches and allergy.

I used what little influence I had, and with the help of the neighbors (and some doctor pals) forced the neighboring "agronomist engineer" to take his poor, dying cattle elsewhere (ideally where they had something to eat). I now tenaciously insisted that he spray his poisons elsewhere, away from the populated urban zone. My arguments and letters became sharper, less obviously vicious, more bureaucratically correct, until finally he was ordered to quit spraying. He kept spraying anyway. I brought authorities to catch his workers in the act. Another official order was issued prohibiting his spraying. When he tried to get a Ministry of Agriculture permit to spray, he was reprimanded by his superior (who had a kid in our school). After not spraying the fungicides and pesticides for a couple of weeks, the tomatoes began to wilt and deform. My neighbor's partner, *Auxilio* (Help), who reportedly became infamous for burning down the mayor's office (along with the rest of the building) to destroy a document, threatened me and kept appearing, chronically unshaven and in his cockeyed, squashed three-cornered hat, at my fence by the tomato field at 5 a.m., as if he were going to spray it secretly or do me some sort of harm with his poisons. By that time, Molly and I had fairly bad allergies, and Tina swore she would never eat another tomato in her life. After Auxilio got up early every morning to see his tomatoes turn black and rot into the ground for want of toxic, foreign chemicals, our neighbor let his lot go to weeds, and conversation between us became taboo.

The city continued to grow, of course, and with growth came more problems. A discotheque opened 200 meters from our house. Despite no construction permit and an illegally transferred liquor license, the owner, Auxilio's nephew, advertised the grand opening by radio and kicked things off with a sound system the size of a pickup, which he proceeded to blast until 1 a.m. on weekends. The kids seemed resistant enough to tolerate the invasion of privacy, but I kept feeling it in my skull, in my heart, in my ears; the deep bass thumping seemed to proclaim a perverse injustice, one made worse by its blatant illegality and its apparent immunity to law and morality. This was one of the shortcomings of the fine, noble, patient, humble majority of the people of Costa Rica – they often allowed themselves to be stepped on or pushed around by the greedy and inconsiderate and corrupt minority.

We were awakened by intoxicated customers walking and screaming by our house, and one night we heard a shrieking woman being forced into a car, which squealed away. I realized it was time to stick my neck out, again. Through conversations, letters, phone calls, and meetings, I realized that there were many irate and disgusted people like myself, but although I tried to obtain relief from the authorities on the neighborhood's behalf, I had no luck.

When Molly completed the sixth grade, she went to the public high school, moving from a class of 12 students to one of 35. If there'd been sufficient discipline or some type of organization of students by achievement levels it might have been okay. However, there was no such organization, and Molly, who spoke, read, and wrote English as if it were her first language, was forced to enroll in first-year English with a teacher who learned much more from Molly than Molly did from her.

I spoke with the director, but she had been mired in her office and her rules for many years and I got nowhere. Delfina and I advised our frustrated daughter not to correct her teacher in class unless she was asked to. Her other courses were demanding enough that she had to study now and then, but we learned that she was being ostracized because her scores were so much higher than those of the other students. This, coupled with the general physical deterioration of the school and the many disciplinary problems, made us decide we had to get Molly into a better educational environment. I wanted to give her the best, as my parents had given me.

We visited some high schools around San José, which had good reputations, but the environment was generally very distasteful to us – so crowded with people and houses, surrounded by narrow streets, threatened by aggressive drivers, and choked by endless diesel-exhaust belching autos and buses.

While we were growing increasingly disenchanted with the urban environment, my physical condition seemed ironically to be paralleling the deterioration of the city. I developed frustratingly bothersome sinus allergies, and the doctor said I had to stay away from the dream cabin we were building at Cantarana, to stay away from the furniture we were designing and fabricating, to stay away from oils and acrylics I painted with in my spare time. He said my ears could no longer take the pressure-changing abuse of free diving or scuba diving. The ophthalmologist said my eyes, from so much sun and salt, lacked enough natural tears and for that reason became irritated and tired with prolonged reading or writing, and oh, by the way, were in a precataract condition. A dermatologist who treated me in the United States sent a letter reminding me to stay out of the sun, pointing out that, having had one dark and possibly cancerous spot removed, I was at high risk for life-threatening melanoma.

Burned out at 40? I knew the tropics could take their toll, especially on Nordic bodies like mine, but didn't every place have its hazards? Still, the thought of pulling up and finding a healthier place with better educational opportunities for my children began to occupy my mind. We could put Cantarana and the San Cristobal house in trustworthy hands, return a few times a year, and spend the school year in the United States, where my children could presumably go to good schools in a good environment. We could see more of Delfina's son, Geovanny, who was going to the University of Miami, and more of my father in Oregon, who, being alone after my mother died, needed visitors more often. I could stay more out of the tropical sun and sea. Maybe I could find better doctors to help fix my allergies, ears, and eyes.

It would have to be a sparsely populated place, hopefully in a beautiful natural setting, away from big cities, chemical factories, military bases, nuclear power plants, heavy traffic, ghettos, swamps, fault lines, hurricanes, tornadoes, floods, droughts, freezing winters, sizzling summers. Maybe I was hoping for too much in a place.

What would it be like to leave dear, precious Costa Rica for the great unknown? After being booted from The Garden, wasn't it normal and desirable for us humans to keep looking for better circumstances? Wasn't it better to venture out and seek rather than stay and risk stagnation? Would moving be courageous or stupid? I kept reminding myself that mainly I wanted to offer my children superior education and varied opportunities for growth in a different and hopefully healthier environment so that someday they could decide for themselves what they wanted to do with their lives and where they wanted to do it.

I'd been in the same place for 20 years; I'd never been anywhere for 20 years, nor even 10, and personally welcomed a change. I would have preferred somewhere over the rainbow, but the United States would probably be good enough for my family (which was good enough for me). I remembered the peculiar Iranian insurance salesman, our first paying guest at Cantarana, who had said, "You love it here. Yes, you love it. . . . But you'll go back to the States, won't you? Yes, you'll eventually go back." I wondered what became of him, how many times he married and divorced, whether he became rich and powerful or had joined the homeless.

Though friends and family in the United States told me I was a fool to think of leaving Costa Rica, that North America was degenerating quickly into a second-rate country full of horrible social problems, I didn't see it that way. In two decades outside the United States, I came to appreciate deeply the many qualities in its people. They liked pretty flowers and views, they appreciated things that were well constructed and well executed, they believed in punctuality and efficient organization, and they petted their dogs and gave them baths at least once a year. They were often naïve or arrogant, but with basically good intentions. My North American friends were mostly simple, peace-loving individuals seeking security and happiness and spiritual fulfillment for themselves and their families. They made great company for me and my family, and I imagined there must be quite a few other North Americans like them. And when the time came – I felt it eventually would – my family and I could go live happily amongst them.

In the meantime, procrastinating as long as I could, I would build a nice house at the finca, where my family and I, and my Central American and North American friends and relatives could go and be really comfortable.

Building a truly comfortable abode at Cantarana was a refreshingly new and inspiring concept, an exciting challenge, a wonderfully messy and fun pursuit. No longer in the pioneering frontiersman mood, no longer so bothered by the idea of living in a house much nicer than those of the employees' families and neighbors, no longer burdened with so much gringo-in-the-Third World guilt, I considered different materials and designs. For years, I knew that if I ever wanted to "do it right" there, my house would have to have a rot-proof and termite-proof concrete foundation, sunk deep and reinforced to withstand earthquakes and landslides, with either a high ceiling or two stories, to promote cooling ventilation. And if I were going to build something that permanent, I wanted to make sure to do it in the right place.

California Bob, who I think truly belonged in Costa Rica, wanted to help finance a special cabin where he could stay by himself or with his wife Carol during his yearly three-week migratory stop. The problem was that there were only three prime sites, of which I only wanted to use one (keeping the others for future possibilities), and so I convinced him we should join efforts and build something big enough to accommodate my family and his during visits to Cantarana. He agreed, and together with Carol and a mutual-friend, a Costa Rican architect from San José, we filled in the details of the two-story concrete and wood and stone cottage I had in mind.

The spot was easy to choose. I'd known it for years, around 200 meters from the ocean, with a magical view of coastline and forest, Piedra Cachelote, Faro Island, the Terranal River mouths, the Osa Peninsula, Punta Morita, San Andrés, Quepos. It was high enough to see such distances, yet close enough to sea level to appreciate the whooshing waves and enjoy the ocean breezes.

It had been ten years since we'd built anything at Cantarana, and in that time the Municipality of La Palma had cracked down on building permits, especially when they were close to the ocean. Except for tourist destinations – and then only with special permission from various government departments – building within 200 meters of the high tide line was prohibited. It was a great idea, intended to avoid the horrible coastal development chaos typical in the United States and other countries.

Before we could even begin the time-consuming bureaucratic process of getting the plans approved in San José and submitted to the municipality and obtaining the accident insurance and Social Security policies, we had to prove the site was outside the 200-meter

Maritime Zone. According to our unofficial measurement using a long metric tape, it was a bit close for comfort, and I didn't know how strict the inspector would be.

Before he came, a few people advised me to bribe him, just in case, since "all officials from La Palma expected it." But when he finally came, I wasn't in a bribing mood. He went to work, measured the distance, and although I expected him to return and say he was sorry, his judgment was pleasantly surprising: "Right on the line."

All he wanted for his favorable verdict was $40, just to cover his transportation costs, which seemed entirely reasonable. He said he saw nothing wrong with going ahead with the construction while waiting for official approval of plans and permit. What a guy!

It took eight men with picks and shovels and wheelbarrows more than a week to more or less level the construction site, and it was nice to know they didn't have to start over again farther back from shore.

A friend put me in touch with "Cullo" (Coo-yo), a short, smiling young man with a crewcut, who was regionally famous for hauling heavy cargoes in and out of the most indecent places. With his ancient orange remnant of a Ford 4-wheel-drive pickup, he agreed to haul the cement, sand, gravel, rebar, wood, nails, tools, and whatever else needed for the construction. Delfina recommended her niece's husband Carlos to start the construction. Another friend of mine, who worked at a hardware store, recommended another man, León, to do the overseeing. León had a couple of favorite helpers, and along with the farm employees, everyone joined to make a great team that worked hard and well for seven full months.

The perennially on-again, off-again highway construction had fizzled out and washed out long before we decided to go ahead with the house project; the road wasn't fit even for oxcarts. The rainy season was just beginning, but Cullo, with chains on four of his truck's six tires, somehow made it even through deep mud and across rapid rivers, when necessary directing Cantarana's employees to remove obstacles and fill in holes and ruts. He earned about $100 for each six-hour round-trip from San Cristobal, and when he made enough money to change his mutilated tires, replace his twice-welded axle, buy a new starter, and have his engine overhauled, he treated me as if I were his best friend in the world. Among all his brothers, he now had the best vehicle, which made him and his family proud. When the rain kept coming and the road kept deteriorating, instead of saying "impossible," like everyone else, he hauled and enterprisingly placed big flat rocks, one by one, to build his own passages through the most unlikely sections.

Witnessing Cullo's enthusiastic and heroic labor, and watching Carlos and León and Antonio and Miguel hand-mixing tons of concrete and pouring the tall columns and setting beams, and seeing Jenkin and Julio cutting and shaping and sanding the heavy hardwood lumber, I couldn't stand idly by. Soon I was spending as much time at the construction as I was in San Cristobal – and changing my muddy, sweat-drenched clothes three times a day. I took charge of all the stonework around the house, using large, rounded basalt rocks from the boulder beach, and oversaw work on the drainage and antierosion system, the retaining wall, and woodwork design.

My enthusiasm and joy for the project kept increasing, probably because I thought I was doing a lot of things right (and not that many wrong), and because I felt more like a competent, welcome, and respected member of the team than like the patrón. Neither my chronic allergy (from the sawdust, wood sealants, and maybe fresh cement) nor the steady pain in my lower back could keep me away for more than a few days.

As soon as the house was habitable, we inhabited it, and we instantly loved it – the rock- and shell-covered concrete work in the open living room downstairs, the adjoining tiled and wood-paneled kitchen, the rich, dark hardwood walls and ceiling in the two large rooms upstairs, and large tiled bathrooms. Everyone had only superlatives for our house, and of course that made us feel very nice. "Better than my best expectations," Bob said, fully pleased with the important part he played in the house's creation. Without his initial and constant encouragement and enthusiasm, I might not have attempted such a project.

The quality of life at Cantarana definitely seemed to improve tremendously with the $60,000 "dream cottage," and all members of my family vastly preferred the finca without television to San Cristobal with, which to me was the best proof that we had become well-adapted to Cantarana. Finally, we had a very comfortable and pretty place to stay, and I could be proud to offer it to family and friends, knowing it was something very good.

Perhaps the thing I most liked about the new house was the way it was integrated into Cantarana. Trees grew up quickly around the stone walls, vines climbed up, birds and bats, iguanas, and butterflies took up residence around the house, and from the cool, breezy main living area downstairs you could view an ever-changing panorama of ocean, sky, and animals. I'd been afraid that building with concrete, and incorporating so many creature comforts would diminish my sense of Cantarana's power. If anything, it was enhanced.

For many years, I'd looked forward to the day I could start doing some detailed landscaping, not just the haphazard planting of fruit and shade trees here and there, but actually planting some colorful flowers where they were free of danger from zealous machete men, hungry horses or cows, or the wheels of passing oxcarts. Converting areas that had been pasture to purely impractical uses, such as jungle to attract wildlife or gardens to please human eyes and noses, marked the long-awaited time when Cantarana was finally thought out and organized, at least for awhile. At last, with Delfina or a child by my side, I could wander around the house with a long hose and water our flowers in the dry-season afternoons without much, if anything, on my mind.

Though I could probably still afford to sit back and watch the plants grow for a few years, I wanted to achieve financial "success" sooner with the small furniture business I had long planned; for the sake of profit; for the sake of proving to myself that I could do better than just break even; and for the sake of proving locally and regionally that reforestation could be worthwhile and profitable. I kept Carlos and Julio on after they finished with the new house and had them repair Cantarana's other buildings. We rigged up a small gasoline motor with a couple of belts to run a circular saw and began cutting 12-inch-diameter logs culled as we thinned the reforestation plantings.

Though several people tried to convince me to export exclusively the beautiful tables, chairs, and benches we began producing, I always thought people nearby should benefit first from the products made in their region. Surely, there were plenty of fine woods and furniture makers in other countries. I would first try the local markets, pursuing the people with money to spend who would soon build cabins and hotels along the Coastal Highway. As soon as the bridge over the Morita River was in and the highway had gravel, maybe I could have someone out by the road showing and hopefully selling furniture to the passersby. I had a confident feeling that somehow the business would do all right without any slick marketing. And when I was in the United States, I could trust Carlos and Julio to run the business honestly if not efficiently.

After my older brother Kevin accepted my invitation to visit and see for himself some of the fruits of many years' efforts, I felt tremendous satisfaction. The last time he had come, in 1979, he had to swim his suitcase across a crocodile-infested river and walk a couple of miles of beach before I found him and gave him a horse. Nicaragua was in full revolution then (in the late 1970s and early 1980s), and Cantarana was mostly untamed jungle with a bunch of wild cows running around. I was so happy he returned to appreciate the vast differences and to give his approval.

I realized it was important for me to show off Cantarana, to win the approval of the family that had supported me for so long in my risky (not to say, crazy) endeavor. It was too late for my dear mother, whose presence on Earth my family and I missed a lot, or for my white-haired father. He no longer liked to leave his home in Oregon, so my brother's visit was all the more important.

I realized that all along I'd been working at Cantarana in large part to gain others' approval: from my parents who backed me psychologically and financially; from the local people, who expressed strong ideas on what to do with the place; from my brothers, who all successfully completed their educational careers at prestigious universities and who helped me enormously with my own financial responsibilities; from visitors to Cantarana, whom I wanted to appreciate the extraordinary natural beauty; and from people of the future, whom I wanted to say of me, "Yeah, he wasn't such a bad guy to have planted all these different indigenous hardwoods, knowing they would take between 20 and 50 years to mature, and to have protected the old-growth forest, the animals, the watersheds, and the streams."

I realized, too, that all my projects, my false starts and failures, had simply been part of a continuing effort to adapt harmoniously to the place and people. This willingness to experiment, to fail and try again, was the main factor in my relatively successful effort to squeeze into a suitable niche. Surely the same dynamics operated all over the Earth, creatures including humans changing and adapting to the demands of the environment, but they were especially amplified in the tropics, where life, growth, decay, and death were so accelerated, so obvious.

It seemed too bad to me that not everyone shared my belief that adaptation – not exploitation and destruction – was the key to long-term, mutually successful symbiosis between humans and the environment. I tried hard to teach that lesson but didn't make much progress. As the earth-moving highway advanced, I protested futilely against the merciless destruction of primary forest, the total disregard for the streams, the wanton dumping of dirt in the ocean that resulted in the disastrous sedimentation of the offshore reefs. The government representatives, however, said they couldn't afford both the construction *and* an environmental conscience.

Land and resources continued to be managed, not for long-term benefit, but strictly for short-term gain. Loss of soil, habitat, biomass, and biodiversity were secondary considerations, pesky afterthoughts. Terracing would work beautifully in tropical agriculture as I'd seen in Bali and Sri Lanka, but the Costa Rican farmers apparently weren't aware of the advantages of terracing or could not afford such labor-costly methods. Maintaining biological corridors was an extremely valuable concept in preserving biodiversity, intact ecosystems, and habitats, but who was going to foot the bill for the private lands that had to be purchased?

The international community, if it really wanted to, could accomplish miracles in the tropics by purchasing and protecting such lands; paying decent prices for renewable local products, eliminating the destructive activities of corrupt and greedy multinational corporations, controlling pesticide sales and use, and being more conscientious about not providing loans for environmentally and socially disastrous projects. The Costa Rican government could do wonders by encouraging small scale local agriculture instead of importing staples of inferior quality and persuading farmers to raise strictly cash crops for export.

It seemed the right things were rarely done. Though I really didn't want to be a bad sport or an elitist, I increasingly found myself unable to accept the actions of animal-hungry, lumber-hungry, seafood-hungry, and money-worshipping exploiters. I was becoming constantly outraged by what seemed to me inept, ignorant, and bizarre decisions made by invisible bureaucrats. Sometimes, it seemed as if nearly every government agency and official was dedicated to preserving and promoting mediocrity, disorganization, corruption, and inefficiency, and causing the cheapening of special and favorite places, the demoralization of fine, noble people, and the disappearance of the best neighbors and far superior traditional culture.

Staying on the front line of tropical reality often wore me down physically, emotionally, and spiritually and made mind-numbing whisky, rum, and beer more attractive to me. I really knew then, and not until then, why Native Americans manifested such a high incidence of alcoholism. Strange though it seemed, I, too, experienced how it felt to lose one's habitat, people, and culture.

My father had predicted part of it years before, saying, "You're so lucky, sittin' down there all out of the way in your little hideaway, your little Shangri-la, like some goddamn kahuna or somethin', but don't forget, someday they're gonna discover you, and when that ol' Pan Am Highway opens you wide up, you're not goin' to be so happy anymore, because the world's goin' to flood in all around you, and when those bureaucrats got you by the yang-yang and won't let go, buddy, you ain't gonna feel like a king no more."

Cantarana, no matter how successfully I developed it toward becoming a comfortable model of adaptation and compromise, was certainly not a kingdom, nor was it an island capable of isolating me from the rest of my species.

Canopé del bosque lluvioso primario
(climax rainforest canopy)

Chapter Eighteen

Too heavy

Throughout the 70s, 80s, and 90s, it struck me as strange how, in newspapers, magazines, books, and on TV, people kept doomsaying about the future. "If present trends continue, there will be so many more people and so many more problems and so many more extinctions, so much less wilderness and biodiversity and so much more human tragedy and suffering." It was always a projection into the future; no one seemed to acknowledge it was all happening in the present and had been for quite some time.

I noted the same sort of mentality in many of our North American visitors. Either they ignored what they could see so as not to concern themselves – it wasn't socially acceptable to talk about very serious things, especially when people were on vacation – or they didn't sense the world disintegrating all around them the way most of my neighbors and I did.

The effects of change could be seen and felt. We could *see* the extinction of species and *feel* the loss of biodiversity. We were *witnessing* the end of a local culture – the ill-considered flight from country to city, the foundering of human spirit, the ominous swelling of the hungry, uneducated masses. We were right there to see the epidemic increase in tuberculosis, malaria, measles, whooping cough, hepatitis, cholera, and AIDS infections. We were witnessing the sacrifice of the best parts of the "Third World" on the altars of "First World" consumption and demand, which kept growing.

In exchange for oxygen-producing, carbon-sequestering, genetically priceless tropical forests; for its topsoil, fisheries, social stability and culture, and health, the Third World was getting from the First World its climate-altering greenhouse gases, toxic wastes, banned agrochemicals, weapons systems, fast-food chains, and TV and movie psycho-thrillers. Still, even with strict programs of social austerity, these "underdeveloped" countries could barely pay back even the interest on the ruinous loans that enabled others to exploit their resources.

There was some justice, perhaps, when the toxic chemicals dumped on the Third World began to return to haunt First World consumers, in the beef and seafood, in the fruits and vegetables; and when the foreign-supplied weapons fueled bloody and otherwise inconvenient revolutions costly to the innocent Northern taxpayers and consumers. Who would grow the bananas for their breakfast cereal if the plantation laborers were being poisoned or were busy killing one another?

It shocked me when I realized that some of my U.S. investments that were supporting our family and farm were involved in activities that I otherwise protested against. Upon discovering that our broad-spectrum mutual fund was possibly involved in the production or use of toxic chemicals, gas and oil exploration, weapons development, tobacco, alcohol, gambling, nuclear energy, and biotechnology, I liquidated the fund, tried some "socially responsible" alternatives, and consequently lost a lot of money – not because socially responsible investments were necessarily losers, but because I wasn't very savvy about picking the right ones.

It was obvious that most people, educated or not, worried almost exclusively about things only to the degree that they were personally affected by them. Arguments to protect the rainforests focused exclusively on their usefulness to residents of industrialized nations: their ability to help remove *our* enormous output of carbon dioxide (reducing the threat of global warming created by *our* huge consumption of fossil fuels) and produce oxygen (good for *our* breathing); for their use in *our* paints, resins, pharmaceuticals, manufacturing (good, good, good for US).

In Africa, the gorillas were being saved because people paid to go see them, not necessarily because they deserved to live on this planet, or because they were our close relatives. The national forests of the United States seemed to warrant preservation because of their value to loggers, sheepherders and cattle-grazers, not because of their own true value.

But weren't all these things worth more than just what people could get out of them? Weren't there more profound issues to consider? Why didn't anyone come out and say that some creatures and places and indigenous peoples should be left alone just for the sake of letting them be?

I hoped that most of the enemies of Earth and humanity were merely ignorant and not actually evil. Surely the leaders of the world could understand that most natural resources were finite (or, if renewable, were not being renewed), and that every day there were more humans to nourish and nurture and educate. Expecting that constant expansion of economies and population could continue on a shrinking resource base was totally absurd and guaranteed that the future would be characterized by mass famines, plagues, and pestilence, as described in <u>Revelation</u>. Population control and family planning were not being given adequate consideration, even though it seemed clear to people like Jacques Cousteau and Paul Ehrlich that uncontrolled human reproduction was the greatest threat to the planet. The subject of human overpopulation seemed taboo at the overcrowded 1992 Rio de Janeiro World Eco-Summit.

Not all the First World exports to developing nations were in the form of technology, chemicals, guns, and economic exploitation. How well would my Moritan friends react or adapt to the approaching onslaught of foreign ideas and thought processes as presented by Pee Wee Herman, Tammy Faye Bakker, Jimmy Swaggart, Michael Jackson, and Madonna, whose words and acts seemed to emit a flood of potentially hazardous cultural waste?

I had gotten a chance to experience a benign kind of clash of cultures a couple of years before the new house was built when my oldest brother James, whom I'd been inviting for years, finally visited me at Cantarana in 1992 with his tall, smiling, pretty wife, Suzanne, and another couple. I enjoyed their company tremendously, but at the same time thought to myself, "These people are really different." They were all highly educated in psychology (normal and paranormal); my brother had a Ph.D. from Harvard and was living in the New Age capital of Boulder, Colorado, and Ron and Karin, I believed, were practicing professionally in New York. They hugged unfamiliar dogs (you didn't hug unfamiliar dogs in the tropics), they swung on vines in the forest (and brought down all kinds of canopy debris), they walked up to cows and horses to pet them, even from behind (ill-advised: I once saw Macho the jackass kick a cow so hard the cow fell down unconscious for five minutes), and they got away with everything they did, as if they were being protected by invisible forces or entities (which is something they might easily have believed).

These people were successful, professionally brilliant, and wonderful, but they scared the hell out of me. They tinkered with crystals and spoke of previous lives and the deeper significance of chigger bites. I loved it! It was all so new! But when Ron wanted me to get all the employees and their families together one night "for some fun," I winced, not knowing what to expect.

The local people were still rather sheltered from imported notions, and I thought it desirable for them to maintain their relative cultural innocence as long as possible. Television, I thought, wasn't *too* bad an influence yet, since the local viewers only got one local channel and seemed to understand the difference between what went on in the box and real life.

But what did I know about Ron? What might he have in mind? His radiant smile and his pleasant Neil Diamond-like voice made him a real charmer. James, whom I hadn't seen in years, had warned me about his own unconventionality and that of his friends, but what harm could they do? Ron came into the kitchen, his smile shining and eyes wandering inquisitively, searching for something. Amariles, Delfina's beautiful young mestizo niece, who helped out in the kitchen and laundry departments, looked at me with that, "Hey, what's this one up to?" look, but kept silent.

Ron picked up a pot and hit the bottom of it with his hand while cocking his head like a curious bird to keenly savor the tone. Then he picked up another pot and tried it out. His long fingers seemed experienced in tapping such objects. Then he went for the garbage can, then the milk pail. With each tom-tom, tin-tin, bum-bum, Amariles looked at me wondering what it would all lead to. I could only shrug that I had no idea either. We had seen some strange visitors, and so far Ron hadn't come close to the level of weirdness we'd encountered in some of them. He hadn't insisted on eating his rice and beans uncooked like the German people with the shaved heads; he hadn't taken all of his clothes off in public like the lone Canadian; he hadn't kissed any mangy local dogs.

Ron seemed to appreciate all the instruments he discovered but seemed particularly pleased with the medium-sized green plastic laundry bucket with the deep tone. That's when he said to me, "I'd like to put on a little entertainment for the people here, do a little drumming or something."

I didn't know whether to trust this gringo, a representative of my culture. Would he perform some unimaginable act in front of the Cantarana community, which had such vastly different traditions and expectations regarding social behavior? Would I be responsible? Could I get out of it? How could I say no to that gigantic smile? And *why* would I say no? I was normally suspicious with fellow gringos, but I liked this charismatic person and felt somehow comfortable enough with him to risk accepting some unknown consequences from his actions. Besides, it was time we locals started loosening up to the outside world, and maybe Ron was a good agent for that. I consulted my brother, and James smiled and said, "Sure, let him do his thing – he's good at that sort of thing."

When the time came for "his thing," Ron directed the group of about 15 Central Americans and North Americans, ages 5 to 45, to sit in a circle in the main dining area, where the tables and chairs had been removed. I sat by his side to interpret. He began with a simple rhythm, repeating it without changing tempo, and after a while I had to admit it generated some primitive inner excitement. But the initial embarrassed looks all around the circle of initiates made me fear the worst, especially since I was set up to be the mad New Yorker's spokesman.

But it was too late to retreat, and I found myself sitting there translating short sentences that seemed ridiculous, while Ron beat his drum. It was hard to carry out my responsibility without laughing.

> "There was a leaf-cutting ant
> Looking for the hole of his colony,
> But a leaf had fallen over it,
> So he tapped his feet on the ground
> And listened for a change in sound.
> And when he tapped the leaf,
> It sounded good to him,
> And he forgot about finding the hole
> Because he liked the sound so much,
> And he tapped and tapped,
> And it sounded like this."
> (Ron beat his drum alone a short while.)
> "But then along came an anteater

Hungry for leaf-cutting ants.
But when he heard the drumming,
He liked it so much
That he too began to dance."

Now Ron wanted somebody to dance the anteater's part, which his wife Karin offered to do, making everyone laugh even harder. When I saw some of the people moving and swaying to the dancing anteater and Ron's hypnotic drumming, I thought, "Oh my God, where will all this end up?"

"*And then a snake came along,*
A poisonous fer-de-lance,
And the snake also began to dance."

Seven-year-old Marcela stood up wiggling and giggling, and moved to the center of the ring with Karin, the anteater.

"*Then an iguana came and he too began to dance.*'

My brother obviously took this thing seriously because he jerked his head up and down in such a perfect iguana imitation (where had he learned that? Did people learn that kind of thing at Harvard?) that everyone rolled with uncontrollable laughter.

"*Then an ox heard the drumming*
And went into the forest
And began to dance with the forest animals."

That is when the truly incredible occurred. Raúl, a serious and skilled worker who tackled the most difficult farm jobs, a 38-year-old father of several children who spent his days driving oxen, operating a chainsaw, working as a carpenter and cowboy, smiled broadly and without coaxing stepped into the center of the circle where he began dancing with his arms curved around his head like the horns of Cantarana's oxen. His wife Lisa was astounded, but that didn't interrupt her own dancing.

Then followed the jaguar and the rooster and the toucan, but when Ron got to the jet planes and potentially delicate subjects such as the Pope, I decided to abort, declining to serve any longer as the mouthpiece. The dancing ended slowly, somewhat gracefully, although it had gained a momentum all its own and the others would have been happy to go on and on.

I was astonished at the scenes that somehow transpired in the dining room of Cantarana's main house, where nothing remotely similar had ever taken place. People so vastly different that they may as well have been from different planets met, communicated, and had fun, lowering their inhibitions without booze, exposing themselves to ridicule and loving it! Ron's show was like bringing electricity and TV to Cantarana – a positive introduction to new ideas from the outside world, not just for the local people, but for me, too. It was the challenge of opening up to a strangeness, newness, to changes of attitude, of perception, of imagination. How much freedom did we dare allow ourselves? How much were we willing to explore with open minds? How much fun would we let ourselves have in life? How much would we let ourselves laugh?

Ron and James helped me see things differently, less seriously, more openly, and that was an extremely valuable asset at Cantarana – and anywhere. Maybe it would have been even more therapeutic to have let Ron bring the jet planes and the Pope into the leaf-cutting ant's dance. Maybe I really missed out on something. How would one dance like the Pope? Would anyone have dared to try?

Cusinga (fiery-billed aracari) in *guarumo* (cecropia tree)

Gavilán blanco (white hawk)

Chapter Nineteen

The spirit of the storm

Whenever I returned from a trip (scuba diving on live-aboard boats in different parts of the world or with my family on slightly safer vacations or visiting family in the United States), I was astounded by how much had changed at Cantarana in such a short time, and it always took me a while to reestablish myself. Over the years, I grew accustomed to this sense of dislocation, however, and found it easier to sink my roots again into the local environment. Instead of feeling overwhelmed and panicky as I had before, by 1992 I found it exciting and usually survived the trauma with a smile – sometimes a sad smile, but maybe sad smiles weren't so bad.

I returned this time two days after the full moon in May, the month of pests, plagues, diseases, flowers, fruits, and fragrance, the transition between dry and rainy seasons, the month when the local world and people get ready for major change. "Macho," our favorite taxi driver from San Cristobal, ingeniously got me and my cargo in his 4-wheel-drive Toyota all the way into Cantarana, which was green and lively from recent rains.

On the drive, I could see that nature was quickly recovering from damage done by the earthmovers who had ceased another of their fitful bursts of activity months earlier. The highway people again ran out of money, millions mysteriously disappearing in a typical scandal that enriched apparently legally immune politicians. Taking advantage of the break in the destruction and construction activities, *balsos* (balsa trees) were sending out millions of tiny seeds in little cloud-fine puffs. With their admirable ability to sprout and grow incredibly quickly in the very worst clay and rock, the balsa trees reforested themselves in apparent moonscapes in a year's time. Other plants moved in around them; cecropia trees (the sloths' favorite); leafy vines sending out long, thick runners; thorny weeds with elaborate orange-and-red flowers. Together with the balsos, the lush undergrowth helped cover the damage that had previously sickened me, and I felt immense relief. Tropical nature was not so easily defeated.

Later the same day, I received news to counter partially this triumphant development. Antonio, the foreman, informed me he had discovered a campsite high up on his forested land where hunters had come and killed the last white-tailed peccaries in the area, leaving the heads of the animals behind. A neighbor had obviously aided the hunters in their poaching, the same neighbor who had also sacrificed his best forest to loggers that year, a man I used to consider a good friend.

Antonio told me that some of the local farmers in Cachelote were using poison bait to kill all the animal "pests" eating their chickens, corn, rice, or beans. Thus, the agoutis, chachalacas, raccoons, opossums, parrots, monkeys, squirrels, coatimundis, hawks, doves, curassows, and how many other creatures were dying at a faster rate than ever before.

This folly was not only murderous, but suicidal. Mankind could not hope to achieve long-term success within the ecosystem as long as our voracious appetites led to this kind of competition-to-the-death with other creatures over land and food. Poisoning and killing was not the way, and whether we understood our interconnectedness or not, by damaging the biosphere we were also precipitating our own doom.

News like Antonio's would usually stir up a torment of disgust, protest, and anger within me, but the day had finally come when I preferred to act as if, besides being balder, I was also wiser. Fighting was not always the answer; if I were going to be good for anything or anybody, I couldn't afford to waste time in quixotic martyrdom. I must try to focus my energy on positive things, and leave the negative ones for later. It was as simple as that.

Never in my life had it actually been simple, but I had learned that there wasn't much good in prolonged negative action or reaction. A plant whose roots ran into a rock needn't sicken or be stunted or die as long as there were alternatives for its roots. I often had trouble dealing with obstacles that, with a little imagination and positive attitude, could easily have been circumvented or even pushed out of the way or ignored.

There was good news, however. Tina's mare had given birth to a beautiful, strong colt, who pranced elegantly beside his proud first-time mother. And the large iguana that lived among the outcropping of black basalt boulders was still there. No one had killed and eaten him even though he was such an easy target and was considered so tasty. Flocks of noisy parakeets descended upon wild fruit trees. Shiny blue morpho butterflies larger than my open hand fluttered through my house; white-faced monkeys leaped through nearby trees; gaudy, fiery-billed aracaris and yellow-and-black toucans hopped around confidently; the dark-green forest trees branched out with deep-purple flowers; there were ripe pineapples, bananas, mangoes, avocados – everything testified that Cantarana was doing very well.

That morning I walked through the reforested areas and cacao groves, and the new growth surpassed my expectations. When I saw the workers preparing the new tree-planting area, all working hard even without the foreman or me with them, I knew Cantarana was functioning nicely.

The first day back after a lengthy absence was always a roller-coaster ride, so when I experienced the highs, I prepared for the lows. Lisa, my sister-in-law, was a reliable source of information concerning the lows. Problems and complications always seemed to accompany her and her family, wherever they were. She suffered from rheumatism in her right arm and needed an operation on the varicose veins in both legs. The doctor had told her to stay off her feet more, but that was impossible. Who would prepare the meals and wash the clothes?

Already her husband, Raúl, had grown so angered by the inability of his 14- and 20-year-old sons to care for the family's pig that he killed the animal, butchered it in a hurry, and gave away most of its meat. Raúl told me his sons didn't bother to collect and chop the firewood or pound the chaff off the rice or wash their own clothes to help out Lisa. And Raúl himself was not well. While I was in the United States, he had worked so hard to finish the 30-foot fishing boat he was building from scratch that he ate irregularly or not enough, causing his ulcer to flare up and sending him to the hospital. Antonio didn't like to give Raúl's sons work because they were lazy and unreliable. Lisa's condition worsened so that she had to lie down every now and then. She put 14-year-old Quino (who liked onions and garlic) to cook, but Francisco, the 20-year-old (who hated onions and garlic) refused to eat it.

Lisa was very glad to see me, and I was glad to help out however I could, which seemed to be enough for the time being. I never liked meddling in other peoples' personal affairs, but sometimes, when the family members were open to me and trusted me, I didn't do so badly, and I thought my simple attempts at reparation were almost always better than not intervening at all.

Other families had more severe complications. Antonio and his wife Marta were suffering with their beautiful 17-year-old daughter Luz, who no longer wanted to attend high school in La Palma, where she had to work for room and board. During vacation, she got involved with a handsome 20-year-old squatter from Morita; her parents approved as long as she didn't get pregnant. But she did.

Even though I had made it very clear to Antonio that I didn't want any squatter sleeping on the farm, he and Marta had let Gerardo move in with them. I understood their reasoning; Gerardo's neighbors were violent and dangerous. But when Antonio confided in me that this quasi-son-in-law rarely wanted to work or chop firewood or even help pay for the family's food bills, I felt tempted to ask Antonio to reconsider the wisdom of handing his relatively well educated daughter to a penniless squatter of dubious character. I wisely kept my mouth shut. Antonio somehow sensed the gist of what was going on in my mind, and he smiled and said, "You have three daughters yourself, you just wait and see – it's not easy, it's not easy at all." It would be too soon when I learned, unfortunately, how right Antonio was.

That afternoon, I sat in my house with my old dog Chito gazing out at the ocean and sandy beach of Punta Morita as the sky grew dark, a wind picked up, and rain began to fall. It was one of those surprise storms that even the local animals hadn't predicted, or maybe I had just been out of tune with their signs. Around 3:00, whitecaps formed in the ocean, trees swayed drunkenly, showing the gray-green undersides of their leaves, and swallows and vultures practiced wild maneuvers in the shifting gusts. Hopping hunch-backed around a stinking mess of rotten flesh, a bald-headed vulture bore little resemblance to its wind-borne self, when it was miraculously converted into a majestic creature of outstanding grace and beauty. I loved to watch the vultures fly in a strong wind and disliked them when they were perched, especially when they perched in the black hawk's formerly reserved place high up in the giant dead ajo tree on the other side of the stream.

I remembered how, during foul weather like this, the black hawk with the clean white tailband would be up there and we'd keep each other company, him way over there, me on my porch, both alone – similar, kindred spirits. He probably didn't think of me much, or much of me, but I thought a lot of him, and it was important to me that he was there. But the people of Cantarana had pressured me to help them protect their chickens by killing my friend. The black hawk, "the gringo's hawk," was gone from his throne, and when I looked over there on that stormy afternoon, I felt lonely and sad and guilty even after so many years. Life would never be quite the same for me. I burned inside over grave errors that couldn't be undone. Were these the coals of hell or the tough lessons required on the way to heaven?

I would catch myself in this too-heavy mood, reason differently, and rephrase my questioning. Why, for example, was it a bigger deal to kill the chicken-eating hawk than it was to kill the equally innocent chicken-killing skunk? Just because I personally liked the hawk better? What was the cosmic truth or divine verdict on this? The dolphin- and whale- (and everything else, it seemed) eating Japanese used this exact same kind of reasoning to justify their appetite for Flipper, Free-Willy, and other cetacean meat, just as we Americans casually devour many other wild and domestic mammals. Are there creatures that are okay to kill and others that are not? How can we know which ones to slaughter and which ones to protect? Who can say with authority? Will we eventually acquire this wisdom? Will we eventually obey it?

Cantarana could be so astonishing. The rain fell out of the dark clouds so hard that I figured it would just be a short-lived downpour, but the rain kept coming. Lightning ripped trees nearby. Falling branches crashed down into the forest. I could still see the black hawk's tree, with the vines whipping out almost horizontally. The hawk would have been there facing the storm, magnificent in his rightful place, the place only he could occupy. The vultures had long since flown away in search of safety.

Inches of rain fell in hours. The same precious water that, in moderate amounts, nourished the young corn plants now – too much, too fast – threatened to wash them away. The dry-season road would have been rendered impassable; hopefully the big logs in the stream would wash over the little dam and not smash into its sides. Where would the emerald snake I'd seen that day hide during the storm? Or the big iridescent blue butterflies? In the last light of that spectacular afternoon I saw the water, too much water, forming rivulets of muddy soil, washing the land of cow dung and decomposed leaves and grass and twigs, scouring, cleansing, sterilizing, the ditch overflowing, all erosion controls overloaded, the Quebrada Chica raging and roaring, uncrossable and dangerous, a presence to respect and keep a safe distance from.

A thick lightning bolt seemed to paralyze the sky as it streaked down by the sandy Punta Morita, near where Raúl was building his fishing boat. I thought right away, "That was the killer type," having no idea what a "killer type" lightning bolt looked like. I hoped it hadn't gotten poor Raúl or destroyed his boat. Chito shivered under the table with fear.

The rainfall kept pounding without letting up in intensity. Giant boulders in the stream rumbled deeply, resonantly, and made the land around the stream tremble. Trees with tremendous gashes in their trunks crashed and banged in the violent stream and washed out to sea, which was orange-clay-colored out to half a mile from shore. More rain fell in three hours than many people saw in three years.

The storm gave me an ecstatic sense of awe, seeming to encapsulate all my feelings for the tropics and for life in general. There was so much energy and grandeur in that storm that it knocked most of my own inflated delusions right out of me. No contest! "Who am I?" I mumbled to Chito, who seemed to be trying to hide his head under his paws in a comparatively dry corner of the porch. "Who are we with all our pettiness next to this?" I'd experienced similar fleeting moments of enlightenment, of being overwhelmed by the immense presence of nature's power and beauty. A hurricane, an earthquake, a mountain, a twinkling starry night, a lively reef in clear water, a giant tree, a tribal dance, a symphony, a clean glassy wave, a campfire, a cool drink when truly thirsty, a baby smiling, a tiger running, a fragrant flower, a smoothed piece of driftwood, a stone, a shell – there were many things as awesome as the storm, as magnificent, as inspiring, as nourishing in the deepest ways. All we needed to appreciate them was to let go of our self-imposed dedication to pettiness and to open our minds and hearts, explore, smile, be ourselves.

The storm dissipated, and I slept in the cool clean night wondering about Raúl and that lightning bolt and about those who had been stranded on the other side of the Morita River, which was at least five times the size of the Quebrada Chica.

I usually loved the mornings after storms, but this time was different. The news came that although Raúl and his boat had narrowly escaped the bolt of lightning, his companion had not. While Raúl's partner Mino and his wife were eating dinner in their beach choza, the powerful electric charge hit the roof and descended a post, shattering it and sending a thick splinter into the fisherman's temple, knocking him down in what appeared to be death. His wife, who at that instant was touching the post, took the blast more directly. The five sons and daughters shook their parents in a desperate attempt to revive them. The father regained consciousness but remained delirious all night. Their mother was dead.

They couldn't get to a hospital until the next day, when the fisherman learned he had lost his mate. Everyone commented on the same thing: that that couple had been so happy, that the woman who died had been a fine wife, mother, person. "Why does God seem to always bring tragedy to people like that?" they asked.

I was troubled, too. Yes, the storm was magnificent, but it killed a woman and seriously damaged a poor fisherman's family. Did that make it a bad thing, despite its awesome beauty? Sitting on my porch the next afternoon, looking out at the peaceful mountains and ocean and sky, I decided most things were too complex to judge in such terms as good and bad. This one fit in both categories. Classifying it was like describing the appearance and location of an electron, or explaining light in terms of waves or particles, proving whether gravity pulled or was the absence of push, debating whether the man-eating Bengal tigers or the encroaching humans had more right to territory and life.

The storm was mostly damaging, I supposed, yet it marked the spectacular end of a harsh dry season. It filled and cleaned the waterways, dispelled any fears of drought, washed away a lot of debris. It also filled people with awe, and through the tragedy of the fisherman's wife, it taught us all some very important lessons: that life and nature and God were mysterious and powerful and worthy of great respect, that humans and their lives were vulnerable to sudden and drastic change, that death often came without warning, and that our loved ones would not always be with us.

The powerful storm served as a catalyst to opening my mind wider than normal, and in that relatively more enlightened state, cleansed out a lot of clutter. I pleasantly and surprisingly experienced a much needed peace as I – at least temporarily – felt acceptance, forgiveness, and compassion for those I had once considered enemies – the barbaric squatters, disrespectful poachers, unscrupulous bureaucrats, and corrupt politicians. Might they have classified me as an arrogant, meddlesome, self-righteous foreigner? We were all only human, and hating each other was such a stupid waste of time. I was tired of it.

Everything was relative. It was important to view personal, social, and planetary things from different perspectives. Even though, if Earth were the size of a soccer ball and we held it in our hand, arm outstretched, we could not detect any sign of life with our naked eye; even though our thin film of a biosphere, including us, was apparently insignificant amidst the chaos; even though this same biosphere had suffered five known major cataclysmic events that destroyed millions of species – could we still be complacent about our own ushering in and riding the sixth and possibly final great wave of mass extinctions? Didn't astronomers, biologists, and theologians all agree that we, our fellow creatures, and our water planet were unique in the universe? Weren't we worth protecting?

"We simply cannot *afford* to continue destroying the rainforests!" I complained, perhaps childishly, to my dog and to the pounding rain. The Minoans of Crete learned this about their forests only after it was too late. They had no more trees for building boats, and rains washed their topsoil away, and who knows, maybe even Thera's devastating eruption was somehow linked to deforestation. The Easter Islanders also became extinct after cutting down their forests. The extensive and sophisticated Mayan and Incan civilizations mysteriously vanished after apparently severe droughts that some believe to be related to their own deforestation. With thousands of years of experience, and now numbering in the billions, shouldn't we be wiser and more concerned? Did we necessarily have to trash our forests, wetlands, oceans, and selves?

Part and parcel of the universe, the storm was beyond us, not subject to our questioning or reasoning, not subject to our tampering. Instead, we were subject to it. Aloof from all our fears and hopes and joys, our jobs, our families, our projects, our plans, our problems, our ideas, our histories, the storm was itself, and its passing left me exhilarated, awed, and humbled, and I felt fortunate and grateful for the experience.

A few years later, I found myself riding another kind of storm, one that I was having much more difficulty with. I walked one muddy morning out along the orange dirt and gray broken boulder desolation of construction and highway, which was to bring speeding cars and buses and trucks and people and garbage and flies and the rest of modern Western civilization. I was amused by the continued impotence of man's efforts to break through "The Stopper." Already financed by international banks several times, each effort ended in failure. Rudely sculptured remnants of dead foreign bulldozers lay in the mud, rusting monuments to entropy.

Did it always have to be such a struggle? I enjoyed imagining being able to blame my personal feelings of insecurity on the defeated metallic monsters. I wanted to believe they were responsible for severing my roots, which had taken so many years to send out and take hold. It was a very satisfactory image, but only partly true. Though I often felt like a member of an indicator species or a displaced tribesman in danger of extinction, I actually was just a mix-blooded, mix-cultured, generally mixed-up gringo hungry for some convenient, ego-building, soul-asserting drama. It was rather fun assuming the role of heroic victim, eco-warrior battling the forces of evil. I'd daydreamed of attacking the highway machinery with my shotgun in a glorious "High Noon" shootout, proving something to everyone, achieving some sort of lasting triumph.

Sometimes I felt like the whole world bore down on me like the college psychologist, proclaiming that *I* was the self-absorbed narcissist, that *I* was the lost one, *I* was the mistaken, *I* was the one needing to adapt to *them*. The dozers and their drivers (no, not the drivers; they were too nice) were "them." The "them" were indiscriminate hunters, the exploiters, the poachers, the loggers, the invaders, the banana companies, the bureaucrats allowing deforestation and poisoning – enemies of nature, mankind, family, country, planet, neighbors, me. Unwell daydreams – I felt embarrassed to be so easily taken by them, but I knew they still formed a true part of my darker self, the part of which I was growing tired. I no longer wanted to fight. My grandiose dreams of creating "a harmonious agricultural community nestled between pristine tropical ocean and rainforest" did not come true, but I didn't regret having them. I no longer wanted to blame or be blamed. I'd always thought I was pretty smart about some things, but I really could not understand who should be responsible for putting themselves between the bulldozers and the rainforests. Where were the respective human representatives whose job it was to save our biosphere and species from extinction?

We are such a young species, such a unique one – surely it isn't going to be easy for us to learn to accept the limits of our world and universe. Surely it isn't so much a matter of "me versus them" as it is "we're all in it together." If I didn't want to be chummy with certain people, or if I didn't like a particular place or government or system, that was fine, but I need not fall into naïve and ludicrous self-righteous indignation. If I liked being warm and mostly vegetarian, it would not be wise to go and live with the Aleuts. If I wished excellent opportunities for my children, in a beautiful rural, clean, crimeless, diseaseless, nukeless, hazardless setting, I might have to do some very serious traveling or, more likely, reconsider my Edenic aspirations.

Life in the tropics (or anywhere) was never simply standard, linear, and black and white, as most of us modern, programmed humans seemed to expect or require. It was curvy and connected, and relative; there were always so many variables to consider, and surprises. Seeking the best circumstances and most favorable compromises for myself and my family was natural and praiseworthy, as long as I didn't expect more than reality had to offer. Successful compromising, trading, sharing, symbiosis, benign selfishness – these were perhaps the keys to happiness and survival for everyone, for every creature on earth.

Out there among the agents of construction/destruction that were performing vivisection on Cantarana, I witnessed how the whole area's once primitive scenario was changing drastically. As soon as they completed the bridge over the Morita River, no one would have to swim their cargoes or families across. No one would be stuck on one side or the other. No one would have to know how to judge the river or wait for it to subside. People would no longer cure with plants, but with pills they could go and get at the pharmacy. Intimate knowledge of the rainforest would be lost. Hunting and gathering would phase out. There would be no more mention of "el tigre" or "the old Tuli." The oxen trainers, oxen, and oxcarts would become scarce, as would the entire horse culture. Most exploitable things would be exploited. Farmers would sell their trees and lands and waste the money and move to the city and regret losing their past lifestyles. The elders would no longer meet and exchange legends and stories and wisdom that younger listeners might have passed on to their children. Along with many of the wild animals that would disappear, so too would the people of the old culture. This was the story already unfolding in most of tropical America, and Africa and Asia and the rest of the world.

Gazing dysfunctionally at the horrifying spectacle of the once pristine Quebrada Chica stream being ravaged by many men and machines, straightened out and forced through a 3-meter-diameter, 50-meter-long aluminum culvert buried under 15 meters of dirt and rock, I noticed it was snowing.

Floating slowly down from high in the sky came little cottony clouds of air and fluffy fuzz, landing on me, and the bare dirt, and the men and their machines. Millions of them, each carrying a tiny, perfect, roundish seed. They came down so soundlessly, so softly, so humbly, so patiently, so surely, these timeless messages of new life, of God's continuing creation sent out by Cantarana's numerous balsos. On the road they had no chance for a future, but all along the sides they did. Balsos could somehow take hold and prosper, even in the most sterile circumstances. New trees were guaranteed. Highway or not. Me or not. The silent news made me smile.

Maybe the highway was okay, I thought. Maybe everything was okay and someday we would understand. Maybe it was less a matter of struggling so much with nature and man than it was of just trying to do our little part wherever we were, trying to be nice, positive, aware and helpful – trusting more in God and surrendering . . . or maybe I was just getting old.

Gavilán negro (black hawk)

About the Author

Jon Marañón (a nom de plume) has lived a remarkable life with which many readers may identify or appreciate. He came of age in America during the turbulent 1960s of Civil Rights marches and opposition to the Vietnam War. He always felt himself to be a poor fit for the consumerism/materialism, conformity, racism, and environmental destructiveness of his own country. A college psychologist told him he'd have to learn to adjust, but he persisted in seeking a place where, and people with whom, he might fit.

This young, blond, blue-eyed college dropout became a Latin American landowner and patrón. He tried numerous schemes to make a living off the land and became a significant observer of both the environmental and social changes in Costa Rica. Marañón listened to local elders tell tales about them, and he passes on some of these and other tales to readers.

The Gringo's Hawk represents the culmination of Mr. Marañón's social struggles and the roles he has played in marine biology conservation and in establishing national parks and marine reserves in his area.

Marañón, almost as a sideline, has had a long-time fascination with whales and worked with scientists and researchers to establish an entirely new understanding of the migratory habits of Northern and Southern hemisphere humpback whales. At the time of publication of The Gringo's Hawk this research is ongoing.

Made in the USA
San Bernardino, CA
08 December 2018